The Career of John Wayne

Films | Radio | Television

Randy Bonneville

The Career of John Wayne
©2025 Randy Bonneville

Published in the USA by:
BearManor Media
1317 Edgewater Dr. #110
Orlando FL 32804
www.BearManorMedia.com

ISBN-10: 979-8-88771-687-9 Career of John Wayne
ISBN-13: 979-8-88771-688-6 Career of John Wayne hb

Art, Design, and Layout: Mark Bailey

About the author

Randy Bonneville became interested in old-time movies, radio and television during the 'nostalgia boom' of the 1970s, when popular culture of the 1930s, '40s and '50s was being discussed and revisited in magazine articles, books and television. In addition to *The Career of John Wayne*, he has authored several e-books for BearManor Media detailing the film, radio and television credits of stars such as Veronica Lake, James Cagney, Audrey Totter and Lucille Ball. He has also contributed material to ten books, including *Gale Gordon: From Mayor of Wistful Vista to Borrego Springs*, *Frances Langford: Armed Forces Sweetheart* and *Mel Blanc: The Man of a Thousand Voices*. Randy resides in Isle la Motte, Vermont, one of Lake Champlain's beautiful islands.

Acknowledgments

Thank you, God, for all our blessings and talents. This book would not be possible without the generosity of Ben Ohmart, who took a chance on publishing my work and asking me to contribute to several of his books; Mark Bailey, whose patience working with me through the editing process went beyond the "call of duty"; Jim Manago, for allowing me to contribute to his valuable and informative books; and most of all, to my mother, Geraldine, whose efforts with a young pre-teen son (guess who) to pull in a far-away television station--which broadcast old movies--started a lifelong interest in vintage film, old-time radio and classic TV.

John Wayne

The film actor who became an American icon was born Marion Robert Morrison on May 26, 1907 in Winterset, Iowa.

Moving with his family to California and settling in Glendale when he was a child, young Marion--nicknamed Duke-became a breadwinner for the struggling family, finding work in nearby orchards and assuming a newspaper route delivering *The Los Angeles Examiner*. Duke was also a member of the Boy Scouts and the YMCA while attending Glendale Union High School. Just prior to graduation, the strapping Morrison was offered a football scholarship to the University of Southern California; his academic focus was on law.

In the summer of 1926, Duke was one of a group of USC football players who gained employment on the Fox Film studio lot in exchange for home game box seats to be used by cowboy star Tom Mix. Duke became interested in the movie industry, managing to make his film debut in **Brown of Harvard** for *Metro-Goldwyn-Mayer*. He received a screen test at Hollywood's most prestigious studio, but failed.

Back at Fox, where he worked behind the scenes handling props for various films, Duke was spotted by one of the company's regular movie directors, John Ford. Their friendship starts when Duke refuses to be intimidated by Ford's forceful demeanor and topples the director in a brief football scrimmage. Ford offered him bit roles in some of his films, at the time seeing Duke only as a prop department employee. It was another notable director, Raoul Walsh, who moved Duke's movie career forward after Walsh saw him moving furniture back into storage. Walsh was preparing to shoot **The Big Trail**, a large-scale sound western, and was in need of a leading man. Duke filled the bill in Walsh's mind, but the final decision rested with production executive Winfield Sheehan. A total of three screen tests were made with Duke before Walsh finally convinced Sheehan they had found the picture's star. However, there was one more matter to settle-they had to change Duke's name. Sheehan wanted something more *American sounding*. Walsh picked *Anthony*

Wayne (the director was a Revolutionary War history buff), but Sheehan didn't like 'Anthony'. How about John Wayne? *Fine*, answered Sheehan. Duke Morrison became John Wayne without benefit of their new star being present at the meeting.

Unfortunately, **The Big Trail** (1930) did not perform at the box office as the studio expected and one of the 'casualties' was Wayne. Hitting a dead end at Fox, he found work at other studios, but initially not in lead roles. For that, he turned to the low-end Poverty Row movie factories which churned out B-westerns by the wagonload. It was in these modest 'oaters' and other 'second features' that Wayne spent the remainder of the decade, honing his natural acting skills.

By 1938, Wayne was working at Republic Pictures, the lot that turned out a better grade of B-western. Even so, Wayne desired to break out of the 'B hive' and become an A-list actor and he finally was given his chance when pal John Ford handed Wayne a motion picture script during one of their sailing jaunts. Ford offered him the role of the Ringo Kid in **Stagecoach**. Wayne accepted and scored in a film which elevated the western from Saturday matinee fodder to a respectable movie genre alongside historical, romantic and literary dramas, sophisticated comedies, grand-scale musicals and the like. Also, Wayne's role as Ringo catapulted him into the ranks of leading Hollywood stars. From here on, he continued to build his reputation as a film actor. In addition to the ever-present westerns, Wayne starred in war pictures and stretched his acting muscles in other genres. Notable examples include **The Long Voyage Home** (1940, a sea-going character study), **The Shepherd of the Hills** (1941, a dramatic vendetta tale set in the mountains), **Reap the Wild Wind** (1942, playing an unsympathetic role as an accused ship-wrecker), **They Were Expendable** (1945, war drama of PT boat commanders fighting the Japanese), **Red River** (1948, a cattle drive western with a hard-bitten Wayne opposing his ward Montgomery Clift over control of the herd) and **Sands of Iwo Jima** (1949, an Oscar-nominated performance with Wayne as a tough Marine sergeant).

The 1950s saw Wayne lead the exhibitors' polls of top box office stars and it was the decade which solidified his status as an enduring star. In addition to John Ford, he made films for top-notch directors Howard Hawks and William A. Wellman. Some top vehicles for Wayne during this decade include ***The Quiet Man*** (1952, a romantic drama about an Irish American looking to settle on his family's homestead in Ireland), ***The High and the Mighty*** (1954, as a co-pilot trying to save a seemingly-doomed aircraft and its passengers) and ***The Search-ers*** (1956, a western quest to locate a young girl captured by Indians). His career continued through the 1960s and '70s, finally rewarding him with an Academy Award for Best Actor in 1969 for his portrayal of the cantankerous veteran marshal Rooster Cogburn in ***True Grit***.

Wayne's final role was perhaps his most poignant, as a gunfighter dying of cancer in ***The Shootist*** (1976). Himself suffering from the disease, John Wayne died at the age of 72 on June 11, 1979.

Chronology

May 26, 1907 - Born Marion Robert Morrison in Winterset, Iowa, of Scotch-Irish descent, to Clyde Leonard Morrison and Mary Alberta ('Molly') Brown.

1918 - Residing in Glendale, Marion--nicknamed 'Duke'-goes to work in the nearby orchards, picking apricots and oranges. He also acquires a newspaper route delivering *The Los Angeles Examiner*. His income helps the family pay its bills.

1919 - Joins Troop Four of the Boy Scouts, as well as the YMCA in Glendale.

1921 - Enters Glendale Union High School.

1925 - Just prior to his high school graduation, is offered a football scholarship to the University of Southern California.

1926 - Film cowboy star Tom Mix agrees to get some USC football players on the Fox movie studio's payroll in exchange for a group of box seats at USC football games. 'Duke' Morrison is one of those play-ers. He is assigned extra parts in films and meets director John Ford.

May 2, 1926 - Makes his film debut as a Yale football player in ***Brown of Harvard***.

March 5, 1928 - Plays an unbilled bit part in *Mother Machree*, premiering at the Globe Theater in New York City. Stars are Victor McLaglen and Belle Bennett. It is Wayne's initial film for director John Ford (even though his second collaboration with Ford, *Four Sons*, is released first).

1930 - Fox executive Winfield Sheehan and director Raoul Walsh rename 'Duke' Morrison, the star of their upcoming western *The Big Trail*, John Wayne.

October 24, 1930 - Has his first starring role as Breck Coleman in *The Big Trail*, opening at the Roxy Theater in New York City.

December, 1930 - Tells *Photoplay* magazine he will not "go Hollywood".

April 5, 1931 - Following the poor performance of *The Big Trail* at the box office, Fox drops his film contract.

June 24, 1933 - Marries Josephine Saenz.

October 10, 1933 - Stars in *Riders of Destiny*, beginning a run of sixteen B-westerns for Lone Star/Monogram Pictures. Along with stuntman Yakima Canutt and director Robert N. Bradbury, Wayne develops the choreographed techniques that make fistfights look more realistic on film.

November 23, 1934 - Son Michael Wayne is born.

February 25, 1936 - Daughter Mary Antonia 'Toni' Wayne is born.

March 2, 1939 - Plays the Ringo Kid in *Stagecoach* as it opens at the Radio City Music Hall in New York City. The film, directed by John Ford, also stars Claire Trevor and Thomas Mitchell.

April 13, 1939 - Makes his radio debut on a broadcast of *Kraft Music Hall*, starring Bing Crosby, on NBC.

July 15, 1939 - Son Patrick Wayne is born.

August 8, 1940 - Participates in the annual charity baseball game benefit for Mount Sinai Hospital and free medical clinic. The game takes place before a crowd of 37,700 people at Wrigley Field in Los Angeles. Wayne is on the Leading Men team with co-players Gary Cooper, Tyrone Power, Errol Flynn, Fred Astaire, Randolph Scott, Roy Rogers, Peter Lorre, Boris Karloff and others. They vie against the Comedians (Jack Benny, Fred Allen, Andy Devine, Buster Keaton, The Ritz Brothers, Edgar Kennedy and Leo Carrillo). Honorary captains are Paulette Goddard (for the Comedians) and Marlene Dietrich for the Leading Men. Milton Berle acts as game announcer; umpires are Kay Kyser, James Gleason, Chico Marx and Thurston Hall. A 'skirmish' during the game is broken up by the Keystone Kops. Karloff, dressed as the Frankenstein monster, hits a home run for the Leading Men, but they still lose to the Comedians 5 to 3.

December 3, 1940 - Daughter Melinda Wayne is born.

February 4, 1944 - The Motion Picture Alliance for the Preservation of American Ideals is founded to oppose liberals and radicals in Hollywood by Sam Wood, King Vidor and Walt Disney. Active members include Gary Cooper, Wayne, Ward Bond, Robert Taylor, Ayn Rand and Hedda Hopper.

November, 1944 - Divorced from Josephine Saenz.

September 12, 1945 - Plays Colonel Joseph Madden in ***Back to Bataan***, opening at the RKO Palace Theater in New York City. His co-star is Anthony Quinn.

December 20, 1945 - Plays Lieutenant Rusty Ryan in ***They Were Expendable***, premiering at the Capitol Theater in New York City. His co-star is Robert Montgomery; the film is directed by John Ford. The stage show features bandleader Tommy Dorsey.

January 17, 1946 - Marries Esperanza 'Chata' Baur.

June 24, 1948 - Plays Captain Kirby York in ***Fort Apache***, co-starring Henry Fonda, Shirley Temple, Pedro Armendariz and John Agar. It premieres at the Capitol Theater in New York City with a stage show headlined by Lena Horne.

September 30, 1948 - Plays Thomas Dunson in ***Red River***, co-starring Montgomery Clift, opening at the Capitol Theater.

1949 - Ranks fourth in Quigley Publications' exhibitors' poll of top box office stars. The remaining nine: Bob Hope, Bing Crosby, Bud Abbott & Lou Costello (as a team), Gary Cooper, Cary Grant, Betty Grable, Esther Williams, Humphrey Bogart and Clark Gable.

November 17, 1949 - Plays Captain Nathan Brittles in ***She Wore a Yellow Ribbon***, co-starring Joanne Dru, John Agar, Ben Johnson, Harry

Carey Jr. and Victor McLaglen. The film is directed by John Ford and opens at the Capitol Theater in New York City.

December 14, 1949 - Plays Sergeant John M. Stryker in *Sands of Iwo Jima*, premiering at the Fox Theater in San Francisco, California.

1950 - Is the number one box office star in the United States, according to the Quigley Poll. Filling out the top ten are Bob Hope, Bing Crosby, Betty Grable, James Stewart, Bud Abbott & Lou Costello (as a team), Clifton Webb, Esther Williams, Spencer Tracy and Randolph Scott.

January 25, 1950 - Becomes the 125th star to leave his hand and foot-prints outside Grauman's Chinese Theater.

May 15, 1950 - Makes his television debut on *Cowboy Slim Theater* over KTTV-Los Angeles, Channel 11.

July 19, 1950 - As president of the Motion Picture Alliance, announces that his organization has asked the Los Angeles City Council to require the registration of all communists.

November 1, 1950 - Plays Lieutenant Colonel Kirby Yorke in *Rio Grande*, premiering at the Majestic Theater in San Antonio, Texas. Wayne also makes a personal appearance with director John Ford and co-star Maureen O'Hara, who lay a wreath at the Alamo.

1951 - Maintains his standing as the number one box office star in the United States, according to the Quigley Poll. The remaining nine: Dean Martin & Jerry Lewis (as a team), Betty Grable, Bud Abbott & Lou Costello (as a team), Bing Crosby, Bob Hope, Randolph Scott, Gary Cooper, Doris Day and Spencer Tracy.

1952 - Places third in the Quigley Poll of top box office stars, which includes Dean Martin & Jerry Lewis (as a team), Gary Cooper, Bing Crosby, Bob Hope, James Stewart, Doris Day, Gregory Peck, Susan Hayward and Randolph Scott.

August 21, 1952 - Plays Sean Thornton in *The Quiet Man*, directed by John Ford and co-starring Maureen O'Hara and Victor McLaglen. The three stars attend the film's premiere at the Capitol Theater in New York City.

1953 - Places third on the Quigley Poll of top box office stars, which includes Gary Cooper, Dean Martin & Jerry Lewis (as a team), Alan

Ladd, Bing Crosby, Marilyn Monroe, James Stewart, Bob Hope, Susan Hayward and Randolph Scott.

October, 1953 - During his divorce trial from wife Esperanza 'Chata' Baur, is accused by Baur of having an affair with actress Gail Russell. He counters with the statement that Baur had Nicky Hilton as a house guest while he was away.

October 28, 1953 - Is granted a divorce from Esperanza Baur.

1954 - Regains his number one standing on the Quigley Poll of top box office stars. The remaining nine: Dean Martin & Jerry Lewis (as a team), Gary Cooper, James Stewart, Marilyn Monroe, Alan Ladd, William Holden, Bing Crosby, Jane Wyman and Marlon Brando.

May 27, 1954 - Plays Dan Roman in *The High and the Mighty*, premiering at the Paramount Theater in San Francisco and the Egyptian Theater in Hollywood.

June, 1954 - Films the movie *The Conqueror* in the Utah desert, near a government atom bomb testing area.

November 1, 1954 - Marries Pilar Pilette.

1955 - Places third on the Quigley Poll of top box office stars. The remaining nine are James Stewart, Grace Kelly, William Holden, Gary Cooper, Marlon Brando, Dean Martin & Jerry Lewis (team), Humphrey Bogart, June Allyson and Clark Gable.

January 17, 1955 - Replaces Robert Mitchum as star of *Blood Alley* after a bit of horseplay-which lands a crew member in San Francisco Bay-gets Mitchum fired.

September 10, 1955 - In a filmed prologue, introduces viewers to the western television series *Gunsmoke*, making its debut on CBS.

1956 - Places second on the Quigley Poll of top box office stars. The remaining nine: William Holden, James Stewart, Burt Lancaster, Glenn Ford, Dean Martin & Jerry Lewis (as a team), Gary Cooper, Marilyn Monroe, Kim Novak and Frank Sinatra.

March 8, 1956 - Joins Ginger Rogers, Susan Hayward, Lana Turner and Charles Boyer on television's *Climax!* in the episode *The Louella Parsons Story*. Teresa Wright stars as the noted gossip columnist.

March 31, 1956 - Daughter Aissa Wayne is born.

May 16, 1956 - Plays Ethan Edwards in *The Searchers*, premiering at the Chicago Theater in the Windy City. The film also stars Jeffrey Hunter and Natalie Wood. Wayne makes a personal appearance at the premiere with co-star Ward Bond.

1957 - Places second on the Quigley Poll of top box office stars. The remaining nine: Rock Hudson, Pat Boone, Elvis Presley, Frank Sinatra, Gary Cooper, William Holden, James Stewart, Jerry Lewis and Yul Brynner.

1959 - Places eighth on the Quigley Poll of top box office stars. The remaining nine: Rock Hudson, Cary Grant, James Stewart, Doris Day, Debbie Reynolds, Glenn Ford, Frank Sinatra, Jerry Lewis and Susan Hayward.

March 18, 1959 - Plays Sheriff John T. Chance in *Rio Bravo*, which opens at the Roxy Theater in New York City. His co-stars are Dean Martin, Angie Dickinson and Ricky Nelson.

April, 1959 - Is accused by the Panamanian government of involvement with the country's politics when it is discovered that Wayne made a payment of $500,000 to rebel leader Roberto Arias. Wayne explains the money was for a shrimp-buying business deal.

1960 - Places tenth on the Quigley Poll of top box office stars. The remaining nine: Doris Day, Rock Hudson, Cary Grant, Elizabeth Taylor, Debbie Reynolds, Tony Curtis, Sandra Dee, Frank Sinatra and Jack Lemmon.

January 9, 1960 - Finishes work on *The Alamo* and comments on other films: *Suddenly Last Summer*-deals with "distasteful" subject matter; *They Came to Cordura*-"degrading the Medal of Honor"; *On the Waterfront*-has a "defeatist attitude".

May 14, 1960 - Is confronted by Frank Sinatra at a costume benefit party over his criticism of Sinatra hiring blacklisted screenwriter Albert Maltz.

October 24, 1960 - Plays Davy Crockett in *The Alamo*, premiering at the Woodlawn Theater in San Antonio, Texas, where a three-day holiday ensues. Wayne attends the premiere along with co-stars Richard Widmark, Laurence Harvey, Frankie Avalon, Richard Boone and Linda Cristal.

November 10, 1960 - Plays Sam McCord in *North to Alaska*, opening at the Paramount Theater in New York City. Co-star Fabian is in the lobby hosting an 'after-school Coke party' (Coke as in Coca-Cola).

1961 - Places fourth on the Quigley Poll of top box office stars. The remaining nine: Elizabeth Taylor, Rock Hudson, Doris Day, Cary Grant, Sandra Dee, Jerry Lewis, William Holden, Tony Curtis and Elvis Presley.

March 27, 1961 - Via Hollywood trade press, disowns the ads of *Alamo* co-star Chill Wills: "We of *The Alamo* cast are praying harder-than the real Texans prayed for their lives in the Alamo-for Chill Wills to win the Oscar".

October 16, 1961 - Joins Roy Rogers, Walt Disney, John Ford, Rock Hudson, Ozzie & Harriet Nelson, Ronald Reagan, Donna Reed, Jane Russell and James Stewart in leading the Pledge of Allegiance at the *Hollywood's Answer to Communism* rally in the Hollywood Bowl.

1962 - Places fourth on the Quigley Poll of top box office stars. The remaining nine: Doris Day, Rock Hudson, Cary Grant, Elvis Presley, Elizabeth Taylor, Jerry Lewis, Frank Sinatra, Sandra Dee and Burt Lancaster.

February 22, 1962 - Son John Ethan Wayne is born.

May 23, 1962 - Plays Tom Doniphon in *The Man Who Shot Liberty Valance*, opening at the Capitol Theater in New York City. His co-stars are James Stewart and Lee Marvin.

October 4, 1962 - Plays Lieutenant Colonel Benjamin Vandervoort in *The Longest Day*, making its US premiere at the Warner Theater in New York City. Co-stars are Robert Ryan and Henry Fonda. Cardinal Spellman and General Omar Bradley attend the premiere.

1963 - Places second on the Quigley Poll of top box office stars. The remaining nine: Doris Day, Rock Hudson, Jack Lemmon, Cary Grant, Elizabeth Taylor, Elvis Presley, Sandra Dee, Paul Newman and Jerry Lewis.

February 20, 1963 - Plays General William Tecumseh Sherman in *How the West Was Won*, making its American premiere at the Warner Cinerama Theater in Hollywood. Also attends the premiere with co-stars Walter Brennan, Debbie Reynolds, James Stewart, Karl Malden, Carolyn

Jones, Lee J. Cobb, Carroll Baker, George Peppard and Russ Tamblyn.

1965 - Places second on the Quigley Poll of top box office stars. The remaining nine: Sean Connery, Doris Day, Julie Andrews, Jack Lemmon, Elvis Presley, Cary Grant, James Stewart, Elizabeth Taylor and Richard Burton.

February 15, 1965 - Plays the Centurion at the Crucifixion in *The Greatest Story Ever Told*, premiering at the Warner Cinerama Theater in Hollywood. Co-stars include Charlton Heston, Max von Sydow and Carroll Baker. Lady Bird Johnson attends the premiere accompanied by Adlai Stevenson.

June 23, 1965 - Plays John Elder in *The Sons of Katie Elder*, premiering at the Roosevelt Theater in Chicago, Illinois.

1966 - Places seventh on the Quigley Poll of top box office stars. The remaining nine: Julie Andrews, Sean Connery, Elizabeth Taylor, Jack Lemmon, Richard Burton, Cary Grant, Doris Day, Paul Newman and Elvis Presley.

February 22, 1966 - Daughter Marisa Wayne is born.

June 21, 1966 - Is in Vietnam signing autographs for US soldiers when a sniper's bullet hits the ground thirty feet away.

1967 - Places eighth on the Quigley Poll of top box office stars. The remaining nine: Julie Andrews, Lee Marvin, Paul Newman, Dean Martin, Sean Connery, Elizabeth Taylor, Sidney Poitier, Richard Burton and Steve McQueen.

February 1, 1967 - Appears in a cameo on TV's *The Beverly Hillbillies*. In lieu of salary, he asks for a fifth of Jack Daniels bourbon.

June 19, 1968 - Plays Colonel Mike Kirby in *The Green Berets*, premiering at the Warner Theater in New York City.

1969 - Places second on the Quigley Poll of top box office stars. The remaining nine: Paul Newman, Steve McQueen, Dustin Hoffman, Clint Eastwood, Sidney Poitier, Lee Marvin, Jack Lemmon, Katharine Hepburn and Barbra Streisand.

June 11, 1969 - Plays Rooster Cogburn in *True Grit*, premiering at Grauman's Chinese Theater in Hollywood. His co-stars are Kim Darby and Glen Campbell.

1970 - Places fourth on the Quigley Poll of top box office stars. The remaining nine: Paul Newman, Clint Eastwood, Steve McQueen, Elliott Gould, Dustin Hoffman, Lee Marvin, Jack Lemmon, Barbra Streisand and Walter Matthau,

February 2, 1970 - Wins the Golden Globe Award for Best Actor-Drama Film for his performance in *True Grit*.

1971 - Ranked as the top box office star in America on the Quigley Poll. Rounding out the roster are Clint Eastwood, Paul Newman, Steve McQueen, George C. Scott, Dustin Hoffman, Walter Matthau, Ali McGraw, Sean Connery and Lee Marvin.

1972 - Places fourth on the Quigley Poll of top box office stars. The remaining nine: Clint Eastwood, George C. Scott, Gene Hackman, Barbra Streisand, Marlon Brando, Paul Newman, Steve McQueen, Dustin Hoffman and Goldie Hawn.

1973 - Places ninth on the Quigley Poll of top box office stars. The remaining nine: Clint Eastwood, Ryan O'Neal, Steve McQueen, Burt Reynolds, Robert Redford, Barbra Streisand, Paul Newman, Charles Bronson and Marlon Brando.

1974 - Places tenth on the Quigley Poll of top box office stars. The remaining nine: Robert Redford, Clint Eastwood, Paul Newman, Barbra Streisand, Steve McQueen, Burt Reynolds, Charles Bronson, Jack Nicholson and Al Pacino.

January 15, 1974 - Rides into Harvard Square aboard an armored personnel carrier to receive the Harvard Crimson's *Brass Balls* Award.

February 19, 1976 - Wins the People's Choice Award for Favorite Movie Actor.

August 11, 1976 - Plays J.B. Books in *The Shootist*, opening at the Astor Plaza in New York City. His co-stars are Lauren Bacall, Ron Howard, James Stewart and Richard Boone.

February 10, 1977 - Wins the People's Choice Award for Favorite Motion Picture Star.

1978 - Receives 150,000 letters from fans and well-wishers in the two months following his cancer surgery.

April 9, 1979 - During the Academy Awards ceremony at the Dorothy

Chandler Pavilion in the Los Angeles Music Center, presents the Oscar for 1978's Best Picture winner, *The Deer Hunter*, to producer Michael Cimino.

May 26, 1979 - Receives a letter from the White House explaining a special medal approved by the US Congress and signed by President Jimmy Carter, *John Wayne, American.*

June 11, 1979 - Dies of stomach cancer at age 72.

Feature Films

John Wayne is ranked #13 on the American Film Institute's list of *50 Greatest American Screen Legends.*

Brown of Harvard (1926) Directed by Jack Conway.

William Haines, Jack Pickford, Mary Brian, Francis X. Bushman Jr., Mary Alden, David Torrence, Edward Connelly, Guinn Williams, Donald Reed, Marion 'Duke' Morrison [John Wayne], Richard Alexander, Robert Livingston, Doris Lloyd, Grady Sutton, Daniel G. Tomlinson, Percy Williams.

Outspoken university athlete Haines is attracted to pretty Brian, daughter of a college professor…and so is his roommate (Pickford). In his film debut, Wayne can be seen as a Yale football player (and he also doubled for Bushman Jr.). Screenplay by Donald Ogden Stewart; scenario by A.P. [Andrew Percival] Younger, from the 1906 play by Rida Johnson Young. Produced by Harry Rapf and (uncredited Irving Thalberg). Portions filmed at Los Angeles City College, California and Cambridge, Massachusetts. Remake of a 1917 film from Essanay Studios.

Released on May 2 | 85 minutes/silent/video | Metro-Goldwyn-Mayer

A devil with the women! A terror with the men!

Bardelys the Magnificent (1926) Directed by King Vidor.

John Gilbert, Eleanor Boardman, Roy D'Arcy, Lionel Belmore, Emily Fitzroy, George K. Arthur, Arthur Lubin, Theodore Von Eltz, Karl Dane, Edward Connelly, Fred Malatesta, John T. Murray, Joseph [Joe Smith] Marba, Daniel G. Tomlinson, Emile Chautard, Max Barwyn, Marion 'Duke' Morrison [John Wayne], Gino Corrado, Lou Costello, Joan Crawford, Lon Poff, Rolfe Sedan, Carl Stockdale, Ellinor Vanderveer.

In 1600s France, swordsman and libertine Gilbert pursues maiden Boardman while clashing with a dastardly member of King Louis XIII's court. Wayne is a spear-carrying guard. Screenplay by Dorothy Farnum, from the 1906 novel by Rafael Sabatini. Portions filmed in Pasadena, California.

Released on September 30 | 91 minutes/silent/DVD | Metro-*Goldwyn*-Mayer

The foremost western thriller of the greatest western star!

The Great K & A Train Robbery (1926) Directed by Lewis Seiler.

Tom Mix, Tony the Wonder Horse, Dorothy Dwan, William Walling, Harry Grippe, Carl Miller, Edward Peil [Sr.], Curtis McHenry, Marion 'Duke' Morrison [John Wayne], Sammy Cohen, Duke R. Lee.

Railroad detective Mix goes undercover to catch the outlaws who are committing robberies against the line. Wayne is an unbilled extra; he also served behind the scenes as a prop man. Scenario by John Stone, from a novel by Paul Leicester Ford. Produced by Lew [Lewis] Seiler. Portions filmed at these Colorado locations: Shoshone Dam, Glenwood Springs; and Royal Gorge.

Released on October 17 | 53 minutes/silent/video/DVD | Fox

A thundering drama of Scottish Highlands! A spectacle of never-ending wonder! You'll love it as you love the song!

Annie Laurie (1927) Directed by John S. Robertson.

Lillian Gish, Norman Kerry, Creighton Hale, Joseph Striker, Hobart Bosworth, Patricia Avery, Russell Simpson, Brandon Hurst, David Torrence, Frank Currier, Marion 'Duke' Morrison [John Wayne], Richard Alexander, Mary Gordon, Carmencita Johnson, Henry Kolker, Margaret Mann, Carl 'Major' Rolf.

The feud involving two clans in Scotland becomes violent and deadly despite a romance between a girl and boy from the opposite factions. Wayne is an unbilled extra in a crowd. Story and screenplay by Josephine Lovett; titles by Marian Ainslee and Ruth Cummings.

Released on May 11 | 97 minutes/silent/2-strip Technicolor sequence | Metro-Goldwyn-Mayer

The All-American screen star in a picture for all Americans!

The Drop Kick (1927) Directed by Millard Webb.

Richard Barthelmess, Barbara Kent, Dorothy Revier, Eugene Strong, Alberta Vaughn, James Bradbury [Jr.], Brooks Benedict, Hedda Hopper, Mayme Kelso, George C. Pearce, Marion 'Duke' Morrison [John Wayne], Al Hill, Bill Elliott.

College football player Barthelmess is accused of murder when his coach dies. Complicating matters is the fact that the coach's widow is infatuated with the lad. Unbilled Wayne appears as a USC player and also a spectator in the stands. Scenario by Winifred Dunn from the short story *Glitter* by Katharine Brush. Produced by Richard A. Rowland and Ray Rockett. Portions filmed on the Berkeley campus of the University of California.

Released on September 25 | 62 minutes/silent/DVD | First National

Big as the heart of humanity!

Four Sons (1928) Directed by John Ford.

Margaret Mann, James Hall, Charles Morton, Francis X. Bushman Jr., George Meeker, June Collyer, Earle Foxe, Albert Gran, Frank Reicher, Archduke Leopold of Austria, Ferdinand Schumann-Heink, Jack Pennick, Hughie Mack, Michael Mark, Marion 'Duke' Morrison [John Wayne], Robert Parrish, Ruth Mix, August Tollaire, Frank Baker, George Blagoi, Stanley Blystone, Carl Boheme, Harry Cording, Constant Franke.

The sons of a German mother go into battle during World War One, but one of them (Hall) has journeyed to America and ends up serving with US forces and is called a traitor in his former homeland. Wayne plays the uncredited role of an officer. Screenplay by Philip Klein, from the 1926 *Saturday Evening Post* magazine story *Grandmother Bernie Learns Her Letters* by I. A. R. Wiley; (uncredited writing contribution by Herman Bing). Produced by (uncredited John Ford).

Song: *Little Mother* (Erno Rapee; Lew Pollack) | Winner of *Photoplay* magazine's Gold Medal of Honor Award | #4 on *Film Daily*'s Ten Best List | Music by (uncredited Erno Rapee and Carli Elinor)

Released on February 13 | 100 minutes/silent, with Movietonemusic and sound effects/video/ DVD | Fox

The touching story of a mother's love and self-denial.

Mother Machree (1928) Directed by (uncredited John Ford).

Victor McLaglen, Belle Bennett, Neil Hamilton, Ethel Clayton, Philippe DeLacey, Ted McNamara, William [Billy] Platt, Eulalie Jensen, Constance Howard, Pat Somerset, John MacSweeney, Vondell Darr, Aggie Herring, Wallace MacDonald, Jacques Rollens, Rodney Hildebrand, Joyce Wirard, Robert Parrish, Marion 'Duke' Morrison [John Wayne].

An Irish widow, looking for a better life in America, is only concerned for her son's happiness-and she makes many sacrifices so he can achieve it. Wayne appears in an unbilled bit. Scenario by Gertrude Orr, from *The Story of Mother Machree* by Rida Johnson Young. Produced by John Ford. Only reels one, two, five and seven survive.

Song: *Mother Machree* (Chauncey Olcott; Ernest Ball; Rida Johnson Young) | Music by Erno Rapee.

Released on March 5 | 75 minutes/silent, with Western Electric Movietone music, singing sequence and sound effects/tinted | Fox

Hangman's House (1928) Directed by (uncredited John Ford).

Victor McLaglen, Larry Kent, June Collyer, Earle Foxe, Hobart Bosworth, Baron O'Brien, Joseph Burke, Mary Gordon, Brian Desmond Hurst, Jack Pennick, Belle Stoddard, Marion 'Duke' Morrison [John Wayne].

The daughter of a retired Irish judge saw her father condemn many men to the gallows; now, on his deathbed, the old man asks that she marry a wealthy-but no-good-suitor…even though she loves another man. Wayne can be spotted among a crowd of horse race enthusiasts in one scene and as the silhouette of a condemned man in another. Scenario by Marion Orth; adaptation by Philip Klein, from the novel by Donn Byrne [Brian Oswald Donn-Byrne]; inter-titles written by Malcolm Stuart Boylan; uncredited writing contribution by Willard Mack. Produced by John Ford.

Released on May 13 | 72 minutes/silent/video/DVD | Fox

Noah's Ark (1928) Directed by Michael Curtiz and (uncredited Darryl F. Zanuck).

Dolores Costello, George O'Brien, Noah Beery [Sr.], Louise Fazenda, Gwynn [Guinn] Williams, Paul McAllister, Myrna Loy, Anders Randolf, Armand Kaliz, William V. Mong, Malcolm Waite, Nigel De-Brulier, Noble Johnson, Otto Hoffman, Marion 'Duke' Morrison [John Wayne], Rosita Delmar, Ward Bond, Joe Bonomo, Andy Devine, Torben Meyer.

O'Brien is in Europe, just prior to World War I, when he falls in love with German girl Costello after they are thrown together during a train wreck. In a parallel story, O'Brien and Costello portray lovers in biblical days just before the Great Flood. Wayne is an extra seen during the deluge. Screenplay by Anthony Coldeway, from a story by Darryl F. Zanuck (who also produced, uncredited). Portions filmed at these California locations: Garden of the Gods, Iverson Ranch, Chatsworth; and Big Basin.

Songs: *Heart o' Mine* (Louis Silvers; Billy Rose), *Du Liegst Mir Im Herzen* (German traditional, composer unknown), *Old Timer* (Silvers; Rose) | Music by Louis Silvers and (uncredited Alois Reiser).

Released on November 1 | (75-minute,108-minute versions/silent; Western Electric Vitaphone Sound sequences/video/laserdisc/DVD) Note: the 108-minute version contains sound sequences | Warner Brothers-First National

A college pug and a plucky newspaper girl take a fling at life behind the scenes of Broadway's fast and furious night life.

Speakeasy (1929) Directed by Benjamin Stoloff.

Paul Page, Lola Lane, Henry B. Walthall, Helen Ware, Sharon Lynn, Warren Hymer, Stuart Erwin, James Guilfoyle, Erville Alderson, Joseph Cawthorne, Ivan Linow, Marjorie Beebe, Sailor Vincent, Helen Lynch, Robert Wilbur, Marion 'Duke' Morrison [John Wayne].

Prizefighter Page's upcoming bout is covered by newspaper reporter Lane, who follows the story and learns that the boxer's manager has a plan to double-cross him. Wayne plays a speakeasy patron. Scenario by Frederick Hazlitt Brennan and Edwin J. Burke, from a play by Edward Knoblock and George Rosener. Presented by William Fox. Considered a lost film, although seven 16-inch soundtrack discs survive.

Released on March 8 | 62 minutes/Western Electric Movietone Sound | Fox

Face to face with the woman he came to betray...duty urged him on... love held him back...a titanic struggle of power and passion.

The Black Watch (1929) Directed by John Ford.

Victor McLaglen, Myrna Loy, David Torrence, David Rollins, Cyril Chadwick, Lumsden Hare, Roy D'Arcy, David Percy, Mitchell Lewis, Claude King, Walter Long, Francis Ford, Pat Somerset, Marion 'Duke' Morrison [John Wayne], Randolph Scott, Harry Allen, Frank Baker, Arthur Clayton, Gregory Gaye, Mary Gordon, Joyzelle Joyner, Bob Kortman, Tom London, Jack Pennick, Phillips Smalley, Lupita Tovar.

British soldier McLaglen is sent on a mission to infiltrate a dangerous rebel faction in India and rescue soldiers held there. The leader of the rebels turns out to be fetching Moslem-Hindu princess Loy. Wayne is a member of the 42nd Highlanders. Screenplay by John Stone, from the 1916 novel *King of the Khyber Rifles* by Talbot Mundy; James Kevin McGuinness contributed dialogue. Produced by (uncredited Winfield R. Sheehan).

Songs: *Flower of Delight* (William Kernell; Harlan Thompson), *Auld Lang Syne* (Scottish traditional; lyrics by Robert Burns) | Music by William Kernell.

Released on May 8 | 93 minutes/Western Electric Movietone Sound | Fox

A ripping romance of college cuties and their boyfriends.

Words and Music (1929) Directed by James Tinling.

Lois Moran, Tom Patricola, David Percy, Helen Twelvetrees, Frank Albertson, Elizabeth Patterson, Duke Morrison [John Wayne], William Orlamond, The Biltmore Quartet (Eddie Bush, Paul Gibbons, Bill Seckler, Charles Kirkpatrick), The Collier Sisters, Bubbles Crowell, Vina Gale, Muriel Gardner, Harriet Griffith, John Griffith, Charles Huff, Helen Hunt, Dorothy Jordan, Richard Keene, Helen Parrish, Arthur Springer, Jack Wade, Dorothy Ward, Ward Bond, Frances Dee.

A college musical competition, involving Moran, Percy and Wayne (as Pete Donahue), becomes less cheerful when a campus vamp (Twelvetrees) blackmails Moran into giving up the lead role. Screenplay by Andrew Bennison, from a story by Frederick Hazlitt Brennan and Jack McEdwards. Choreography by Edward Royce. Produced by Chandler Sprague. Considered a lost film.

Songs: *Steppin' Along* (William Kernell), *Too Wonderful for Words* (Dave Stamper; Kernell; Edmund Joseph; Paul Gerard Smith), *Shadows* (Archie Gottler; Con Conrad; Sidney D. Mitchell), *Good Old Mary Brown* (Kernell), *The Hunting Song* (Stamper; Harlan Thompson), *Beauty Waltz* (Stamper; Thompson), *Yours Sincerely* (Stamper; Thompson), *Take a Little Tip* (Stamper; Thompson) | Music by Con Conrad, Archie Gottler, Sidney D. Mitchell and Dave Stamper.

Released on August 18 | 81 minutes/silent and Western Electric Movietone Sound versions | Fox

Hear! See! The Army-Navy football classic in this all talking Fox Movietone!

Salute (1929) Directed by (uncredited John Ford and David Butler).

George O'Brien, Helen Chandler, William Janney, Stepin Fetchit, Frank Albertson, Joyce Compton, David Butler, Lumsden Hare, Clifford Dempsey, Ward Bond, Duke Morrison [John Wayne], John Breeden, Rex Bell, Lee Tracy, Ben Hall, Jack Pennick, Harry Tenbrook.

O'Brien and Janney are brothers attending West Point Military Academy and Annapolis, who develop an antagonism towards each other over pretty Chandler. They settle matters during the classic Army-Navy football game. Wayne plays Midshipman Bill, who takes part in a hazing. Screenplay by James K. McGuinness, from a story by John Stone and Tristram Tupper. Produced by John Ford. Portions filmed at the US Naval Academy, Annapolis, Maryland.

Song: *Anchors Aweigh* (Charles A. Zimmerman)

Released on September 1 | (84 minutes/Western Electric Movietone Sound | Fox

Real Harvard-Yale thrills brought to vivid life!

The Forward Pass (1929) Directed by Eddie [Edward F.] Cline.

Douglas Fairbanks Jr., Loretta Young, Guinn Williams, Marion Byron, Phyllis Crane, Bert Rome, Lane Chandler, Allen [Allan] Lane, Floyd Shackelford, Duke Morrison [John Wayne], Marjorie Kane, Rae Samuels.

College student Fairbanks falls for pretty Young while he is singled out for punishment by opposing players on the football field. Wayne is an extra. Screenplay by Howard Emmett Rogers, from a story by Harvey Gates. Considered a lost film; however, the Vitaphone Sound discs survive.

Michael H. Cleary, Herb Magidsen and Ned Washington songs: *One Minute of Heaven, I Gotta Have You, H'lo, Baby, Huddlin', Give It!, I Love to Hit Myself on the Head with a Hammer, Nobody But You.*

Released on November 10 | 78 minutes/Vitaphone Sound | First National

16 men trapped at the bottom of the sea...how they talked about women!

Men Without Women (1930) Directed by John Ford.

Kenneth McKenna, Frank Albertson, [J.] Farrell MacDonald, Warren Hymer, Paul Page, Walter McGrail, Stuart Erwin, George Le Guere, Charles [K.] Gerard, Ben Hendricks [Jr.], Harry Tenbrook, Warner Richmond, Duke Morrison [John Wayne], Pat Somerset, Roy Stewart, Robert Parrish, Frank Baker, Wong Chung, Ivan Lebedeff, Alberto Morin, Frank Richardson.

Tensions mount on board a sinking submarine as the men wonder who, if any of them, will be saved. Wayne is a radioman on the rescue crew. Screenplay by Dudley Nichols, from the story *Submarine* by James Kevin McGuinness and John Ford. Produced by Ford. Portions filmed in the waters between Long Beach, California, and Catalina Island, as well as in San Diego, California.

Voted one of the *10 Best Films* of 1929-30 by the *National Board of Review*.

Music by Carli Elinor and (uncredited Peter Brunelli, Glen Knight and R. H. Bassett).

Released on January 31 | 73 minutes/Western Electric Sound/DVD | Fox

The mastermind of gangdom gets a change of heart!

Born Reckless (1930) Directed by John Ford.

Edmund Lowe, Catherine Dale Owen, Lee Tracy, Marguerite Churchill, Warren Hymer, William Harrigan, Frank Albertson, Ilka Chase, Ferike Boros, Paul Porcasi, Joe Brown, Ben Bard, Pat Somerset, Eddie Gribbon, Mike Donlin, Paul Page, Roy Stewart, Jack Pennick, Ward Bond, Yola d'Avril, Duke Morrison [John Wayne], Stanley Blystone, Edwards Davis, Bill Elliott, Dick Gordon, Robert Homans, James A. Marcus, Randolph Scott.

Bootlegger Lowe is convicted then sent to war. When he returns, he begins a battle with rival gangster Hymer and falls in love with socialite Owen. Wayne plays Soldier. Screenplay by Dudley Nichols, from the novel *Louis Beretti* by Donald Henderson Clarke. Produced by James

Kevin McGuinness.

Music by (uncredited Peter Brunelli, George Lipschultz, Albert Hay Malotte and Jean Talbot).

Released on May 11 | 82 minutes/Western Electric Movietone Sound/DVD | Fox

William Fox presents a Movietone drama of the snowlands.

Rough Romance (1930) Directed by A.F. Erickson and (uncredited Benjamin Stoloff).

George O'Brien, Helen Chandler, Antonio Moreno, Roy Stewart, Harry Cording, David Hartford, Eddie Borden, Noel Francis, Frank Lanning, Duke Morrison [John Wayne].

Rugged woodsman O'Brien witnesses a murder and becomes the next target of the thieves who did the killing. Wayne plays a lumberjack. Screenplay by Elliott Lester and Donald Davis, from the novelette *The Girl Who Wasn't Wanted* by Kenneth B. Clarke. Produced by A.F. Erickson.

George A. Little and Johnny Burke songs: *The Song of the Lumberjacks, She's Somebody's Baby, Nobody Knows* | Music by (uncredited Peter Brunelli, R.H. Bassett and George Lipschultz).

Released on June 15 | 55 minutes/Western Electric Sound | Fox

Cheer Up and Smile (1930) Directed by Sidney Lanfield.

Arthur Lake, Dixie Lee, Olga Baclanova, 'Whispering' Jack Smith, Johnny Arthur, Charles Judels, John Darrow, Sumner Getchell, Franklin Pangborn, Buddy Messinger, Duke Morrison [John Wayne], J. Carrol Naish, Ward Bond, Joyce Compton, Eddie Kane, George Magrill, Ray Turner.

College boy Lake gets into trouble when he is hazed by a fraternity and tries to follow his ambitions as a musician. Wayne appears as Roy, a college student. Screenplay by Howard J. Green, from the story *If I Was Alone with You* by Richard Connell. Produced by Al Rockett.

Raymond Klages and Jesse Greer songs: *The Scamp of the Campus,*

Released on June 22 | 76 minutes/ Western Electric Movietone Sound | Fox

Wayne (here with Marguerite Churchill) was given an initial chance at stardom in *The Big Trail*, but it did not pan out due to the film's underperformance at the box office. Wayne had to wait nearly a decade to gain bonafide status as a star.

Youth, love and courage blaze through to glory!

The Big Trail (1930) Directed by Raoul Walsh and (uncredited Louis R. Loeffler).

John Wayne, Marguerite Churchill, El Brendel, Tully Marshall, Tyrone Power [Sr.], David Rollins, Frederick Burton, Ian Keith, Charles Stevens, Louise Carver, Ward Bond, Helen Parrish, DeWitt Jennings, Russ Powell, William V. Mong, Dodo Newton, Jack Peabody, Marcia Harris, Marjorie Leet, Frank Rainboth, Emslie Emerson, Andy Shuford, Gertrude Van Lent, Lucille Van Lent, Alphonse Ethier, Chief John Big Tree, Victor Adamson, Walter Bacon, Nino Cochise, Iron Eyes Cody, Don Coleman, Jack Curtis, Dannie MacGrant, Marilyn Harris, Marion Lessing, Pete Morrison, Robert Parrish, Apache Bill Russell.

Western about the first wagon train to set out for the West Coast by way of the Oregon Trail, with hundreds of miles and scores of Indians along the dangerous route. Wayne stars as frontiersman Breck Coleman, searching for his old trapper friend's murderer. Screenplay by Jack Peabody, Marie Boyle, Florence Postal, from a story by Hal G. Evarts; uncredited writing contribution by Raoul Walsh. Produced by Winfield R. Sheehan. Portions filmed in Oregon; California (Sacramento River; Sequoia National Park; Buttercup Dunes, Imperial County); Wyoming (Teton Pass; Jackson Hole; Yellowstone National Park); Arizona (Grand Canyon National Park; Yuma); Utah (Zion National Park; St. George); and Montana (Moise-National Buffalo Range).

Quotes: Breck Coleman (John Wayne): *"Say, Zeke, who was that he-grizzly that just went by?"*, Zeke (Tully Marshall): *"That's Red Flack. He's bullwhackin' for Wellmore. He's gonna whack Wellmore's train clear through to Oregon."*, Windy Bill (Ian Keith): *"You reckon you'll ever find out who downed old Ben?"*, Breck: *"It's just possible that a certain low-down coyote left his sign there."*

Music by (uncredited R.H. Bassett, Peter Brunelli, Alfred Dalby, Arthur Kay and Jack Virgil).

Released on October 2 | 122 minutes/Western Electric Sound/Fox 70mm Grandeur Wide Screen/video/DVD/Blu-Ray/National Film Registry 2006 | Fox

She wanted excitement and stopped at nothing to get it!

Girls Demand Excitement (1931) Directed by Seymour Felix.

Virginia Cherrill, John Wayne, Marguerite Churchill, Edward J. Nugent, Helen Jerome Eddy, Terrance Ray, Martha Sleeper, William Janney, Ralph Welles, George Irving, Winter Hall, Marion Byron, Addie McPhail, Jerry Mandy, Ray Cooke, Carter Gibson, Emerson Treacy.

Comedy-romance about a group of college men, led by Wayne (as Peter Brooks), who wish to banish all females from the university. His attitude softens after he meets pretty co-ed Cherrill. Screenplay by Harlan Thompson. Produced by Ralph Block.

Song: *"(There's Something About an) Old Fashioned Girl"* (Ray Henderson; B.G. DeSylva; Lew Brown)

Released on February 8 | 69 minutes/Western Electric Sound | Fox

Three Girls Lost (1931) Directed by Sidney Lanfield.

Loretta Young, Lew Cody, John Wayne, Joan Marsh, Joyce Compton, Paul Fix, Hank Mann, Kathrin Clare Ward, Bert Roach, Brooks Benedict, George Beranger, Ward Bond, Willie Fung, Sherry Hall, Charles Sullivan, Tenen Holtz, Robert Emmett O'Connor.

Urban architect Wayne (as Gordon Wales) befriends a trio of young women who have come to the city in search of their fortunes. When Wayne is accused of murdering a racketeer, one of the girls (Young) tries to help him clear his name. Screenplay by Bradley King, from a story by Robert D. [Hardy] Andrews.

Music by (uncredited R. H. Bassett).

Released on April 19 | 80 minutes/Western Electric Sound | Fox

Arizona/Men Are Like That (1931) George B. Seitz.

Laura LaPlante, John Wayne, June Clyde, Forrest Stanley, Nena [Nina] Quartero, Susan Fleming, Loretta Sayers, Hugh Cummings, Jack Cheatham, Geneva Mitchell, Adrian Morris, Harry Northrup, Charles Sellon.

Army lieutenant Bob Denton (Wayne), assigned to a southwest outpost, learns that his one-time girlfriend (LaPlante) is married to his mentor and commanding officer. LaPlante decides to further 'get back' at Wayne when he begins a romance with her sister (Clyde). Screenplay by Robert Riskin and Dorothy Howell, from the 1899 play *Arizona* by Augustus Thomas. Produced by Harry Cohn.

Music by (uncredited Mischa Bakaleinikoff).

Released on June 27 | 70 minutes/Western Electric Sound/DVD | Columbia

You'll be baffled and thrilled by this exciting story of love, intrigue, murder and mystery behind the scenes of a New York stage show!

The Deceiver (1931) Directed by Louis King.

Lloyd Hughes, Dorothy Sebastian, Ian Keith, Natalie Moorhead, Richard Tucker, George Byron, Greta Granstedt, Murray Kinnell, DeWitt Jennings, Allan Ernest Garcia, Harvey Clark, Sidney Bracey, Frank Holliday, Colin Campbell, Nick Copeland, John Wayne.

When a lecherous Shakespearean actor (Keith) is murdered, cast and crew in a Broadway theater set out to discover who committed the crime. Wayne appears as the corpse of Richard Thorpe, the victim of a stabbing. Screenplay by Jo Swerling, Jack Cunningham and Charles Logue, from the story *It Might Have Happened* by Abem Finkel and Bella Muni.

Released on November 21 | 66 minutes/Western Electric Sound | Columbia

Riding like a whirlwind-fighting like a fiend-enduring like a man!

The Range Feud (1931) Directed by D. Ross Lederman.

Buck Jones, John Wayne, Susan Fleming, Ed LeSaint, William Walling, Wallace MacDonald, Harry Woods, Frank Austin, Glenn Strange, Lew Meehan, Jim Corey, Bob Reeves, Frank Ellis, Hank Bell, Jack Curtis, Al Taylor, Blackjack Ward.

Jones has recently become sheriff and one of his first acts is to arrest his foster brother (Wayne, as Clint Turner) for the murder of Fleming's father. Screenplay by George Plympton and Milton Krims, from a story by Krims. Produced by Irving Briskin. Portions filmed at these California locations: Vasquez Rocks, Agua Dulce and Walker Ranch, Newhall.

Quote: Clint Turner (John Wayne): (On his way to be hanged for a crime he didn't commit) *"Kinda expected Buck'd be standing by me on my last ride."*

Music by (uncredited Irving Bibo and Dan Dougherty).

Released on December 1 | 58 minutes/Western Electric Sound/video/DVD | Columbia

He wanted power-she wanted love!

Maker of Men (1931) Directed by Edward Sedgwick.

Jack Holt, Richard Cromwell, Joan Marsh, Natalie Moorhead, Walter Catlett, John Wayne, Robert Alden, Richard Tucker, Ethel Wales, Paul Hurst, Corbet Morris, Ward Bond, Sidney Bracey, Buster Crabbe, Joe Sawyer.

Holt is a college football coach who does not get along too well with his son (Cromwell), a gridiron star who ends up playing for an opposing team. Wayne is Dusty, who sells out his team to a pack of gamblers. Screenplay by Howard J. Green, from a story by Green and Edward Sedgwick.

Released on December 18 | 71 minutes/Western Electric Sound | Columbia

A crashing adventure serial!

The Shadow of the Eagle (1932/serial) Directed by Ford Beebe and (uncredited B. Reeves Eason).

John Wayne, Dorothy Gulliver, Walter Miller, Kenneth Harlan, Richard Tucker, Pat O'Malley, Edmund Burns, Yakima Canutt, Roy D'Arcy, Billy West, Edward Hearn, Lloyd Whitlock, Little Billy [Rhodes], Ivan Linow, James Bradbury Jr., Ernie S. Adams, Bud Osborne, Monty [Monte] Montague, Murdock MacQuarrie.

An anonymous pilot writes messages in the sky attacking a large airplane corporation. As people begin to disappear, another pilot (Wayne, as Craig McCoy)-himself a suspect-is hired to find the mysterious airborne rogue. Screenplay by Ford Beebe, Colbert Clark and Wyndham Gittens. Produced by Nat Levine. Portions filmed in these California locations: Antelope Valley, Bronson Canyon, Lancaster and Los Angeles.

Chapters: 1. The Carnival Mystery, 2. Pinholes, 3. The Eagle Strikes, 4. The Man of a Million Voices, 5. The Telephone Cipher, 6. The Code of the Carnival, 7. Eagle or Vulture?, 8. On the Spot, 9. When Thieves Fall Out, 10. The Man Who Knew, 11. The Eagle's Wing, 12. The Shadow Unmasked

Music by (uncredited Lee Zahler).

Released on February 1 | 218 minutes/Disney Recording/video/DVD | Mascot

Afraid of nothing!

Texas Cyclone (1932) Directed by D. Ross Lederman.

Tim McCoy, Shirley Grey, Wheeler Oakman, John Wayne, Wallace MacDonald, James [Jim] Farley, Harry Cording, Vernon Dent, Walter Brenan [Brennan], Mary Gordon, Al Haskell, Monte Montague, Bud Osborne, F.R. Smith, Glenn Strange, Al Taylor, Bob Reeves, Tex Palmer, Bud McClure, Jack Kirk, Alfred P. James, Jack Hendricks, Herman Hack, Jack Evans, Ken Cooper.

McCoy rides into a frontier town and is immediately mistaken for a man believed to have died years before. He also pits himself against rustlers as he tries to find out the mystery behind the mistaken identity. Wayne plays Steve Pickett, an honest cowpoke. Screenplay by Randall Faye, from a story by William Colt MacDonald. Produced by Irving Briskin. Portions filmed at these California locations: Iverson Ranch, Chatsworth; and Santa Clarita.

Quotes: Texas Grant (Tim McCoy): *"These rustlers got you buffaloed too?"*, Steve Pickett (John Wayne): *"Nope, they ain't. There ain't nobody got me buffaloed!"*

Released on February 24 | 63 minutes/Western Electric Sound/video/DVD | Columbia

His latest and greatest outdoor romance!

Two Fisted Law (1932) Directed by D. Ross Lederman.

Tim McCoy, Alice Day, Wheeler Oakman, Tully Marshall, Wallace MacDonald, John Wayne, Walter Brennan, Richard Alexander, Bud Osborne, Arthur Thalasso, Merrill McCormack, Jack Hendricks, Jack Evans, Rube Dalroy, Hank Bell.

McCoy loses his ranch to crooked banker Oakman when rustlers (hired by Oakman) steal his cattle, leaving him unable to repay money he borrowed. McCoy then turns to silver mining and finds the means to get back at Oakman and his gang when they try to swindle Day's ranch. Wayne plays Duke, a cowhand. Screenplay by Kurt Kempler, from a story by William Colt MacDonald. Produced by Irving Briskin. Portions filmed at the following California locations: Andy Jauregui Ranch, Newhall; Trem Carr Ranch, Newhall; Walker Ranch, Newhall; and Santa Clarita.

Quotes: Tim Clark (Tim McCoy): (Regarding his eviction from his ranch) *"Just remember, Russell was acting within his legal rights."*, Duke (John Wayne): *"Legal be hanged! He promised to renew that note of yours and then wouldn't. It may be legal, all I can wish for Russell is a rough horse, a cactus saddle and a long journey."*

Music by (uncredited Mischa Bakaleinikoff, Sam Perry, Irving Bibo and Milan Roder).

Released on June 8 | 64 minutes/Western Electric Sound/video/DVD | Columbia

Right smack on the ol' button! It's a sock on the chin...in the heart.

Lady and Gent (1932) Directed by Stephen Roberts.

George Bancroft, Wynne Gibson, Charles Starrett, James Gleason, John Wayne, Morgan Wallace, James Crane, William Halligan, Billy Butts, Joyce Compton, Frank McGlynn Sr., Charles [Charley] Grapewin, Lew Kelly, Syd Saylor, Russ Powell, Frank Darien, Hal Price, A.S. 'Pop' Byron, John Beck, Tom Kennedy, Frank Dawson, Sheila Bromley, Eddy Chandler, Robert Homans, Sidney Miller, Frank Mills, Bob Perry, Philip Sleeman, Phil Tead, Fred Wallace, Carolyn Spahn.

A veteran prizefighter and his nightclub-singer girlfriend are entrusted with the care of his dead manager's son. They retire to a small town and see the boy grow up to become a success at college. When the young man desires to become a boxer, his foster parents have trouble dissuading him. Wayne plays another pugilist, Buzz Kinney. Written by Grover Jones and William Slavens McNutt.

Song: *Everyone Knows But You* (Arthur Johnston; Sam Coslow) | Academy Award Nomination | (Writing-Original Story) Grover Jones and William Slavens McNutt. | Music by (uncredited John Leipold).

Released on July 15 | (84 minutes/Western Electric Noiseless Recording) | Paramount

A thriller of the roaring rails in twelve crashing episodes!

The Hurricane Express (1932/serial) Directed by J.P. McGowan and Armand Schaefer.

John Wayne, Shirley Gray [Grey], Conway Tearle, Tully Marshall, Edmund Breese, Lloyd Whitlock, Alan [Al] Bridge, Mathew [Matthew] Betz, Joseph [W.] Girard, James [P.] Burtis, Ernie S. Adams, Charles King, J. Farrell MacDonald, Al Ferguson, Glenn Strange, Victor Adamson, Yakima Canutt, Henry Hall, Rodney Hildebrande, Eddie Parker, Fred Parker, Fred 'Snowflake' Toones.

A masked villain, who is able to assume the identity of anyone he chooses, is out to destroy the L & R Railroad. It is up to one man (Wayne, as Larry Baker) to stop him before he is framed for the crime himself. Screenplay by George Morgan, J.P. McGowan and (uncredited Harold Tarshis), from a story by Colbert Clark, Barry [A.] Sarecky and Wyndham Gittens. Produced by (uncredited Nat Levine). Portions filmed at these California locations: Santa Clarita, Bronson Caves, Bronson Canyon, Los Angeles, Newhall and Saugus.

Chapters: 1. The Wrecker, 2. Flying Pirates, 3. The Masked Killer, 4. Buried Alive, 5. Danger Lights, 6. The Airport Mystery, 7. Sealed Lips, 8. Outside the Law, 9. The Invisible Enemy, 10. The Wrecker's Secret, 11. Wings of Death, 12. Unmasked

Quote: Larry Baker (John Wayne): (After his father's fatal crash) *"Whoever's back of it means my father was murdered, and I'll bring that man to justice if it takes the rest of my life."*

Music by (uncredited Lee Zahler).

Released on August 1 | 227 minutes/Disney Film Recording/video/DVD | Mascot

Yipee! Here comes the ridin', fightin' king of the range!

Ride Him, Cowboy (1932) Directed by Fred Allen.

John Wayne, Duke (a horse), Ruth Hall, Henry B. Walthall, Otis Harlan, Harry Gribbon, Edmund Cobb, Lafe McKee, Bud Osborne, Charles Sellon, Glenn Strange, Frank Hagney, Chuck Baldra, Bob Burns, Edward Burns, Fred Burns, Ben Corbett, Jim Corey, Helen Dickson, Adabelle Driver, Frank Ellis, Frank Fanning, William Gillis, Tiny Jones, Jack Kirk, Murdock MacQuarrie, Bud McClure, Rose Plumer, Hal Price, F.R. Smith, Blackjack Ward, Slim Whitaker. Screenplay by Scott Mason, adapted from a 1923 novel by Kenneth Taylor Perkins.

Produced by Leon Schlesinger and Sid Rogell. Remake of the 1926 film *The Unknown Cavalier*, which provided stock footage for this picture.

Wayne (as John Drury) rescues a horse that has been accused of killing a rancher and sets out to find the real (two-legged) murderer. However, the culprit-known as the Hawk-turns the tables and leaves Wayne on the desert to die. The Hawk makes his mistake when he does not figure on the resourcefulness of the equine Duke.

Quote: John Drury (John Wayne): *"Where I come from we don't shoot horses when they get ornery; we tame 'em"*.

Songs: *She'll Be Comin' 'Round the Mountain When She Comes* (traditional, composer unknown) (played on the harmonica by Wayne), *Till We Meet Again* (Richard A. Whiting; Ray Egan)

Released on August 27 | Box Office: $220,000 | 55 minutes/Western Electric Sound/video/DVD | Vitagraph/Warner Brothers

A new kind of football story! He became a great gridiron star-but he forgot to be himself!

That's My Boy (1932) Directed by Roy William Neill.

Richard Cromwell, Dorothy Jordan, Mae Marsh, Arthur Stone, Douglass Dumbrille, Lucien Littlefield, Leon Waycoff [Ames], Russell Saunders, Sumner Getchell, Otis Harlan, Oscar 'Dutch' Hendrian, Elbridge Anderson, Crilly Butler, Douglas Haig, Oscar Apfel, Ward Bond, Buster Crabbe, Rolfe Sedan, Robert Warwick, John Wayne, Harrison Greene, Frank LaRue, Joan Marsh.

Cromwell becomes a football whiz at Bedford University, but is almost undone by his involvement in a shady stock scheme. Gridiron drama with Wayne seen as a Harvard player named Taylor. Screenplay by Norman Krasna, from the novel by Francis Wallace. Produced by Roy William Neill. Portions filmed at these California locations: Los Angeles Memorial Coliseum and the University of Southern California at Los Angeles.

Music by Charles Kisco.

Released on October 6 | 71 minutes/Western Electric Sound | Columbia

Quick on the trigger...lightning fast on the draw!

The Big Stampede (1932) Directed by Tenny Wright.

John Wayne, Duke (a horse), Noah Beery [Sr.], Paul Hurst, Mae Madison, Luis Alberni, Berton Churchill, Sherwood Bailey, Lafe McKee, Joseph [W.] Girard, Iron Eyes Cody, John Ince, Bud Osborne, Glenn Strange, Slim Whitaker, Chuck Baldra, Tom Bay, Hank Bell, Edward Burns, Fred Burns, Jim Corey, Frank Ellis, Bob Fleming, Al Haskell, G. Raymond Nye, Henry Otho, Tex Phelps, Rose Plumer, S.S. Simon, Al Taylor, Leonard Trainor, Blackjack Ward.

The Big Stampede was typical of the Saturday matinee westerns Wayne toiled in for nearly a decade after failing to gain stardom in *The Big Trail* (1930)

Undercover lawman Wayne (as John Steele) joins a wagon train herding 5,000 head of cattle into lawless territory where two rustling gangs operate unchallenged. Wayne splits the factions by deputizing the less dangerous outlaws to go after deadly Beery's outfit. Screenplay by Kurt Kempler, from the story *Land Beyond the Law* by Marion Jackson. Produced by Leon Schlesinger and Sid Rogell. Remake of **Land Beyond the Law** (1927) which provided stock footage for this film.

Music by (uncredited Bernhard Kaun).

Released on October 8 | 55 minutes/Western Electric Sound/video/DVD | Vitagraph/Warner Brothers

There's more than gold at stake in this battle to the death!

Haunted Gold (1932) Directed by Mack V. Wright.

John Wayne, Duke (a horse), Sheila Terry, Harry Woods, Erville Alderson, Otto Hoffman, Martha Mattox, Blue Washington, Bud Osborne, Tom Bay, Bob Burns, Edward Burns, Ben Corbett, Jim Corey, Charles LeMoyne, John T. Prince, Blackjack Ward, Slim Whitaker.

Wayne (as John Mason), Terry and Woods converge on a ghost town in search of gold. Wayne already owns a half-share of a mine, but Terry has lost her half-share to no-good Woods. Wayne suspects Woods of illegally holding his claim and moves to rectify the situation, but the arrival of a mysterious 'Phantom' complicates matters. Screenplay by Adele Buffington. Produced by Leon Schlesinger and Sid Rogell. Animated title sequence directed by (uncredited Hugh Harman and Rudolf Ising). Portions filmed at these California locations: Iverson Ranch, Chatsworth; Lasky Mesa, Los Angeles; Warner Ranch, Calabasas. Portions also filmed in Yuma, Arizona.

Quotes: Joe Ryan (Harry Woods): *"And who invited you into this game?"*, John Mason (John Wayne): *"Looked to me like someone was getting a dirty deal. Just thought I'd cut in."*, Ryan: *"Cutting in here ain't the healthiest thing you could do."*, Mason: *"Well, I'll take that chance. You boys better get moving."*

Songs: *She'll Be Comin' 'Round the Mountain* (traditional, composer unknown) (played by Wayne on the harmonica), *Sweet Genevieve* (Henry Tucker) | Music by (uncredited Leo F. Forbstein and Bernhard Kaun).

Released on December 17 | (58 minutes/Western Electric Noiseless Recording/video/DVD | Vitaphone/Warner Brothers

The story of how the telegraph was laid from East to West, with plenty of hardships and Indian attacks.

The Telegraph Trail (1933) Directed by Tenny Wright.

John Wayne, Duke (a horse), Frank McHugh, Marceline Day, Otis Harlan, Albert J. Smith, Yakima Canutt, Lafe McKee, Bud Osborne, Chuck Baldra, Chief John Big Tree, Bob Burns, Ben Corbett, Frank Ellis, Bob Fleming, Clarence Geldert, Jack Jones, Jack Kirk, Arie Ortego, Al Taylor, Blackjack Ward, Slim Whitaker, Bud McClure.

Cavalry scout John Trent (Wayne) is assigned to see that telegraph lines are completed on the frontier, but discovers that scheming businessman Smith has enlisted an Indian tribe to attack the operation and keep the lines from going up. Screenplay by Kurt Kempler. Produced by Leon Schlesinger and Sid Rogell. Wayne's singing voice was dubbed by Jack Kirk.

Songs: *Oh, Susanna* (Stephen Foster) (played by Wayne on the harmonica), *Mandy Lee* (Thurland Chattaway) | Music by Leo F. Forbstein.

Released on March 18 | 54 minutes/Western Electric Sound/video/DVD | Vitagraph/Warner Brothers

A story of the modern escapades of the most famous adventurers in all fiction!

The Three Musketeers (1933/serial) Directed by Colbert Clark and Armand Schaefer.

Jack Mulhall, Raymond Hatton, Francis X. Bushman Jr., John Wayne, Ruth Hall, Creighton Chaney [Lon Chaney Jr.], Hooper Atchley, Gordon DeMain, Robert Frazer, Noah Beery Jr., Al Ferguson, Edward Piel [Peil, Sr.], William Desmond, George Magrill, Robert Warwick, Emile Chautard, Yakima Canutt, Wilfred Lucas, Kermit Maynard, Ken Cooper, Frank Ellis, Rodney Hildebrand, Tracy Layne, Merrill McCormick, Charles Middleton.

This action film casts the Musketeers in a modern setting as Foreign Legionnaires fighting for truth, justice and brotherhood as they strive to capture El Shaitan--the leader of a sinister group out to destroy the Legion. Wayne plays Lieutenant Tom Wayne, an aviator who comes to the aid of the trio. Screenplay by Norman [S.] Hall, Colbert Clark, Barney [A.] Sarecky, Ben [Bennett] Cohen and Wyndham Gittens, based loosely on the 1844 novel by Alexandre Dumas. Produced by Nat Levine. Portions filmed at these California locations: Imperial County; Bronson Caves and Canyon, Los Angeles; Buttercup Valley; and Griffith Park, Los Angeles. Portions also filmed in Yuma, Arizona.

Chapters: 1. The Fiery Circle, 2. One for All and All for One, 3. The Master Spy, 4. Pirates of the Desert, 5. Rebel Rifles, 6. Death's Marathon, 7. Naked Steel, 8. The Master Strikes, 9. The Fatal Circle, 10. Trapped, 11. The Measure of a Man, 12. The Glory of Comrade.

Music by Lee Zahler.

Released on April | (210 minutes/International Film Recording/video/DVD | Mascot

Desperately he courted death because he loved an unfaithful girl!

Central Airport (1933) Directed by William A. Wellman and (uncredited Alfred E. Green).

Richard Barthelmess, Sally Eilers, Tom Brown, Grant Mitchell, James Murray, Claire McDowell, Willard Robertson, Arthur Vinton, Irving Bacon, Louise Beavers, Dick Elliott, James Ellison, Charles Lane, Chris-Pin Martin, Sam McDaniel, J. Carrol Naish, Jed Prouty, John Wayne, Charles Williams, Toby Wing, Harry C. Bradley, James Bush, Harry Depp, James Donlan, Lester Dorr, Betty Jane Graham, Harrison Green, Frances Miles, John 'Skins' Miller, Walter Miller, Bert Moorhouse, Bradley Page, Russ Powell, George Regas, Fred 'Snowflake' Toones.

The romantic rivalry between adventurous pilots (and brothers) Barthelmess and Brown-over parachuting daredevil Eilers-leaves Barthelmess bitter and wounded…but he is the only hope for saving Brown when his plane goes down in the Gulf of Mexico. Wayne is Brown's co-pilot in the ill-fated plane. Screenplay by Rian James and James Seymour, from the story *Hawk's Mate* by John C. 'Jack' Moffitt. Produced by (uncredited Hal B. Wallis). Portions filmed at Glendale Grand Central Air Terminal, California.

Song: *Remembering* (Rosetta Duncan; Vivian Duncan | Music by (uncredited Howard Jackson, Bernhard Kaun and Cliff Hess).

Released on April 15 | Box Office: $747,000 | 75 minutes/Vitaphone Sound/DVD | Warner Brothers-First National

Reach for a piece of sky, stranger-or you'll get six feet of earth!

Somewhere in Sonora (1933) Directed by Mack V. Wright.

John Wayne, Duke (a horse), Henry B. Walthall, Shirley Palmer, Ann Faye [Fay], J.P. McGowan, Paul Fix, Ralph Lewis, Frank Rice, Billy Franey, Bud Osborne, Glenn Strange, Dick Botiller, Tommy Coats, Joe Dominguez, Frank Ellis, Bob Fleming, Pat Harmon, Cactus Mack, Slim Whitaker, Blackie Whiteford, G. Raymond Nye, William McCall, Charles LeMoyne, Jack Hendricks, Jack Evans, Art Dillard, Jim Corey, Barney Beasley, Sam Appel.

Wayne is John Bishop, who gets out of a tight spot thanks to help from Walthall. In return, Wayne goes to Mexico in search of Walthall's missing son-who has reluctantly joined McGowan's deadly gang. In order to get the young man free of the outlaws, Wayne joins the gang himself. Screenplay by Joe [Joseph Anthony] Roach, from the 1924 *Saturday Evening Post* magazine story *Somewhere South in Sonora* by Will Levington Comfort. Produced by Leon Schlesinger and Sid Rogell. Portions filmed at these California locations: Alabama Hills, Lone Pine; and Sonora. Remake of a silent 1927 Ken Maynard western of the same name.

Music by Leo F. Forbstein.

Released on May 27 | (57 minutes/Western Electric Noiseless Recording/video/DVD | Vitagraph/Warner Brothers

Too strange to be fiction.

The Life of Jimmy Dolan (1933) Directed by Archie Mayo.

Douglas Fairbanks Jr., Loretta Young, Aline MacMahon, Guy Kibbee, Lyle Talbot, Fifi Dorsay [D'Orsay], Harold Huber, Shirley Grey, George Meeker, John Wayne, Arthur Hohl, Dawn O'Day [Anne Shirley], Edward Arnold, Mickey Rooney, Joan Barclay, Robert Barrat, Don Brodie, George Chandler, Billy Coe, Arthur De Kuh, James Donlan, David Durand, Sam Godfrey, Allen 'Farina' Hoskins, Mike Lally, Clarence Muse, Bradley Page, Sammy Stein, Arthur Vinton.

Prizefighter Fairbanks goes on the run after accidentally killing a man and finds refuge at a farm for physically-challenged children. He gains a renewed interest in life when he meets Young, one of the women who run the farm. Wayne is a boxer named Smith. Screenplay by David Boehm and Erwin Gelsey, from the 1933 play *Sucker* by Bertram Millhauser and Beulah Marie Dix. Produced by Hal B. Wallis.

Music by (uncredited Cliff Hess and Bernhard Kaun).

Released on June 3 | (89 minutes/Vitaphone Sound | Warner Brothers

He was a sucker for women-and she knew her fish!

His Private Secretary (1933) Directed by Philip H. Whitman.

Evalyn Knapp, John Wayne, Reginald Barlow, Alec B. Francis, Arthur Hoyt, Natalie Kingston, Patrick Cunning, Al St. John, Hugh Kidder, Mickey Rentschler.

Wayne (as Dick Wallace) is the playboy son of a banker who would rather chase women than pay attention to work. He becomes seriously smitten with Knapp, a minister's granddaughter, and finally settles down. However, his father assumes she is just another gold-digger and refuses to meet her. Screenplay by Jack Francis Natteford, from a story by Lewis D. Collins; (uncredited writing contribution by Sam Katzman). Produced by (uncredited Sam Katzman), Al Alt and D.J. Mountan. Portions filmed in New York City.

Quotes:Jenkins-Digges, the butler (Hugh Kidder): (opens door to admit Dick and friends) *"Shhh!"*, Dick Wallace (John Wayne): (entering loud and inebriated) *"Hello, Diggsy, old boy!"*, Jenkins: *"Your father's trying to sleep, sir."*, Dick: *"Ohhh...better let sleeping dads lie, eh, Diggs?"*

Music by (uncredited Abe Meyer).

Released on June 10 | Box Office: $95,000 | 60 minutes/Freeman Lane Recording/video/DVD | Colam/Screencraft Productions/ Showmen's Pictures/Marcy

She climbed the ladder of success-wrong by wrong!

Baby Face (1933) Directed by Alfred E. Green.

Barbara Stanwyck, George Brent, Donald Cook, Alphonse Ethier, Henry Kolker, Margaret Lindsay, Arthur Hohl, John Wayne, Robert Barrat, Douglas[s] Dumbrille, Theresa Harris, Joan Barclay, Charles Coleman, James Murray, Nat Pendleton, Edward Van Sloan, James Bush, Heinie Conklin, Jack Curtis, Frank Darien, John Elliott, Grace Hayle, Maynard Holmes, Reginald Mason, Spec O'Donnell, Donna Mae Roberts, Matty Roubert, Cliff Saum, Charles Sellon, Sailor Vincent, Toby Wing.

A harsh life has turned Stanwyck into a heartless user of men, regarded by her as sexual stepping stones to success. Wayne is Jimmy McCoy Jr., a filing office clerk who gets cast aside by Stanwyck. Screenplay by

Gene Markey and Kathryn Scola, from a story by Mark Canfield [Darryl F. Zanuck]. Produced by William LeBaron and (uncredited Raymond Griffith).

Quotes: Lily Powers (Barbara Stanwyck): *"Oh, hello, Jimmy."*, Jimmy McCoy Jr. (John Wayne): *"Listen, Baby Face, how 'bout havin' dinner tonight? I've got two tickets for the Vanities."*

Music by Leo F. Forbstein.

Released on July 13 | Box Office: $452,000 | 75 minutes/Vitaphone Sound/National Film Registry 2005/video/laserdisc/DVD | Warner Brothers

He'll out-fight or out-shoot the toughest hombre of the plains!

The Man from Monterey (1933) Directed by Mack V. Wright.

John Wayne, Duke (a horse), Ruth Hall, Luis Alberni, Donald Reed, Nena [Nina] Quartero, Francis Ford, Lafe McKee, Lillian Leighton, Charles [Slim] Whitaker, Tom London, Chris-Pin Martin, Sam Appel, Hank Bell, Ralph Bucko, Roy Bucko, Jim Corey, Joe Dominguez, Frank Ellis, Jack Evans, Charles Geldart, George Hazel, Bud McClure, John T. Prince, Blackjack Ward.

Cavalry officer Wayne (as Captain John Holmes) is sent to have Spanish land grant owners register their property in California before it becomes public domain. With an eye for grabbing a large parcel of land, schemer Ford kidnaps ranch owner McKee so he will forfeit his holdings. Wayne enlists the aid of outlaw Whitaker-who owes him a favor-to fight Ford. Screenplay by Lesley [Leslie] Mason. Produced by Leon Schlesinger and Sid Rogell.

Quotes: Captain John Holmes (John Wayne): *"You know, Felipe, there's something suspicious about all this."*, Felipe (Luis Alberni): *"Senor, we shall consult the cards. They never fail. Ah, they never fail."*, John: *"Aw, stick those cards in your…"*, Felipe: *"Senor!"*, John: *"In your pocket. Come on."*

Music by (uncredited Leo F. Forbstein).

Released on July 15 | Box Office: $193,000 | 57 minutes/Western Electric Noiseless Recording/video/DVD | Vitagraph/Warner Brothers

He wrote the code of justice with a blazing six-gun!

Riders of Destiny (1933) Directed by Robert N. Bradbury.

John Wayne, Cecilia Parker, Forrest Taylor, George [Gabby] Hayes, Al St. John, Heinie Conklin, Yakima Canutt, Earl Dwire, Lafe McKee, Addie Foster, Silver Tip Baker, Horace B. Carpenter, Anne Howard, Si Jenks, Tex Palmer, Hal Price.

A corrupt rancher (Taylor) uses his control of the local water supply to squeeze out his neighbors-until undercover cowboy Wayne (as Singin' Sandy Sanders) rides into the territory to thwart Taylor's schemes. Story and screenplay by R.N. [Robert N.] Bradbury. Produced by (uncredited Paul Malvern). Portions filmed at the following California locations: Andy Jauregui Ranch, Newhall; Kernville; Palmdale; Trem Carr Ranch, Newhall; and Lancaster. John Wayne's singing was dubbed by Bill Bradbury.

Songs: *A Cowboy's Song of Fate* (composer unknown), *Song of the Wild* (composer unknown)

Released on October 10 | 58 minutes/Balsley & Phillips Recording/computer color version/video/DVD | Lone Star/Monogram

College Coach (1933) Directed by William A. Wellman.

Dick Powell, Ann Dvorak, Pat O'Brien, Arthur Byron, Lyle Talbot, Hugh Herbert, Arthur Hohl, Charles C. Wilson, Guinn Williams, Nat Pendleton, Phillip Reed, Donald Meek, Berton Churchill, Harry Beresford, Herman Bing, Joe Sauers [Sawyer], Philip Faversham, Ward Bond, Sammy Fain, John Wayne, William Austin, Jesse Hibbs, Milton Kibbee, Sam McDaniel, Edward McWade, Dave O'Brien, Jed Prouty.

Hard-driving football coach Pat O'Brien spends all his time building Calvert College's gridiron roster, which includes singing chemistry student-player Powell. Wayne has a bit role as a student who greets Powell in an early scene. Story and screenplay by Niven Busch and Manuel Seff. Produced by (uncredited Robert Lord). Portions filmed at these California locations: Los Angeles Memorial Coliseum; Rose Bowl, Pasadena; Los Angeles City College (Millspaugh Hall on the old UCLA campus).

Songs: *Men of Calvert* (Sammy Fain; Irving Kahal), *Lonely Lane* (Fain; Kahal), *Meet Me in the Gloaming* (Arthur Freed; Al Hoffman; Al Goodhart) *What Will I Do Without You?* (Hilda Gottlieb; Johnny Mercer) | Music by (uncredited Bernhard Kaun).

Released on November 4 | (75 minutes/Vitaphone Sound/DVD | Warner Brothers

Romance rides in a drama of thundering hoofs and blazing guns!

Sagebrush Trail/An Innocent Man (1933) Directed by Armand Schaefer.

John Wayne, Nancy Shubert, Lane Chandler, Yakima Canutt, Henry Hall, Wally Wales [Hal Taliaferro], Art Mix, Bob Burns, Ted Adams, Silver Tip Baker, Hank Bell, William Dyer, Tex Palmer, Hal Price, Slim Whitaker, Blackjack Ward, Archie Ricks, Tex Phelps, Julie Kingdon, Jack Jones, Wally Howe, Tommy Coats.

Wayne (as John Brant, also known as Smith), wrongfully convicted of murder, escapes to find the real killer by infiltrating an outlaw gang. Story and screenplay by Lindsley Parsons, from a story by (uncredited Will Beale). Produced by (uncredited Trem Carr and Paul Malvern). Wayne's stunt double was Yakima Canutt. Portions filmed at these California locations: Bronson Caves and Canyon, Los Angeles; Trem Carr Ranch, Newhall; and Kernville.

Released on December 15 | 55 minutes/Balsley & Phillips Recording/computer color version/video/DVD | Lone Star/Monogram

Action all the way, a hundred in a fight for gold and a girl!

The Lucky Texan/Gold Strike Fever (1934) Directed by Robert N. Bradbury.

John Wayne, Barbara Sheldon, Lloyd Whitlock, George ['Gabby'] Hayes, Yakima Canutt, Ed [Eddie] Parker, Gordon DeMain, Earl Dwire, Phil Dunham, Artie Ortego, Tommy Coats, Jack Evans, Wally Howe, John Ince, Philip Kieffer, Julie Kingdon, George Morrell, Tex Palmer, Tex Phelps, Jack Rockwell, Hal Taliaferro.

Wayne (as Jerry Mason) takes on a mining partner (Hayes) and they strike it rich. When Hayes is shot, Wayne is indicted for his murder.

What he doesn't tell the law is that Gabby survived the shooting and they both plan a surprise at Wayne's trial. Story and screenplay by Robert N. Bradbury. Produced by Paul Malvern. Portions filmed at these California locations: Kernville; and Trem Carr Ranch, Newhall.

Released on January 22 | (55 minutes/computer color version/video/DVD | Lone Star/Monogram

A two-gun son of the west takes the law into his own hands!

West of the Divide (1934) Directed by Robert N. Bradbury.

John Wayne, Virginia Faire Brown [Brown Faire], George ['Gabby'] Hayes, Lloyd Whitlock, Yakima Canutt, Lafe McKee, Billie [Billy] O'Brien, Dick Dickinson, Earl Dwire, Hal Taliaferro, Horace B. Carpenter, Philip Kieffer, Blackie Whiteford, Artie Ortego, Tex Palmer, Archie Ricks.

Wayne (as Ted Hayden) poses as dead outlaw 'Gat Ganns' to get near the man who killed his father and kidnapped his younger brother. Screenplay by Robert N. Bradbury, from a story by Bradbury and (uncredited Oliver Drake). Produced by Paul Malvern. Portions filmed in Kernville, California.

Released on February 15 | 54 minutes/Balsley & Phillips Recording/computer color version/video/DVD | Lone Star/Monogram

He turned man-hunter to run down a gang of thieving scoundrels!

Blue Steel/Stolen Goods (1934) Directed by Robert [N.] Bradbury.

John Wayne, Eleanor Hunt, George 'Gabby' Hayes, Edward Peil [Sr.], Yakima Canutt, Lafe McKee, George Cleveland, Earl Dwire, Lane Chandler, Hank Bell, George Nash, Chris Allen, Silver Top Baker, Barney Beasley, Ralph Bucko, Horace B. Carpenter, Jack Evans, Herman Hack, Henry Hall, Theodore Lorch, Bud McClure, Art Mix, Perry Murdock, Herman Newlin, Artie Ortego, Tex Phelps.

After a payroll robbery, sheriff Hayes suspects Wayne (as John Carruthers) of the theft, but Wayne is actually a US Marshal out to get the gang who is crippling area ranchers by stopping all supply wagons from coming into the territory. Story and screenplay by Robert [N.] Bradbury. Produced by Paul Malvern. Filmed at General Service Studios, Hollywood, and these other California locations: Alabama Hills, Lone Pine; Trem Carr Ranch, Newhall; Santa Clarita; Big Pines; and Kernville.

Released on May 10. | 54 minutes/Balsley & Phillips Recording/computer color version/video/DVD | Lone Star/Monogram

Whirling ropes and snarling guns in the galloping grip of a clamorous drama!

The Man from Utah (1934) Directed by Robert [N.] Bradbury.

John Wayne, Polly Ann Young, Anita Compillo [Campillo], Edward Peil [Sr.], George ['Gabby'] Hayes, Yakima Canutt, George Cleveland, Lafe McKee, Tex Phelps, Archie Ricks, Silver Tip Baker, Edward Bilby, Earl Dwire, Herman Hack, Jack Kirk, Bud McClure, Perry Murdock, Artie Ortego, Tex Palmer, Sam Garrett.

Rodeo riders are dying at competitions and marshal Hayes sends in Wayne (as John Weston) to find out who is killing the cowboys. Story and screenplay by Lindsley Parsons. Produced by Paul Malvern. Jack Kirk dubbed Wayne's singing voice. Portions filmed at these California locations: Alabama Hills, Lone Pine; and Owens River.

Quotes: Marshal George Higgins (George Hayes): *"It seems mighty funny to me that every time this gang organizes a rodeo, their own men win all the first prizes. When it begins to look like an outsider is going to win, he gets sick. Two or three have even died from it."*, John Weston (John Wayne): *"Well, you can't arrest them for that, Marshal."*, Higgins: *"No, maybe not. But it's mighty peculiar that when these outsiders fall off them broncs, they're suffering from snake bite. I tell ya, it just ain't natural.* Weston: *"What do you want me to do? Get snake-bit?"*

Song: *Sing Me a Song of the Wild* (Robert N. Bradbury) (sung by Wayne/Kirk) | Music by (uncredited Bernard B. Brown, Norman Spencer, Lee Zahler).

Released on May 15 | 55 minutes/computer color version/video/DVD | Lone Star/Monogram

Fearless-he rode the danger trail!

Randy Rides Alone (1934) Directed by Harry [L.] Fraser.

John Wayne, Alberta Vaughn, George ['Gabby'] Hayes, Yakima Canutt, Earl Dwire, Arthur Artego [Artie Ortego], Tex Phelps, Horace B. Carpenter, Tommy Coats, Perry Murdock, Mack V. Wright, Herman Hack, Tex Palmer.

Wayne (as Randy Bowers) finds himself in jail for murders he did not commit, and is freed due to the efforts of a sympathetic Vaughn. Wayne rides out ahead of the posse and stumbles into the gang responsible for the killings. Gaining both shelter from the pursuing lawmen and an opportunity to clear his name, Wayne joins the outlaws. Story and screenplay by Lindsley Parsons. Produced by Paul Malvern. Portions filmed in Santa Clarita, California. Wayne's singing is dubbed by Bill Bradbury.

Music by (uncredited Bernard B. Brown and Norman Spencer).

Released on July 18 | 54 minutes/Balsley & Phillips Sound/computer color version/video/DVD | Lone Star/Monogram

He dared death in the outlaws' lair!"

The Star Packer (1934) Directed by R.N. [Robert N.] Bradbury.

John Wayne, Verna Hillie, George ['Gabby'] Hayes, Yakima Canutt, Billy Franey, Ed [Eddie] Parker, Earl Dwire, Tom [Thomas G.] Lingham, George Cleveland, Glenn Strange, Davie Aldrich, Artie Ortego, Tex Palmer, Frank Ball, Arthur Millett, Bud Pope, Starlight (a horse).

Wayne (as John Travers) steps in for a murdered sheriff to track down a deadly gang of fugitives which is led by a mysterious outlaw named The Shadow. Story and screenplay by R.N. [Robert N.] Bradbury. Produced by Paul Malvern. Filmed at General Service Studios, Hollywood, and the following California locations: Santa Clarita; Newhall; and Kernville.

Quotes: US Marshal John Travers (John Wayne): *"What did ya find out?"*, Yak (Yakima Canutt): *"Two men gonna hold up stage-Coyote Canyon. Much money on stage."* Travers: *"Well, it looks like we're going to have our hands full."* Yak: *"More trouble-more fun!"* Travers: *That's one way to look at it.*

Music by (uncredited Abe Meyer).

Released on July 30 | 53 minutes/Balsley & Phillips Sound/computer color version/video/DVD | Lone Star/Monogram

"The spell of adventure and the unknown!"

The Trail Beyond (1934) Directed by Robert [N.] Bradbury.

John Wayne, Verna Hillie, Noah Beery Sr., Noah Beery Jr., Robert Frazer, Iris Lancaster, James [A.] Marcus, Eddie Parker, Earl Dwire, Artie Ortego, Tex Palmer.

While on the hunt for a missing miner and his daughter, Wayne (as Rod Drew) gets embroiled in the fight over a gold mine and the predicament of Beery Jr.-who has been framed for murder by card sharks. Screenplay by Lindsley Parsons, from the novel *The Wolf Hunters* by James Oliver Curwood. Produced by Paul Malvern. Portions filmed at these California locations: Devil's Postpile National Monument; King's Canyon National Park; Mammoth Lakes; June Lake; Big Bear Lake and Valley, San Bernadino National Forest; railroad station, Chatsworth; and Trem Carr Ranch, Newhall.

Music by (uncredited Lee Zahler, Sam Perry and Oliver Wallace).

Released on October 22 | (55 minutes/computer color version/video/DVD) | Lone Star/Monogram

We'll shoot it out now-hombre! Draw before I drill you!

The Lawless Frontier (1934) Directed by R.N. [Robert N.] Bradbury.

John Wayne, Sheila Terry, Jack Rockwell, George ['Gabby'] Hayes, Earl Dwire, Buffalo Bill Jr. [Jay Wilsey], Yakima Canutt, Bud Wood [Gordon DeMain], Tommy Coats, Herman Hack, Arthur Millett, Artie Ortego, Tex Phelps, Lloyd Whitlock.

A Mexican outlaw (Dwire) killed Wayne's parents and plans to murder Hayes and kidnap Terry. Wayne (as John Tobin) manages to save the intended victims from death and abduction-intensifying his determination to track down the deadly badman. Story and screenplay by R.N. [Robert N.] Bradbury. Produced by Paul Malvern. Portions filmed at the following California locations: Red Rock Canyon State Park, Cantil;

Kernville; and Trem Carr Ranch, Newhall.

Music by (uncredited Sam Perry).

Released on November 22 | (56 minutes/Balsley & Phillips Sound/computer color version/video/DVD | Lone Star/Monogram

Hair-trigger action!

'Neath the Arizona Skies (1934) Directed by Harry [L.] Fraser.

John Wayne, Sheila Terry, Shirley Jane [Jean] Rickert, Jack Rockwell, Yakima Canutt, George ['Gabby'] Hayes, Buffalo Bill Jr. [Jay Wilsey], Phil Keefer [Philip Kiefer], Weston Edwards [Harry L. Fraser], Earl Dwire, Artie Ortego, Frank Hall Crane, Billy Franey, Herman Hack, George Morrell, Eddie Parker, Tex Phelps, Allen Pomeroy.

When the half-Indian child heiress to a large amount of land is kidnapped, her rough and tough guardian (Wayne, as Chris Morrell) goes after the outlaws while also trying to track down her father. Screenplay by Burl [R.] Tuttle, from his story *Gun Glory*. Produced by Paul Malvern. Portions filmed at these California locations: Placerita Canyon; Santa Clarita and Santa Clarita River; and Newhall.

Quote: Chris Morrell (John Wayne): *"Snakes like you usually die of their own poison."*

Music by (uncredited Paul Van Loan).

Released on December 5 | 53 minutes/Balsley & Phillips Sound/computer color version/video/DVD/Blu-Ray | Lone Star/Monogram

Texas Terror (1935) Directed by R.N. [Robert N.] Bradbury.

John Wayne, Lucille [Lucile] Brown, Leroy Mason, Fern Emmett, George ['Gabby'] Hayes, Buffalo Bill Jr. [Jay Wilsey], John Ince, Henry Roguemore [Roquemore], Jack Duffy, Frank Ball, Bert Dillard, Julia Griffith, Herman Hack, Jack Jones, Jack Kenny, Thomas G. Lingham, Bert O'Hara, George Ovey, Tex Palmer, Tex Phelps, Bud Pope, William Wilkerson.

A shoot-out with robbers leaves one man dead-the best friend of sheriff Wayne (as John Higgins). Wayne thinks it was his bullet that killed his pal, so he turns in his badge. Later, he has a chance to help run the ranch for the dead man's sister-but what will happen if she learns about her father's death? Story and screenplay by R.N. [Robert N.] Bradbury. Produced by Paul Malvern. Portions filmed at these California locations: Jack Garner Ranch, San Bernardino National Forest; and Trem Carr Ranch, Newhall.

Released on February 1 | 51 minutes/Balsley & Phillips Sound/video/DVD | Lone Star/Monogram

Rainbow Valley (1935) Directed by R.N. [Robert N.] Bradbury.

John Wayne, Lucille [Lucile] Browne, George ['Gabby'] Hayes, LeRoy Mason, Lloyd Ingraham, Buffalo Bill Jr. [Jay Wilsey], Frank Ball, Bert Dillard, Lafe McKee, Eddie Parker, Tommy Coats, Art Dillard, Frank Ellis, Fern Emmett, Jack Evans, Olin Francis, Herman Hack, Buck Morgan, Artie Ortego, Tex Palmer, Tex Phelps, Henry Roquemore.

Wayne (as John Martin) agrees to build a much-needed road through the valley, but is opposed by corrupt Mason-who isn't above calling in a hired gunman to finish off Wayne. Story and screenplay by Lindsley Parsons. Produced by Paul Malvern. Portions filmed at these California locations: Trem Carr Ranch, Newhall; Walker Ranch, Newhall; and Kernville.

Released on March 15 | 52 minutes/video/DVD | Lone Star/Monogram

The Desert Trail (1935) Directed by Cullen Lewis [Lewis D. Collins].

John Wayne, Mary Kornman, Paul Fix, Eddy Chandler, Carmen Laroux, Lafe McKee, Al Ferguson, Henry Hall, Frank Ball, Frank Brownlee, Tommy Coats, Silver Tip Baker, Dick Dickinson, Bert Dillard, Frank Ellis, Jack Evans, Olin Francis, Herman Hack, Jack Hendricks, Theodore Lorch, Lew Meehan, Artie Ortego, Tex Palmer, Fred Parker, Archie Ricks, Wally West.

Rodeo riders Wayne (as John Scott) and Chandler are accused of robbery and murder, but they elude the law and ride out for another town-where they hope to corral the guilty party and get a confession. Story and screenplay by Lindsley Parsons. Produced by Paul Malvern.

Portions filmed at these California locations: Santa Clarita; Walker Ranch, Newhall; Kernville; and Trem Carr, Newhall.

Music by (uncredited Jean de la Roche).

Released on April 22 | Box Office: $27,500 | (54 minutes/computer color version/video/DVD | Lone Star/Monogram

The end of the vengeance trail.

The Dawn Rider/Cold Vengeance (1935) Directed by R.N. [Robert N.] Bradbury.

John Wayne, Marion Burns, Denny Meadows [Dennis Moore], Reed Howes, Joe [Joseph] DeGrasse, Yakima Canutt, Earl Dwire, Nelson McDowell, Bert Dillard, Fred Parker, Chris Allen, Chuck Baldra, Barney Beasley, Jack Evans, Herman Hack, Jack Jones, George Morrell, Tex Palmer, Tex Phelps, Archie Ricks, James Sherman.

After his father is killed in a freight office holdup, Wayne (as John Mason) pursues the deadly robbers and is badly wounded. While recuperating, Wayne strikes up a friendship with Burns-whose brother is guilty of killing Wayne's father. Screenplay by (uncredited Robert N. Bradbury), from a story by Lloyd Nosler and (uncredited Wellyn Totman). Produced by (uncredited Paul Malvern). Portions filmed at these California locations: Iverson Ranch, Chatsworth; Santa Clarita; and Trem Carr Ranch, Newhall.

Released on June 20 | (53 minutes/computer color version/video/DVD | Lone Star/Monogram

Where life was raw and might was law!

Paradise Canyon/Guns Along the Trail (1935) Directed by Carl L. Pierson.

John Wayne, Marion Burns, Reed Howes, Earle Hodgins, Gino Corrado, Yakima Canutt, Perry Murdock, Gordon Clifford, Henry Hall, Earl Dwire, Chuck Baldra, Bob Burns, Horace B. Carpenter, Joe Dominguez, Herman Hack, Tex Palmer, James Sheridan, Chris Allen, Joe De La Cruz, George Hazel, Wally Howe, George Morrell, Fred Parker, Tex Phelps, Wally West.

Government agent Wayne (as John Wyatt) tracks a frontier counterfeiting ring to the Arizona-Mexico border when he joins Hodgins' medicine show. Wayne discovers the man who once framed Hodgins is also leader of the fake-money gang. Screenplay by Robert Emmett [Tansey], from a story by Lindsley Parsons. Produced by Paul Malvern. Portions filmed at these California locations: Santa Clarita; Kernville; and Trem Carr Ranch, Newhall.

Songs: *When We Were Young and Foolish* (composer unknown), *Snap Those Old Suspenders Once Again* (composer unknown)

Released on July 20 | 53 minutes/computer color version/video/DVD | Lone Star/Monogram

Romance rides the plains!

Westward Ho (1935) Directed by R.N. [Robert N.] Bradbury.

John Wayne, Sheila Mannors [Bromley], Frank McGlynn Jr., James [Jim] Farley, Jack Curtis, Bradley Metcalfe, Dickie Jones, Mary MacLaren, Yakima Canutt, Hank Bell, Glenn Strange, The Singing Riders (Chuck Baldra, Jack Kirk, Charles Sargent), Earl Dwire, Frank Ellis, Cactus Mack, Eddie Parker, Silver Tip Baker, Bob Burns, Fred Burns, Edward Coxen, Herman Hack, Henry Hall, Edward Hearn, Jack Hendricks, Wally Howe, Lloyd Ingraham, Jack Ingram, Frank LaRue, Clyde McClary, Tex Palmer, Fred Parker, Hal Price, James Sheridan, Al Taylor, Arthur Thalasso.

As a youth, Wayne (as John Wyatt) was part of a wagon train that was attacked and, in the ensuing violence, his parents were killed and his brother kidnapped. Now a man, Wayne forms a vigilante group to hunt for the gang responsible and ends up meeting one of the outlaws-who happens to be his long-lost brother. Story and screenplay by Robert Emmett [Tansey] and Lindsley Parsons. Produced by Paul Malvern. Portions filmed at these California locations: Alabama Hills, Lone Pine; and Owens Valley. Wayne's singing voice was dubbed by Glenn Strange.

Songs: *"Westward Ho"* (Tim Spencer; Glenn Strange), *"The Vigilantes"* (Spencer; Strange), *"The Girl I Loved Long Ago"* (Robert N. Bradbury) (sung by Wayne/Strange) | Music by (uncredited Mischa Bakaleinikoff,

Heinz Roemheld and Clifford Vaughan).

Released on August 19 | Box Office: $500,000 | (62 minutes/video/DVD/Blu-Ray | Republic

A mighty rush of empire builders again sweep on to conquer the West!

The New Frontier (1935) Directed by Carl L. Pierson.

John Wayne, Muriel Evans, Warner Richmond, Alan [Al] Bridge, Sam Flint, Murdock MacQuarrie, Allan Cavan, Mary MacLaren, Theodore Loren [Lorch], Glen[n] Strange, Phil Keefer [Philip Kieffer], Frank Ball, Jack Montgomery, Earl Dwire, John Ince, Cactus Mack, Perry Murdock, Eddie Parker, Fred Parker, Chuck Baldra, Art Dillard, Jack Evans, Herman Hack, Pat Harmon, Jack Kirk, Buck Moulton, Tex Palmer, Tex Phillips.

As honest citizens rush to claim free land in the Oklahoma Territory in 1889, the son (Wayne, as John Dawson) of a wagon master becomes the sheriff of a new town overrun by lawlessness, murder and corruption at the hands of an unethical saloon keeper. Story and screenplay by Robert Emmett [Tansey]. Produced by Paul Malvern. Filmed at Talisman Studios in Hollywood and these California locations: Alabama Hills, Lone Pine; Kernville; and Trem Carr Ranch, Newhall. Wayne's singing voice was dubbed by Glenn Strange.

Glenn Strange songs: *The New Frontier, Outlaw Range* | Music by (uncredited Hugo Riesenfeld, Heinz Roemheld and Clifford Vaughan).

Released on October 24 | (57 minutes/RCA Victor High Fidelity Sound/video/DVD/Blu-Ray | Republic

Western justice! Roaring romance!

Lawless Range (1935) Directed by R.N. [Robert N.] Bradbury.

John Wayne, Sheila Mannors [Bromley], Frank McGlynn Jr., Jack Curtis, Wally Howe, Julia Griffith, Yakima Canutt, Earl Dwire, Glenn Strange, Bob Burns, Sam Flint, John Ince, George Ovey, Tex Palmer, The Wranglers (Chuck Baldra, Charles Sargent), Victor Adamson, Charles Brinley, Fred Burns, Frank Ellis, Herman Hack, Jack Hendricks, Jack Kirk, Bob Kortman, Fred Parker, Pascale Perry, James Sheridan,

Francis Walker, Slim Whitaker.

While looking into a case of cattle rustling, Wayne (as John Middleton) is abducted and imprisoned in a cave to keep him from upsetting the rustlers' plans to also get control of valuable gold mines. Story and screenplay by Lindsley Parsons. Produced by Trem Carr and Paul Malvern. Portions filmed at these California locations: Santa Clarita; Alabama Hills, Lone Pine; and Vasquez Rocks Natural Area Park, Agua Dulce. Wayne's singing voice was dubbed by Jack Kirk.

Songs: *On the Banks of the Sunny San Juan* (The Wranglers) (sung and played on guitar by Wayne/Kirk), *Down That Old Dusty Road* (composer unknown), *The Girl I Loved Long Ago* (Robert N. Bradbury) | Music by (uncredited Sam Perry and Clifford Vaughan).

Released on November 4 | 59 minutes/Balsley & Phillips Sound/video/DVD | Republic

Thrills of the covered wagon days!

The Oregon Trail (1936) Directed by Scott Pembroke.

John Wayne, Ann Rutherford, Joe [Joseph W.] Girard, Yakima Canutt, Frank Rice, E.H. Calvert, Ben Hendricks Jr., Harry Harvey, Fern Emmett, Jack Rutherford, Marian Ferrell, Roland Ray, Gino Corrado, Edward LeSaint, Octavio Giraud, Dave O'Brien, Frances Grant, James Sheridan.

Wayne (as US Army Captain John Delmont) leaves the military to search for his missing father. The trail leads to a wagon train which Wayne takes over as he closes in on the outlaws responsible for his father's disappearance. Screenplay by Lindsley Parsons, Robert Emmett [Tansey] and Jack Natteford, from a story by Parsons and Tansey. Produced by Paul Malvern and Trem Carr. Portions filmed at Alabama Hills, Lone Pine, California. Considered a lost film.

Music by Harry Grey.

Released on January 8 | 59 minutes/RCA Victor High Fidelity Sound | Republic

He's 'G-Man No. 1' waging a one-man war in the new west!

The Lawless Nineties (1936) Directed by Joseph Kane.

John Wayne, Ann Rutherford, Harry Woods, George ['Gabby'] Hayes, Al Bridge, Snowflake [Fred Toones], Etta McDaniel, Tom Brower, Lane Chandler, Cliff Lyons, Jack Rockwell, Al Taylor, Charles King, George Chesebro, Tracy Layne, Chuck Baldra, Sam Flint, Tom London, Lloyd Ingraham, Chris Allen, Bob Burns, Horace B. Carpenter, Steve Clark, Jim Corey, Art Dillard, Curley Dresden, Helen Gibson, Henry Hall, James Harrison, Edward Hearn, Wally Howe, Jack Kirk, Bert Lindley, William McCall, Philo McCullough, Lew Meehan, Jack Montgomery, Bud Osborne, James Sheridan, Blackjack Ward.

When crime and corruption run rampant in old Wyoming, the government sends in federal agent Wayne (as John Tipton) to reel in the crooked politicians who are out to keep Wyoming from becoming a state. Screenplay by Joseph [F.] Poland, from a story by Poland and Scott Pembroke. Produced by Paul Malvern and Trem Carr. Portions filmed at Trem Carr Ranch, Newhall, California. Yakima Canutt was Wayne's stunt double.

Music by (uncredited Arthur Kay and Heinz Roemheld).

Released on February 15 | 56 minutes/RCA Victor High Fidelity Sound/video/DVD/Blu-Ray | Republic

Who dares challenge the rule of the range-who will brave the blazing bandit bullets?

King of the Pecos (1936) Directed by Joseph Kane.

John Wayne, Muriel Evans, Cy Kendall, Jack [Rube] Clifford, Arthur Aylesworth, Herbert Heywood, [J.] Frank Glendon, Edward Hearn, John Beck, Mary MacLaren, Bradley Metcalfe, Yakima Canutt, Earl Dwire, Jack Curtis, Tex Palmer, Bud Pope, Horace B. Carpenter, Wally Howe, Jack Kirk, Tracy Layne, James A. Marcus, William McCall, Tex Phelps.

Wayne (as John Clayborn) totes both a six-gun and a lawbook as a frontier attorney who is out to stop murdering cattle baron Kendall from swallowing up millions of valuable acres in Pecos Valley. Screenplay by Bernard McConville, Dorrell McGowan and Stuart [E.] McGowan, from a story by McConville. Produced by Paul Malvern and Trem Carr. Portions filmed at Alabama Hills, Lone Pine, California.

Music by (uncredited Mischa Bakaleinikoff, Arthur Kay, Hugo Riesenfeld and Milan Roder).

Released on March 9 | 54 minutes/RCA Victor High Fidelity Sound/video/DVD/Blu-Ray | Republic

The Lonely Trail (1936) Directed by Joseph Kane.

John Wayne, Ann Rutherford, Cy Kendall, Bob Kortman, Snowflake [Fred Toones], Sam Flint, Denny Meadows [Dennis Moore], Jim Tony [Toney], Etta McDaniel, Yakima Canutt, Lloyd Ingraham, James [A.] Marcus, Bob Burns, Rodney Hildebrand, Eugene Jackson, Floyd Shackleford, Maude Eburne, Charles King, Lafe McKee, Clifton Young, Leon Lord, Horace B. Carpenter, Oscar Gahan, Henry Hall, Jack Ingram, Nina Mae McKinney, Jack Kirk.

Veteran Union officer Wayne (as Captain John Ashley) returns home after the Civil War only to find his hometown overrun by murderous Confederate sympathizers-stealing from local citizens under the guise of state authority. Screenplay by Bernard McConville and Jack Natteford, from a story by McConville. Produced by Paul Malvern and (uncredited Nat Levine).

Music by (uncredited Heinz Roemheld).

Released on May 25 | (57 minutes/RCA Victor High Fidelity Sound/video/DVD/Blu-Ray | Republic

Wayne rides again on the bullet-studded trail of revenge.

Winds of the Wasteland/Stagecoach Run (1936) Directed by Mack V. Wright.

John Wayne, Phyllis Fraser, Lew Kelly, Douglas Cosgrove, Lane Chandler, Sam Flint, Robert [Bob] Kortman, Ed Cassidy, Charles Locher [Jon Hall], W.M. [Merrill] McCormick, Chris Franke [Christian J. Frank], Jack Rockwell, Arthur Millett, Tracy Layne, Yakima Canutt,

Horace B. Carpenter, Henry Hall, Art Mix, Helen Gibson, Herman Hack, Lloyd Ingraham, Cliff Lyons, Jack Ingram, Joe Yrigoyen.

Ex-Pony Express rider Wayne (as John Blair) and his pal Chandler go into the stage and freight business. They have a chance to secure a $25,000 government mail contract if they can win a stagecoach race against rival Cosgrove-who has no qualms about sabotaging Wayne's chances to win by setting up an ambush. Story and screenplay by Joseph [F.] Poland. Produced by Paul Malvern and Nat Levine. Portions filmed at the following California locations: Agoura Ranch; Sacramento River Valley; and Brandeis Ranch, Chatsworth.

Music by (uncredited James Branson, Arthur Kay, Heinz Roemheld, Leon Rosebrook and Paul Van Loan).

Released on July 6 | 55 minutes/RCA High Fidelity Sound/computer color version/video/DVD | Republic

He-man dynamite in a red-blooded story of the Coast Guard.

Sea Spoilers (1936) Directed by Frank [R.] Strayer.

John Wayne, Nan Grey, William Bakewell, Fuzzy Knight, Russell Hicks, George Irving, Lotus Long, Harry Worth, Ernest Hilliard, George Humbert, Ethan Laidlaw, Chester Gan, Cy Kendall, Harrison Greene, Hal Price, Harry Tenbrook, Don Brodie, Lester Dorr.

Wayne (as Bob Randall) takes temporary command of a Coast Guard ship, only to have his girlfriend (Grey) abducted by seal poachers. However, when Bakewell replaces Wayne as commander of the vessel, they disagree on how to both effect a rescue and capture the poachers. Screenplay by George Waggoner [Waggner], from a story by Dorrell and Stuart E. McGowan. Produced by (uncredited Trem Carr) and Paul Malvern.

Music by (uncredited Arthur Morton, Heinz Roemheld, Marlin Skiles, Clifford Vaughan and Franz Waxman).

Released on September 28 | (63 minutes/RCA Photophone Sound | Universal

Conflict (1936) Directed by David Howard.

John Wayne, Jean Rogers, Ward Bond, Tommy Bupp, Bryant Washburn, Frank Sheridan, Harry Woods, Margaret Mann, Eddie Borden, Frank Hagney, Lloyd Ingraham, Glenn Strange, Edward Peil Sr., Leonard Kibrick, Harry Bowen, Bruce Mitchell, Billie Morris, Fred Parker, Richard Perry, Walter Weems.

Wayne (as Pat Glendon) makes his living by taking 'dives' in the boxing ring for a traveling prizefighter (Bond)-until he meets pretty reporter Rogers. Screenplay by Charles Logue and Walter Weems, from the novel *The Abysmal Brute* by Jack London. Produced by Trem Carr and Paul Malvern. Portions filmed at these California locations: Tuolumne County and Sonora.

Music by (uncredited Howard Jackson, George Parrish, Sam Perry, Charles Previn, Heinz Roemheld, Paul Van Loan, Clifford Vaughan and Franz Waxman).

Released on November 29 | (60 minutes/RCA Sound | Universal

Gasoline and courage challenge steam and steel!

California Straight Ahead (1937) Directed by Arthur Lubin.

John Wayne, Louise Latimer, Robert McWade, Theodore von Eltz, Tully Marshall, Emerson Treacy, Harry Allen, LeRoy Mason, Grace Goodall, Olaf Hytten, Monte Vandergrift, Lorin Raker, Frank Ellis, George Morrell, Oscar Gahan, Donnie Allen, Billy Diamond.

Wayne (as Biff Smith) is a truck driver who endeavors to deliver a shipment of aviation parts to a West Port destination before a trainload of similar cargo can arrive at the same place. Screenplay by W. Scott Darling, from a story by Herman Boxer. Produced by Trem Carr and Paul Malvern. Portions filmed at these California locations: Santa Clarita and Newhall.

Music by (uncredited W. Franke Harling, Arthur Kay, Charles Maxwell, Charles Previn, Heinz Roemheld, Clifford Vaughan, Oliver Wallace, Edward Ward and Franz Waxman).

Released on April 16 | (67 minutes/Western Electric Noiseless Recording | Universal

A shooting war...dodging bullets and stumbling smack into desert love!

I Cover the War (1937) Directed by Arthur Lubin.

John Wayne, Gwen Gaze, Don Barclay, Charles Brokaw, James Bush, Pat Somerset, Richard Tucker, Major Sam Harris, Olaf Hytten, Arthur Aylesworth, Frank Lackteen, Franklyn [Franklin] Parker, Keith Kennedy [Hitchcock], Abdulla, Jack [John] Mack, Earle Hodgins.

Newsreel cameraman Wayne (as Bob Adams) has a hand in quashing an Arab insurrection and saving a regiment of British Lancers when he is assigned to get pictures of a conflict in Mesopotamia. Screenplay by George Waggner, from a story idea by Bernard McConville. Produced by Trem Carr and Paul Malvern. Portions filmed at Alabama Hills, Lone Pine, California.

Music by (uncredited Arthur Morton, Sam Perry, David Raksin, Heinz Roemheld, Clifford Vaughan, Edward Ward and Franz Waxman).

Released on July 4 | 68 minutes/Western Electric Noiseless Recording | Universal

The fastest game on earth!

Idol of the Crowds (1937) Directed by Arthur Lubin.

John Wayne, Sheila Bromley, Charles Brokaw, Billy [Bill] Burrud, Jane Johns, Huntley Gordon, Frank Otto, Russell Hopton, Hal Neiman, Virginia Brissac, George Lloyd, Clem Bevins [Bevans], Wayne Castle, Lloyd Ford, Lee Ford, Edward Peil Sr., Wilfred Lucas, Theodore Lorch.

Hockey player Wayne (as Johnny Hanson) helps his team to the championships, but then racketeers try to force him into throwing the games-and he flatly refuses. His integrity marks him as the target of a gangland hit. Screenplay by George Waggner and Harold Buckley, from Waggner's story *Hell on Ice*. Produced by Trem Carr and Paul Malvern.

Music by (uncredited Arthur Morton, Charles Previn, David Raksin, Heinz Roemheld, Marlin Skiles, Frank Skinner, Dimitri Tiomkin, Alfred Tommasino, Paul Van Loan, Clifford Vaughan, Oliver Wallace, Edward Ward and Franz Waxman).

Released on September 30 | (60 minutes/Western Electric Noiseless Recording | Universal

Adrift on the high seas! The crew gone mad! One lone woman at the mercy of all of them!

Adventure's End (1937) Directed by Arthur Lubin.

John Wayne, Diana Gibson, Montagu Love, Moroni Olsen, Paul White, Maurice Black, George Cleveland, Patrick J. Kelly, Cameron Hall, James T. Mack, Britt Wood, Oscar W. [William] Sundholm, Ben Carter, Wally Howe, Jimmie Lucas, Glenn Strange, Victor Potel, Lynton Brent.

Pearl diver Wayne (as Duke Slade) finds himself eluding a group of angry natives and finds refuge on a whaling ship. He discovers the ship's captain on his deathbed; the dying skipper makes a request of his new crewman-marry his daughter to keep her away from the first mate. Screenplay by Ben Grauman Kohn, Scott Darling and Sidney Sutherland, from a story by Ben Ames Williams. Produced by Trem Carr and Paul Malvern. Considered a lost film.

Music by (uncredited Charles Henderson, Charles Maxwell, George Parrish, Charles Previn, Heinz Roemheld, Clifford Vaughan, Edward Ward and Franz Waxman).

Released on December 5 | 60 minutes/Western Electric Noiseless Recording | Universal

It took six murdering rustlers and a girl to make a reckless rover settle down to love!

Born to the West/Hell Town (1937) Directed by Charles Barton.

John Wayne, Marsha Hunt, John [Johnny] Mack Brown, John Patterson, Monte Blue, Syd Saylor, Lucien Littlefield, James Craig, Jim Thorpe, Henry Wills, Johnny Boyle, Jack Kennedy, Nick Lukats, John Bose, Jack Daley, Earl Dwire, Al Ferguson, Art Mix, Vester Pegg, Lee Prather.

Trailhand Wayne (as Dare Rudd) takes a job on his cousin's ranch and is put in charge of a cattle drive. After he delivers the herd, dishonest gambler Craig attempts to cheat Wayne out of his money. Screenplay by Stuart Anthony and Robert Yost, from the novel by Zane Grey; (uncredited Jack Natteford provided additional dialogue). Produced by (uncredited William LeBaron and William T. Lackey). Portions filmed at these California locations: Alabama Hills, Lone Pine; Kernville.

Quotes: Tom Fillmore (Johnny Mack Brown): *"Why don't you get married and settle down? Why you're running around like a maverick without a brand on."*, Dare Rudd (John Wayne): *"Well, I don't like branding. It hurts in the wrong place!"*

Songs: *Red River Valley* (traditional; composer unknown), *Bury Me Not on the Lone Prairie* (traditional; composer unknown), *You're the One I Crave* (Ralph Rainger; Victor Young) | Music by (uncredited George Antheil, Gerard Carbonara, Hugo Friedhofer, John Leipold, Ralph Rainger and Victor Young).

Released on December 10 | (52 minutes/Western Electric Mirrophonic Recording/video/laserdisc/DVD | Paramount

Peril-packed adventure with dashing devil-may-care John Wayne leading the Mesquiteers into their greatest, most thrilling range exploits!

Pals of the Saddle (1938) Directed by George Sherman.

John Wayne, Ray Corrigan, Max Terhune, Doreen McKay, Josep [Joseph] Forte, George Douglas, Frank Milan, Ted Adams, Harry Depp, Dave Weber, Don Orlando, Charles Knight, Jack Kirk, Yakima Canutt, George Montgomery, Bill Yrigoyen, Joe Yrigoyen, Chris Allen, John Beach, Bob Burns, Art Dillard, Curley Dresden, Olin Francis, Otto Hoffman, Kenner G. Kemp, Philip Kieffer, Monte Montague, Herman Nowlin, Tex Palmer, George Plues.

Wayne (as Stony Brooke) is framed for murder as he and his pards (Corrigan, Terhune) battle munitions-chemicals smugglers in the modern west. Seventeenth entry in the **Three Mesquiteers** series. Screenplay by Stanley Roberts and Betty Burbridge, based on characters created by William Colt MacDonald. Produced by William Berke. Portions filmed at these California locations: Corriganville (Ray Corrigan Ranch), Simi Valley; Red Rock Canyon State Park, Cantil. George Montgomery was Wayne's stunt double.

Music by Cy Feuer and (uncredited Alberto Colombo, William Lava and Victor Young).

Released on August 28 | (55 minutes/RCA High Fidelity Recording/video/DVD/Blu-Ray | Republic

Overland Stage Raiders (1938) Directed by George Sherman.

John Wayne, Ray Corrigan, Max Terhune, Louise Brooks, Anthony Marsh, Ralph Bowman [John Archer], Gordon Hart, Roy James, Olin Francis, Fern Emmett, Henry Otho, George Sherwood, Archie Hall [Arch Hall Sr.], Frank LaRue, Yakima Canutt, Slim Whitaker, Bud Osborne, Burr Caruth, Tommy Coats, Edwin Gaffney, Dirk Thane, Curley Dresden, Milton Kibbee, Chuck Baldra, John Beach, Charles Brinley, Fred Burns, Jack Kirk, Duke R. Lee, Bud McClure, George Morrell, George Plues, Bill Wolfe.

When a gang of hijackers targets a bus carrying gold, Wayne (as Stony Brooke) teams with Corrigan and Terhune to protect the shipment. They then get the idea to form an air freight company to ship valuables by plane. Eighteenth entry in the *Three Mequiteers* series. Screenplay by Luci Ward, from a story by Bernard McConville and Edmond Kelso based on characters created by William Colt MacDonald. Produced by William Berke. Portions filmed at these California Locations: Iverson Ranch, Chatsworth; and Conejo Valley Airport, Thousand Oaks.

Quote: Stony Brooke (John Wayne): *"Hey, Lullaby, wake up. It's time to go to sleep."*

Music by (uncredited Alberto Colombo, Cy Feuer and William Lava).

Released on September 20 | (55 minutes/RCA High Fidelity Recording/video/DVD/Blu-Ray | Republic

Santa Fe Stampede (1938) Directed by George Sherman.

John Wayne, Ray Corrigan, Max Terhune, June Martel, William Farnum, LeRoy Mason, Martin Spellman, Genee Hall, Walter Wills, Ferris Taylor, Tom London, Dick Rush, John F. [James] Cassidy, Richard Alexander, Griff Barnett, Yakima Canutt, Jerry Frank, Charles King, Nelson McDowell, George Morrell, Bud Osborne, George Chesebro, Curley Dresden, Ralph Peters, Marin Sais, Bob Woodward, Horace B. Carpenter, Jim Corey, Tex Driscoll, John Elliott, Chick Hannan, Duke

R. Lee, Bud McClure, Robert Milasch, Charles Murphy, Frank O'Connor, Fred Parker, Cliff Parkinson, Tex Phelps, Russ Powell, George Sowards, Blackjack Ward, Bill Wolfe.

Corrigan and Terhune move against a town boss who frames Wayne (as Stony Brooke) for the murder of a prospector who struck it rich. While his two pards ride out to clear him, Wayne sees a lynch mob form outside the jail. Nineteenth entry in the **Three Mesquiteers** series. Screenplay by Luci Ward and Betty Burbridge, from a story by Ward based on characters created by William Colt MacDonald. Produced by William Berke. Portions filmed at these California locations: Brandeis Ranch, Chatsworth; Corriganville-Ray Corrigan Ranch, Simi Valley. George Montgomery was Wayne's stunt double.

Quotes: Stony Brooke (John Wayne): *"Just a minute! What kind of farce do you call this?"*, Mayor Gil Byron (LeRoy Mason): *"Don't you approve of the way we hold court?"*, Stony: *"This isn't a court, it's a three-ring circus."*, Judge Henry J. Hixon (Ferris Taylor): *"Careful, young man..."* Stony: *"Of what? You're sworn to uphold the laws of this territory and what do you do? Jump like a rabbit every time he cracks a whip."*, Judge: *"One more word from you and I'll fine you for contempt!"*, Stony: *"Words fail to express my contempt for this court."*

Music by William Lava (and uncredited Cy Feuer).

Released on November 28 | (57 minutes/RCA High Fidelity Recording/video/DVD/Blu-Ray | Republic

The Three Mesquiteers make war...on the rustlers!

Red River Range (1938) Directed by George Sherman.

John Wayne, Ray Corrigan, Max Terhune, Lorna Gray [Adrian Booth], Kirby Grant, Polly Moran, Sammy McKim, William Royle, Perry Ivins, Stanley Blystone, Lenore Bushman, Burr Caruth, Roger Williams, Earl Askam, Olin Francis, Fred 'Snowflake' Toones, Al Taylor, Chuck Baldra, Curley Dresden, Robert McKenzie, Jack Montgomery, Ed Cassidy, Theodore Lorch, Frank O'Connor, John Beach, Bert Dillard, Joe Whitehead.

The Three Mesquiteers are recruited by the government to stop a band of organized cattle rustlers who use mobile slaughterhouses and refrigerator vans. Wayne (as Stony Brooke) poses as an outlaw to infiltrate the gang and send word to Corrigan and Terhune about upcoming raids. However, Ivins-the boss rustler-works with the posse chasing his confederates to hatch a plant that will eliminate the Mesquiteers. Twentieth entry in the *Three Mesquiteers* series. Screenplay by Stanley Roberts, Betty Burbridge and Luci Ward, from a story by Ward based on characters created by William Colt MacDonald. Produced by William Berke. Portions filmed at Agoura, California.

Quotes: Lullaby Joslin (Max Terhune): *"Reckon the folks in Red River will kinda be surprised they're gettin' three investigators when they only asked for one?"*, Stony Brooke (John Wayne): *"They're only gettin' one-and his two assistants."*, Tucson Smith (Ray Corrigan): *"And you're the one?"*, Stony: *"Sure!"*, Tucson: *"It's awfully nice of you to take us along for the ride."*

Music by William Lava (and uncredited Alberto Colombo).

Released on December 22 | 56 minutes/RCA High Fidelity Recording/video/DVD/Blu-Ray | Republic

Danger holds the reins as the devil cracks the whip! Desperate men! Frontier women! Rising above their pasts in a west corrupted by violence and gunfire!

Stagecoach (1939) Directed by John Ford.

Claire Trevor, John Wayne, Andy Devine, John Carradine, Thomas Mitchell, Louise Platt, George Bancroft, Donald Meek, Berton Churchill, Tim Holt, Tom Tyler, Chris-Pin Martin, Yakima Canutt, Francis Ford, Franklyn Farnum, Robert Homans, William Hopper, Florence Lake, Jack Pennick, Bryant Washburn, Hank Worden, Brenda Fowler, Cornelius Keefe, Walter McGrail, Kent

After several years of making B westerns, Wayne broke through to stardom as the Ringo Kid in *Stagecoach*.

Odell, Vester Pegg, Joe Rickson, Buddy Roosevelt, Mickey Simpson, Harry Tenbrook, Chief John Big Tree, Nora Cecil, Marga Ann Deighton, Si Jenks, Theodore Lorch, Jim Mason, Louis Mason, Whitehorse.

A diverse group of travelers, including a drunken doctor, a pregnant woman, a corrupt banker, a shady gambler, a meek whiskey drummer, an outcast saloon girl and an outlaw (Wayne, as the Ringo Kid) must band together to fight off a rampaging Indian attack while they attempt to reach a distant settlement in their vulnerable stagecoach. Wayne also has a score to settle with a gang of outlaws who killed his brother. Screenplay by Dudley Nichols, from The *Saturday Evening Post* magazine story *Stage to Lordsburg* by Ernest Haycox; (with an uncredited writing contribution by Ben Hecht). Produced by Walter Wanger and (uncredited John Ford). Portions filmed at these California locations: Lucerne Dry Lake; Kern Rivers, Bakersfield; Santa Clarita; Kernville; Victorville; Muroc Dry Lake; Calabasas; Beale's Cut, Newhall; Iverson Ranch, Chatsworth; RKO Encino Ranch, Los Angeles; The Lot, West Hollywood. Portions filmed at these Arizona locations: Mesa; Agathla Peak; Monument Valley (shared with Utah); Kayenta; Red Mesa; Teec Nos Pos; Mexican Water.

The cast of *Stagecoach*, left to right: Claire Trevor, John Wayne, Andy Devine, John Carradine, Louise Platt, Thomas Mitchell, Berton Churchill, Donald Meek and George Bancroft.

Quotes: Dr. Josiah Boone (Thomas Mitchell): *"Seems to me I knew your family, Henry. Didn't I fix your arm once when you, oh, bumped off a horse?"*, Henry, the Ringo Kid (John Wayne): *"Are you Doc Boone?"*, Boone: *"I certainly am. Ah, let's see…I'd just been honorably discharged from the Union Army after the War of the Rebellion."*, Hatfield (John Carradine): *"You mean the War for the Southern Confederacy, sir."*, Boone: *"I mean nothing of the kind, sir!"*, Ringo: *"That was my kid brother broke his arm. You did a good job, Doc, even if you was drunk."*, Boone: *"Thank you, son. Professional compliments are always pleasing. What happened to that boy whose arm I fixed?"*, Ringo: *"He was murdered."*

Academy Awards

- (Supporting Actor) Thomas Mitchell.
- (Music-Scoring) Richard Hageman, [W.] Franke Harling, John Leipold, Leo Shuken.

Academy Award Nominations

- (Picture) Walter Wanger.
- (Director) John Ford.
- (Cinematography-Black and White) Bert Glennon.
- (Film Editing) Otho Lovering, Dorothy Spencer.
- (Art Direction) Alexander Toluboff.

National Board of Review Award

- (Best Acting) Thomas Mitchell.

National Board of Review Award Nomination

- (Best Picture) Walter Wanger (Third Place).

Faro Island Film Festival Award

- (Golden Train for Best Screenplay) Dudley Nichols.

Faro Island Film Festival Award Nominations

- (Audience Award for Best Actor) John Wayne.
- (Golden Train for Best Film) John Ford.

New York Film Critics Circle Award

- (Best Director) John Ford.

This film was inducted into the Online Film & Television Association Hall of Fame in 2011.

Music by Boris Morros, Louis Gruenberg, Richard Hageman, [W.]

Franke Harling, John Leipold, Leo Shuken (and uncredited Gerard Carbonara).

Released on March 3 | Box Office: $1,103,757 | 96 minutes/Western Electric Mirroscopic Recording/computer color version/video/DVD/Blu-Ray/National Film Registry 1995/AFI Greatest 63/AFI Western 9/AFI Cheers Nominee/AFI Hero Nominee (Ringo Kid) | Walter Wanger/United Artists

Three game guys unite to quell the most daring land-grant swindle in the history of the old west!

The Night Riders (1939) Directed by George Sherman.

John Wayne, Ray Corrigan, Max Terhune, Ruth Rogers, George Douglas, Tom Tyler, Sammy McKim, Kermit Maynard, Doreen McKay, Walter Mills, Ethan Laidlaw, Horace Murphy, Edward Peil Sr., Tom London, Jack Ingram, William [Bill] Nestell, Eily Malyon, Yakima Canutt, George Montgomery, David Sharpe, Hank Worden, Glenn Strange, Bud Osborne, Francis Sayles, Georgia Simmons, Curley Dresden, Jack Kirk, Cactus Mack, David McKim, Bob Card, Allan Cavan, Dick Dickinson, Art Dillard, Olin Francis, Jack Hendricks, Jane Keckley, Frankie Marvin, Eva McKenzie, Frank O'Connor, Fred Parker, Hal Price, Hugh Prosser, Lee Shumway, Al Taylor, Francis Walker, Nellie Walker, Roger Williams.

A crooked gambler holds a cleverly-crafted land grant that allows him to lay heavy taxes on everyone in the territory. He also adds rustling and theft to his outlawry and causes the Three Mequiteers to be dispossessed of their ranch. Wayne (as Stony Brooke), Corrigan and Terhune fight back by becoming vigilantes and attacking the gambler's henchmen. Twenty-first entry in the **Three Mesquiteers** series. Screenplay by Betty Burbridge and Stanley Roberts, based on characters created by William Colt MacDonald. Produced by William Berke. Portions filmed at Agoura Ranch, California. George Montgomery was Wayne's stunt double.

Music by William Lava.

Released on April 12 | 58 minutes/RCA High Fidelity Recording/DVD/Blu-Ray | Republic

They hit the circus trails in a fast-riding, action-thriller that ends in a blaze of glory on the racetrack!

Three Texas Steers (1939) Directed by George Sherman.

John Wayne, Ray Corrigan, Max Terhune, Carole Landis, Ralph Graves, Rosco[e] Ates, Collette Lyons, Billy Curtis, Ted Adams, Stanley Blystone, David Sharpe, Ethan Laidlaw, Lew Kelly, John Merton, Dave Willock, Bob Burns, Jack Kirk, Ted Mapes, Dirk Thane.

Wayne (as Stony Brooke), Corrigan and Terhune aid pretty Landis when her circus is sabotaged-which may force the sale of her ranch to crooked Graves. Twenty-second entry in the **Three Mesquiteers** series. Screenplay by Betty Burbridge and Stanley Roberts, based on characters created by William Colt MacDonald. Produced by William Berke. Portions filmed at Corriganville-Ray Corrigan Ranch, Simi Valley, California. That's Corrigan in the gorilla suit as 'Naba', aka Willie the Gorilla.

Quotes: Lillian (Collette Lyons): *"What's your job around here?"*, Stony Brooke (John Wayne): *"I'm a cowhand, Ma'am. I chase cows."*, Lillian: *"If I could only learn to moo."*

Music by William Lava (and uncredited Cy Feuer, Alberto Colombo, Karl Hajos, Sam H. Stept, Victor Young).

Released on May 12 | 57 minutes/RCA High Fidelity Recording/video/DVD/Blu-Ray | Republic

Gangland drives an innocent to crime!

Wyoming Outlaw (1939) Directed by George Sherman.

John Wayne, Ray Corrigan, Raymond Hatton, Donald Barry, Adele Pearce [Pamela Blake], LeRoy Mason, Charles Middleton, Katherine Kenworthy, Elmo Lincoln, Jack Ingram, David Sharpe, Jack Kenney, Yakima Canutt, Dave O'Brien, Budd Buster, John [Bud] Hiestand, Tommy Coats, Allan Cavan, Curley Dresden, Ralph Peters, John Beach, Bob Burns, George DeNormand, Jack Kirk, Frankie Marvin, Malcolm 'Bud' McTaggart, Ed Payson, Robert Robinson, Jack Rockwell, Al Taylor.

Wayne (as Stony Brooke), Corrigan and Hatton chase cattle thief Barry, only to discover he has been reduced to stealing after his father

(Middleton) lost his job due to a frontier dictator (Mason). The trio work to help the family-which includes pretty Blake. Twenty-third entry in the *Three Mesquiteers* series. Screenplay by Jack Natteford and Betty Burbridge, from a story by Natteford based on characters created by William Colt MacDonald. Produced by William Berke. George Montgomery was Wayne's stunt double. Portions filmed at these California locations: Lancaster; Corriganville-Ray Corrigan Ranch, Simi Valley.

Music by William Lava (and uncredited Cy Feuer, Victor Young).

Released on June 27 | 57 minutes/RCA High Fidelity Recording/DVD/Blu-Ray | Republic

Six-gun adventures…for three pals of the plains!

New Frontier/Frontier Horizon (1939) Directed by George Sherman.

John Wayne, Ray Corrigan, Raymond Hatton, Phylis Isley [Jennifer Jones], Eddy Waller, Sammy McKim, LeRoy Mason, Harrison Greene, Reginald Barlow, Burr Caruth, Dave O'Brien, Hal Price, Jack Ingram, Bud Osborne, Charles [Slim] Whitaker, George Chesebro, Jody Gilbert, John Elliott, Cactus Mack, Helen Gibson, Herman Hack, Betty Mack, Wilbur Mack, Charles Murphy, Chuck Baldra, Bob Burns, Fred Burns, Jim Corey, Victor Cox, Russell Custer, Curley Dresden, Frank Ellis, Oscar Gahan, Walt La Rue, Frankie Marvin, Bud McClure, Bill Nestell, George Plues, Bob Reeves, Bill Wolfe.

New Hope Valley families are shocked when their properties are condemned to make way for a new dam project. The Three Mesquiteers' ranch is also slated to be destroyed, but they rally the valley citizens to fight the ruling-and outlaws who operate the claim-jumping construction company. Wayne is Stony Brooke. Twenty-fourth entry in the *Three Mesquiteers* series. Screenplay by Betty Burbridge and Luci Ward based on characters created by William Colt MacDonald. Produced by William Berke. Wayne's stunt double was George Montgomery. Portions filmed at these California locations: Corriganville-Ray Corrigan Ranch, Simi Valley; Iverson Ranch, Chatsworth; Van Norman Reservoir, Granada Hills, Los Angeles.

Music by (uncredited William Lava, Cy Feuer, Floyd Morgan, David Tamkin and Victor Young).

Released on August 10 | (57 minutes/RCA High Fidelity Recording/video/DVD | Republic

Thrill-romance of the year! Fighting man and wildcat blonde...during the days when Pittsburgh was 'way out west!

Allegheny Uprising (1939) Directed by William A. Seiter.

Claire Trevor, John Wayne, George Sanders, Brian Donlevy, Wilfred Lawson, Robert Barrat, John F. Hamilton, Moroni Olsen, Eddie Quillan, Chill Wills, Ian Wolfe, Wallis Clark, Monte Montague, Olaf Hytten, Eddy Waller, Clay Clement, Ralph Dunn, Charles Middleton, Noble Johnson, Tom London, Douglas Spencer, Stanley Blystone, Horace B. Carpenter, Ethan Laidlaw, Bud Osborne, Jess Cavin, Tom Coleman, Forrest Dillon, Jesse Graves, Lew Harvey, Leyland Hodgson, Charles Knowles, Robert McKenzie, Clive Morgan, Jack O'Shea, Russ Powell, Earl Askam.

Colonial backwoodsman Wayne (as James 'Jim' Smith) squares off against an English loyalist (Sanders) and an unscrupulous trader (Donlevy), who is selling arms to the Indians under the protection of Sanders. Wayne leads his men, 'The Black Boys', against King George III's forces in south-center Pennsylvania. Screenplay by Pandro S. Berman and P.J. Wolfson, based on the 1937 factual novel The First Rebel by Neil H. Swanson. Choreography by David Robel. Produced by P.J. Wolfson. Portions filmed in Pittsburgh, Pennsylvania, and these California locations: Lake Sherwood and Sherwood Forest.

Quotes: James 'Jim' Smith (John Wayne): *"Put that gun down!"*, Janie McDougal (Claire Trevor): *"I won't! I'm not going to be a widow before I'm even a wife!"*

Music by Anthony Collins.

Released on November 10 | Box Office: $750,000 | 81 minutes/RCA Victor Sound/computer color version/video/laserdisc/DVD | RKO Radio

A drama of undying love.

Dark Command (1940) Directed by Raoul Walsh.

Claire Trevor, John Wayne, Walter Pidgeon, Roy Rogers, George [Gabby] Hayes, Porter Hall, Marjorie Main, Raymond Walburn, Joe [Joseph] Sawyer, Helen MacKellar, J. Farrell MacDonald, Trevor Bardette, Richard Alexander, Mildred Gover, Clinton Rosemond, Edmund

Cobb, Harry Cording, Tom London, John Merton, Glenn Strange, Harry Woods, Budd Buster, Walter Long, Ernie Adams, Stanley Blystone, Yakima Canutt, Horace B. Carpenter, Joseph Forte, Ethan Laidlaw, Mike Lally, Hal Taliaferro, Henry Wills, Earl Askam, Hank Bell, Ray Bennett, Ed Brady, Al Bridge, Roy Bucko, Nora Bush, Bob Card, Burr Caruth, Noble 'Kid' Chissell, Tex Cooper, Bobby Crandell, Marvin Davis, Art Dillard, John Dilson, Edward Earle, Betty Farrington, Robert Ferrero, Herman Hack, Frank Hagney, Al Haskell, Edward Hearn, Howard Hickman, Lloyd Ingraham, Jack Kirk, Jack Low, Cactus Mack, Dick Rich, Jack Rockwell, Tom Smith, Harry Strang, Al Taylor, Ferris Taylor, Ethel Wales, Bob Woodward.

In the days before the Civil War, tyrant Pidgeon's reign of terror in Lawrence, Kansas, is sparked by conflicts with new marshal Wayne (as Bob Seton). Pidgeon forms a gang of raiders who rob and attack the settlers in the territory. Wayne and some decent citizens of Lawrence move towards a showdown with Pidgeon's forces. Screenplay by Grover Jones, Lionel Houser and F. Hugh Herbert, from Jan Fortune's adaptation of the 1938 novel by W.R. Burnett. Produced by Sol C. Siegel. Wayne's stunt double was Cliff Lyons. Portions filmed at these California locations: Agoura; Melody Ranch, Newhall; and Sherwood Forest.

Quotes: Mary McCloud (Claire Trevor): *"I thought they bred men of flesh and blood in Texas. I was wrong. You're made of granite!"*, Bob Seton (John Wayne): *"No, Mary, just common clay. It bakes kind of hard in Texas."*

Academy Award Nominations
- (Art Direction-Black and White) John Victor Mackay.
- (Music-Original Score) Victor Young.

Released on April 15 | 94 minutes/RCA High Fidelity Recording/computer color version/video/DVD/Blu-Ray | Republic

What barrier mars the path of their destiny…the fulfillment of their right to happiness?

Three Faces West (1940) Directed by Bernard Vorhaus.

John Wayne, Sigrid Gurie, Charles Coburn, Spencer Charters, Helen MacKellar, Roland Varno, Sonny Bupp, Wade Boteler, Trevor Bardette,

Russell Simpson, Charles Waldron, Wendell Niles, Mary Field, Francis Ford, Byron Foulger, Hank Patterson, Dewey Robinson, Douglas Evans, Frank Brownlee, Jack Montgomery, Si Jenks, Frederick Vogeding, Wolfgang Zilzer, Bob Burns, Horace B. Carpenter, Darwood Kaye, Arthur Millett, Hugh Chapman, Jim Corey, Calvin Ellison, Stuart Holmes, Gretchen Kisker, Lola Milliorn, Bill Nestell, Manuel Paris, Rose Plumer, Victor Potel, John Sheehan, Ted Stanhope, Bill Wolfe.

Wayne (as John Phillips) leads his fellow townsfolk out of a dust bowl-inflicted plain to richer lands in Oregon. Among them is Viennese refugee doctor Coburn and his daughter (Gurie). Wayne is smitten with Gurie, but she is promised to the man who helped her and Coburn escape the Nazis. Screenplay by F. Hugh Herbert, Joseph Moncure March and Samuel Ornitz. Produced by Sol C. Siegel. Portions filmed at Alabama Hills, Lone Pine, California.

Music by Victor Young (and uncredited Harry Grey).

Released on July 3 | (79 minutes/RCA High Fidelity Recording/video/DVD/Blu-Ray | Republic

She's dynamite…tearing through a lawless Pacific paradise!

Seven Sinners (1940) Directed by Tay Garnett.

Marlene Dietrich, John Wayne, Albert Dekker, Broderick Crawford, Anna Lee, Mischa Auer, Billy Gilbert, Richard Carle, Samuel S. Hinds, Oscar Homolka, Reginald Denny, Vince Barnett, Herbert Rawlinson, James Craig, William Bakewell, Antonio Moreno, Russell Hicks, William [B.] Davidson, Noble Johnson, Mamo Clark, Tom Seidel, Willie Fung, Frank Hagney, Tay Garnett, Mike Lally, Rolfe Sedan, Henry Victor, Eric Alden, Al Bain, George Barrows, John Barton, Danny Beck, Ted Billings, Phil Bloom, Paul Bradley, Ralph Brooks, Bing Conley, Helen Dickson, Alphonso Dubois, Jay Eaton, Edgar Edwards, Virginia Engels, Bobbie Hale, Michael Harvey, Al Hill, Kay Leslie.

A sultry singer (Dietrich), deported and chased out of every South Sea port she's worked, enchants rugged Navy officer Wayne (as Lt. Dan Brent) at her latest nightclub job. Danger, violence and romance follow the duo-especially as local gangster Dekker considers Marlene 'his property'. Screenplay by John Meehan and Harry Tugend, from

Sexy singer Marlene Dietrich entrances Navy officer Wayne in *Seven Sinners*.

an original story by Ladislas Fodor and Laslo Vadnai [Laszlo Vadnay]. Produced by (uncredited Joe Pasternak). Portions filmed at Saugus Airfield, Saugus, California.

Quotes: Lt. Dan Brent (John Wayne): *"Imagine finding you here."*, Bijou (Marlene Dietrich): *"I'm the type of girl you're liable to find anywhere."*

Songs: *I've Been in Love Before* (Frederick Hollander [Friedrich Hollaender]; Frank Loesser), *The Man's in the Navy* (Hollander [Hollaender; Loesser), *I Can't Give You Anything But Love* (Jimmy McHugh; Dorothy Fields), *Egga Dagga* (Nick C. Cochrane) | Music by H. [Hans] J. Salter and Frank Skinner.

Released on October 25 | 87 minutes/Western Electric Mirrophonic Recording/computer color version/video/laserdisc/ | DVD/Blu-Ray | Universal

The love of women in their eyes…the salt of the sea in their blood!

The Long Voyage Home (1940) Directed by John Ford.

John Wayne, Thomas Mitchell, Ian Hunter, Barry Fitzgerald, Wilfred [Wilfrid] Lawson, John Qualen, Mildred Natwick, Ward Bond, Arthur Shields, Joseph [Joe] Sawyer, J.M. Kerrigan, Rafaela Ottiano, Carmen Morales, Jack Pennick, Bob E. Perry, Constant Frenke [Franke], David Hughes, Constantine Romanoff, Dan Borzage, Harry Tenbrook, Cyril McLaglen, Douglas Walton, James Flavin, Harry Woods, Guy Kingsford, Billy Bevan, Mary Carewe, Jane Crowley, Lionel Pape, Maureen Roden-Ryan, Bing Conley, Lita Cortez, Carmen D'Antonio, Lowell Drew, Soledad Gonzales, Judith Linden, Elena Martinez, Tina Menard, Art Miles. Luanne Robb, Ky Robinson, Lee Shumway, Leslie Sketchley, Wyndham Standing, Sammy Stein, Blue Washington.

A moody crew of seamen aboard a freighter set sail on a mission to deliver a load of dynamite to Baltimore after a night of revelry in the West Indies. Rough seas and rumors of a German spy aboard leave the crew rattled and uneasy on the voyage. Wayne is Olsen, a lonely Swedish sailor. Screenplay by Dudley Nichols from four one-act plays by Eugene O'Neill: **Bound East for Cardiff** (1916), **In the Zone** (1917), **The Long Voyage Home** (1917) and **The Moon of the Caribee**s (1918) (they were later presented together as **One Act Plays of the Sea** in 1937). Produced by (uncredited Walter Wanger) and John Ford.

Song: *When Irish Eyes Are Smiling* (Ernest Ball; Chauncey Olcott; George Griff)

Academy Award Nominations
- (Picture) John Ford.
- (Special Effects) R.T. Layton, R.O. Binger, Thomas T. Moulton.
- (Writing-Screenplay) Dudley Nichols.
- (Film Editing) Sherman Todd.
- (Cinematography-Black and White) Gregg Toland.
- (Music-Original Score) Richard Hageman.

National Board of Review Award
- (Best Picture) John Ford.

National Board of Review Award Nomination
- (Best Acting) Thomas Mitchell.

New York Film Critics Circle Award
  • (Best Director) John Ford.

New York Film Critics Circle Award Nomination
  • (Best Actor) Thomas Mitchell.

Released on November 22 | Box Office: $580,129 | 105 minutes/Western Electric Mirrophonic Recording/video/laserdisc/DVD | Argosy-Walter Wanger/United Artists

Lobby card for *A Man Betrayed.*

Fearless! Stalking his prey in a stronghold of corruption...daring death for the woman he loves!

A Man Betrayed/Wheel of Fortune (1941) Directed by John H. Auer.

John Wayne, Frances Dee, Edward Ellis, Wallace Ford, Ward Bond, Harold Huber, Alexander Granach, Barnett Parker, Ed [Edwin] Stanley, Tim Ryan, Harry Hayden, Russell Hicks, Pierre Watkin, Ferris Taylor, Joseph Crehan, Eddie Dean, Raymond Bailey, Tristram Coffin, Greta Granstedt, Tom Steele, Minerva Urecal, Wendell Niles, Dick Elliott, Eddie Parker, Jack Carr, Kit Guard, Jack Raymond, Leona Roberts, Jack Roper, Philip Sleeman, Charles Sullivan, Blackie Whiteford, Don Brodie, Joe Devlin, Robert Homans, Patricia Knox, Walter Long, Frances Morris, Harry Strang.

When a small-town lawyer (Wayne, as Lynn Hollister) heads into the city to investigate his friend's alleged suicide, he meets corruption big-city style and butts heads with a crooked politician (Ellis) running a gambling ring. To make matters worse, Wayne falls for Ellis' daughter (Dee). Screenplay by Isabel Dawn, from Tom Kilpatrick's adaptation of an original story by Jack Moffitt. Produced by Armand Schaefer.

Quotes: Lynn Hollister (John Wayne): *"You know, you'd be lovely if you had brown hair."*, Sabra Cameron (Frances Dee): *"I have brown hair."*, Lynn: (fixing his eyes on her) *"Yeah...!"*

Song: *Sunshine for Sale* (Jule Styne; Sol Barzman) | Music by (uncredited Mort Glickman, Paul Sawtell and Cy Feuer).

83 minutes/RCA Sound/video/DVD/Blu-Ray | Republic

The Duke battles corruption down New Orleans way.

Lady from Louisiana (1941) Directed by Bernard Vorhaus.

John Wayne, Ona Munson, Ray Middleton, Henry Stephenson, Helen Westley, Jack Pennick, Dorothy Dandridge, Shimen Ruskin, Jacqueline Dalya, Paul Scardon, Major James H. MacNamara, James C. Morton, Maurice Costello, Lane Chandler, Virginia Farmer, Bob Kortman, Anthony Warde, Stanley Blystone, Howard Hickman, Jesse Graves, Noble 'Kid' Chissell, Heinie Conklin, Ethan Laidlaw, Gino Corrado, Karl Hackett, Harry Holman, Frank Jaquet, George Lloyd, Walter Long, Ted Mapes, Hugh Prosser, Blackie Whiteford, Phyllis Woodward.

Honest Northern lawyer Wayne (as John Reynolds) falls for a Southern belle who happens to be a corrupt politician's daughter. Wayne walks a fine line wooing her, since he has been sent to imprison her father in a bid to clean up New Orleans' crime syndicate. Screenplay by Vera Caspary, Michael Hogan and Guy Endore, from an original story by Edward James and Francis [Edward] Faragoh. Produced by Bernard Vorhaus.

Song: *Tres Bien* (Jule Styne; Eddie Cherkose) | Music by (uncredited Mort Glickman, Cy Feuer, Raoul Kraushaar, William Lava, Paul Sawtell and Victor Young).

Released on April 22 | 82 minutes/RCA Sound/computer color version/video/DVD/Blu-Ray | Republic

He tamed their wild hearts with his courage and won them with his love.

Shepherd of the Hills (1941) Directed by Henry Hathaway.

John Wayne, Betty Field, Harry Carey [Sr.], Beulah Bondi, James Barton, Samuel S. Hinds, Marjorie Main, Ward Bond, Marc Lawrence, John Qualen, Fuzzy Knight, Tom Fadden, Olin Howland, Dorothy Adams, Virita Campbell, Fern Emmett, John Harmon, Henry Brandon, Selmer Jackson, Bob Kortman, Charles Middleton, William Haade, Hank Bell, Jim Corey, Ann Kunde, C.E. Anderson, Nora Bush, Douglas Deems, Carl Knowles, Glen Walters.

A story of passionate love, revenge and secrets within a moonshining family sees Wayne (as Young Matt Matthews) seething with hate for the father he has never met-whom he blames for abandoning Wayne's mother…an action that resulted in her death. Wayne's feelings negatively affect the other mountain folk, until a gentle stranger (Carey) comes to the hills to undo what the dark mood has wrought. Screenplay by Grover Jones and Stuart Anthony, from the 1907 novel by Harold Bell Wright. Produced by Jack Moss. Portions filmed at these California locations: Big Bear Lake, Big Bear Valley, Cedar Lake, Barlett's Lake, San Bernardino National Forest; Moon Ridge, San Bernardino Mountains. Portions also filmed in Branson, Missouri.

Quote: Young Matt Matthews (John Wayne): *"The bigger the man, the deeper the imprint. And when he's in love, he suffers knowing it's a dead end."*

Song: *There's a Happy Hunting Ground* (Sam Coslow) | Music by Gerard Carbonara.

Released on July 18 | (98 minutes/Western Electric Mirrophonic Recording/Technicolor/video/DVD/Blu-Ray | Paramount

Wayne was the protagonist in an offbeat story centering on mountain clans and their emotions spurred by an intense hatred in *Shepherd of the Hills*.

Lady for a Night (1942) Directed by Leigh Jason.

Joan Blondell, John Wayne, Philip Merivale, Blanche Yurka, Ray Middleton, Edith Barrett, Leonid Kinskey, Hattie Noel, Montagu Love, Carmel Myers, Dorothy Burgess, Guy Usher, Ivan Miller, Patricia Knox, Lew Payton, Marilyn Hare, The Hall Johnson Choir, Dolores Gray, Mickey Simpson, Pierre Watkin, Dewey Robinson, Minerva Urecal, Gertrude Astor, Brooks Benedict, Leigh Whipper, Dudley Dickerson, Neely Edwards, Frances Gladwin, Sam Harris, Howard Hickman, Cyril Ring, Blue Washington.

Wealthy Blondell, who co-owns a riverboat gambling casino, leaves business partner Wayne (as Jackson Morgan) and marries a Southern aristocrat for the sole purpose of gaining prestige and status in society. When her husband dies, Blondell is accused of his murder. Screenplay by Isabel Dawn and Boyce Degaw, from a story by Garrett Fort. Choreography by Dave Gould. Produced by Albert J. Cohen. Portions filmed at Paramount Studios, Hollywood, California.

Songs: *Up in a Balloon* (Henry B. Farnie; Sol Meyer) (sung by Blondell, whistled by Wayne), *Has Anybody seen My Man?* (Jule Styne; Sol Meyer), *Ezekiel Saw De Wheel* (traditional, composer unknown), *Ta-Ra-Ra Boom-Der-E* (Henry J. Sayers; Sol Meyer) | Music by David Buttolph (and uncredited Cy Feuer, Raoul Kraushaar).

Released on January 5 | 87 minutes/RCA Sound/video/DVD/Blu-Ray | Republic

Reap the Wild Wind (1942) Directed by Cecil B. DeMille.

Ray Milland, John Wayne, Paulette Goddard, Raymond Massey, Robert Preston, Lynne Overman, Susan Hayward, Charles Bickford, Walter Hampden, Louise Beavers, Martha O'Driscoll, Elisabeth Risdon, Hedda Hopper, Victor Kilian, Oscar Polk, Janet Beecher, Ben Carter, William Davis, Lane Chandler, Davison Clark, Lou Merrill, Frank M. Thomas, Keith Richards, Victor Varconi, J. Farrell MacDonald, Harry Woods, Raymond Hatton, Milburn Stone, Dave Wengren, Tony Paton, Barbara Britton, Julia Faye, Ameda Lambert, D'Arcy Miller, Bruce Warren, Frank Ferguson, Byron Foulger, Fred Graham, Ethan Laidlaw, Akim Tamiroff (voice), Dale Van Sickel, Stanley Andrews, Gertrude Astor, Monte Blue, James Flavin, William Haade, Mildred Harris, Sam Harris, Eugene Jackson, Frank Lackteen, Elmo Lincoln, John Merton, Nestor Paiva, Emory Parnell, Frank Shannon, Richard Alexander, Robert Homans.

As salvagers in the 1840s recover cargo from wrecked ships, Wayne (as Captain Jack Stuart) falls in love with a pretty female salvage company owner (Goddard). While trying to help Wayne secure the command of a steam vessel, Goddard befriends lawyer Milland-who also falls for her. The romantic rivalry causes Wayne to make a fateful choice. Screenplay by Alan Le May, Charles Bennett and Jesse Lasky Jr., from a 1940 *Saturday Evening Post* magazine story by Thelma Strabel (uncredited writing contributions were made by Strabel, Jeanie Macpherson and Theodore St. John). Produced by (uncredited Buddy G. DeSylva), Cecil B. DeMille and William H. Pine. Portions filmed at these California locations: Columbia/Warner Brothers Ranch, Burbank; Little Old New York set at 20th Century-Fox Studios, Los Angeles; Tank, Pan Pacific Marine Museum, Santa Monica; Santa Catalina Island; United Artists Studios, West Hollywood. Portions filmed at these Florida locations: Key West; Coast; New Iberia. Portions also filmed at Charleston, South Carolina.

Quote Captain Jack Stuart (John Wayne): *"If I thought that wreck was planned, I'd make a topsail out of Cutter's hide!"*

Songs: *Sea Chanty (The Nellie B)"* (Victor Young; Frank Loesser), *Bye and Bye* (Troy Sanders), *'Tis But a Little Faded Flower* (John Rogers Thomas; Frederick Enoch), *When I'm Gone Away* (Sanders) | Music by Victor Young.

Academy Award
- (Special Effects) Farciot Edouart, Gordon Jennings, William L. Pereira, Louis Mesenkop.

Academy Award Nominations
- (Cinematography-Color) Victor Milner, William V. Skall.
- (Art Direction-Interior Decoration-Color) Hans Dreier, Roland Anderson; George Sawley.

Released on March 18 | Box Office: $4,000,000 | 124 minutes/Western Electric Mirrophonic Recording/Technicolor/video/DVD/Blu-Ray | Paramount

Crashing fists in the gold-crazed Alaska of '98!

The Spoilers (1942) Directed by Ray Enright.

Marlene Dietrich, Randolph Scott, John Wayne, Margaret Lindsay, Harry Carey [Sr.], Richard Barthelmess, George Cleveland, Samuel S. Hinds, Russell Simpson, William Farnum, Marietta Canty, Jack Norton, Ray Bennett, Forrest Taylor, Art Miles, Charles McMurphy, Charles Halton, Bud Osborne, Drew Demorest, William Haade, Irving Bacon, Harry Cording, Willie Fung, Earle Hodgins, Emmett Lynn, Paul Newlan, Mickey Simpson, Glenn Strange, Matt Willis, Harry Woods, Chester Clute, John Elliott, Lloyd Ingraham, Gibson Gowland, Robert Homans.

Yukon miner Wayne (as Roy Glennister) attempts to save his gold-mining claim from unscrupulous commissioner Scott as they vie for the affections of saloon girl Dietrich. Events escalate and erupt in a brutal barroom brawl. Screenplay by Lawrence Hazard and Tom Reed, from the 1906 novel by Rex Beach. Produced by Charles K. Feldman, Frank Lloyd and Lee [S.] Marcus. Portions filmed at Lake Arrowhead, San Bernardino National Forest, California; and Yukon, Canada.

Quote: Roy Glennister (John Wayne): *"I imagine that dress is supposed to have a chilling effect. Well, if it is, it isn't working, 'cuz you'd look good to me, baby, in a burlap bag."*

Music by H. [Hans] J. Salter.

Academy Award Nomination
- (Art Direction-Interior Decoration) John B. Goodman, Jack Otterson; Russell A. Gausman, Edward R. Robinson.

Released on May 8 | Box Office: $1,100,000 | 87 minutes/Western Electric Mirrophonic Recording/computer color version/video/laserdisc/DVD | Frank Lloyd Productions/Charles K. Feldman Group/Universal

In Old California (1942) Directed by William [C.] McGann.

John Wayne, Binnie Barnes, Albert Dekker, Helen Parrish, Patsy Kelly, Edgar Kennedy, Dick Purcell, Harry Shannon, Charles Halton, Emmett Lynn, Bob [Robert] McKenzie, Milt [Milton] Kibbee, Paul Sutton, Anne O'Neal, Donald Curtis, Robert Homans, Minerva Urecal, Chester Conklin, Olin Howland, Matt Willis, Rex Lease, Frank McGlynn Sr., Bud Osborne, Richard Alexander, Hooper Atchley, Jim Corey, Pearl Early, Fern Emmett, Esther Estrella, Martin Garralaga, Karl Hackett, Frank Jaquet, Emily LaRue, Michael Miller, James C. Morton, Jose Portugal, Ruth Robinson, Fred Walburn, Cecil Weston, Stanley Blystone, Zeke Canova, Dorothy Granger, Harry McKim.

A Boston pharmacist (Wayne, as Tom Craig) comes west to set up his drug store in Sacramento, but clashes with crooked town boss Dekker-who demands protection money from the merchants. Wayne also lures away Dekker's lady-friend Barnes. Screenplay by Gertrude Purcell and Frances Hyland, from a story by J. Robert Bren and Gladys Atwater. Produced by Robert North. Portions filmed at these California locations: Big Tujunga Canyon, San Gabriel Mountains; and Kernville.

Songs: *There's Gold in the Hills* (David Buttolph; Sol Meyer), *She Was a Heavenly Sight* (Johnny Marvin; Fred Rose), *California Joe* (Marvin; Rose) | Music by David Buttolph (and uncredited David Raksin).

Released on May 31 | 88 minutes/RCA Sound/Sepiatone/computer color version/video/DVD/Blu-Ray | Republic

Flying Tigers (1942) Directed by David Miller.

John Wayne, John Carroll, Anna Lee, Paul Kelly, Gordon Jones, Mae Clarke, Addison Richards, Edmund MacDonald, Bill Shirley, Tom Neal, Malcolm 'Bud' McTaggart, David Bruce, Chester Gan, James [Jimmie] Dodd, Gregg Barton, John James, Willie Fung, Charles Lane, Richard Loo, Tom Seidel, Richard Crane, Anne Jeffreys, Nestor Paiva, Dave Willock, Eddie Dew, Lotus Long.

Wayne (as Captain Jim Gordon) heads up a squadron of American pilots (the American Volunteer Group) who fly for China against the Japanese during World War Two. He allows an old friend (Carroll) to join the team, but the buddy turns out to be a reckless and avaricious adventurer without much discipline-who develops a yen for Wayne's girlfriend (Lee). Screenplay by Kenneth Gamet and Barry Trivers, from a story by Gamet. Produced by Edmund Grainger. Sid Davis was Wayne's stunt double. Portions filmed at these Arizona locations: Flagstaff; Coolidge Army Airfield; and Marana Army Air Field. Portions also filmed at Russell Ranch, Thousand Oaks, California; Santa Fe, New Mexico; and Curtiss-Wright Aircraft Company, Buffalo, New York.

Academy Award Nominations
- (Sound Recording) Daniel Bloomberg.
- (Special Effects) Howard Lydecker, Daniel J. Bloomberg.
- (Music-Scoring of a Dramatic or Comedy Picture) Victor Young.

Released on October 8 | Box Office: $1,500,000 | 102 minutes/RCA Sound/computer color version/video/laserdisc/DVD/Blu-Ray | Republic

They made Pittsburgh's roaring '20s roar!

Pittsburgh (1942) Directed by Lewis Seiler.

Marlene Dietrich, Randolph Scott, John Wayne, Frank Craven, Louise Allbritton, Shemp Howard, Thomas Gomez, Ludwig Stossel, Samuel S. Hinds, Paul Fix, William Haade, Charles Coleman, Nestor Paiva, Douglas Fowley, Kay Linaker, Virginia Sale, Hobart Cavanaugh, Harry Cording, Tom Steele, Anthony Ward, Karen X. Gaylord, Brooks Benedict, John Dilson, William Gould, Nolan Leary, Alphonse Martel, Johnny Marvin, Mira McKinney, Paul McVey, Edmund Mortimer, Lorin Raker, Cyril Ring, John Sheehan, Jack C. Smith, Sammy Stein, Ray Walker, Charles Arnt, Don Barclay, Wade Boteler, Grace Cunard, Bess Flowers, Sam Harris, Ethan Laidlaw, Dale Van Sickel.

A rags-to-riches tale of friendship, love and power among ambitious coal miners fighting for the same girl. Wayne is Charles 'Pittsburgh' Markham, who climbs his way to success in the steel industry-but with a cost. Screenplay by Kenneth Gamet and Tom Reed, from a story by George Owen and Reed; additional dialogue by John Twist (and uncredited writing contributions from Robert Fellows and Winston Miller). Produced by Charles K. Feldman and Robert Fellows. Portions filmed in Pittsburgh, Pennsylvania.

Song: *Oh, My Darling Clementine* (Percy Montrose) (sung by Wayne and Scott) | Music by H. [Hans] J. Salter, Frank Skinner (and uncredited Sam Perry).

Released on December 11 | Box Office: $1,100,000 | (90 minutes/Western Electric Recording/ video/laserdisc/DVD | Charles K. Feldman Group/Universal

What a thrill! Startling drama of a stranded Yankee flier and a Parisian beauty!

Reunion in France (1942) Directed by Jules Dassin.

Joan Crawford, John Wayne, Philip Dorn, Reginald Owen, Albert Bassermann, John Carradine, Ann Ayars, J. Edward Bromberg, Moroni Olsen, Henry Daniell, Howard Da Silva, Charles Arnt, Morris Ankrum, Edith Evanson, Ernst Dorian [Deutsch], Margaret Laurence, Odette Myrtil, Peter Whitney, Barbara Bedford, Ann Codee, Ava Gardner, Jody Gilbert, Henry Kolker, Natalie Schafer, Arthur Space, John Considine, Ludwig Donath, Claudia Drake, Peter Leeds, Angelo Rossitto, Henry Rowland, Philip Van Zandt, James Craven, Michael Visaroff, Jacqueline White, Leatrice Joy Gilbert, Harry Adams, Oliver Blake, George Calliga, Larry Gremer, Greta Keller, Sandra Morgan, Gayne Whitman, Walter O. Stahl, Robert R. Stephenson, George Travell.

A wealthy, patriotic French woman (Crawford) living in occupied Paris begins to think that her fiancé is a Nazi collaborator. However, after he helps her save a downed American pilot (Wayne, as Pat Talbot), she learns the truth about his allegiance. Screenplay by Jan Lustig, Marvin Borowsky and Marc Connelly, from a story by Leslie Bus-Fekete; (uncredited writing contribution by Charles Hoffman). Produced by Joseph L. Mankiewicz.

Songs: *Concerto for Violin in D Minor* (Felix Mendelssohn), *I'll Be Glad When You're Dead (You Rascal You)* (Spo-De-Odee [Samuel Allen Theard]) | Music by Franz Waxman (and uncredited Earl K. Brent, Mario Castelnuovo-Tedesco, David Snell, Edward Ward and Eric Zeisl).

Released on December 25 | Box Office: $1,863,000 | 104 minutes/Western Electric Sound/video/DVD | Metro-Goldwyn-Mayer

It's screwy…and so funny! It's riotous…and romantic!

A Lady Takes a Chance (1943) Directed by William A. Seiter.

Jean Arthur, John Wayne, Charles Winninger, Phil Silvers, Mary Field, Don Costello, John Philliber, Grady Sutton, Peggy Carroll [Jean Stevens], Grant Withers, Hans Conried, Ariel Heath, Sugar Geise, Joan Blair, Tom Fadden, Ed [Eddy] Waller, Nina Quartero, Alex Melesh, Cy Kendall, Paul Scott, Charles D. Brown, Butch & Buddy [Billy Lenhart, Kenneth Brown], The Three Peppers, Lane Chandler, Patsy Moran,

Wayne with popular 1930s and '40s star Jean Arthur.

Hank Worden, Benny Bartlett, Armand Cortez, Frank Melton, Clarence Straight, Hank Bell, Roy Bucko, Monte Collins, Eddie Dew, Clem Fuller, Fred Graham, Dorothy Granger, Ralf Harolde, Sam Harris, Syd Saylor, Bud Geary.

A rough-riding rodeo star (Wayne, as Duke Hudkins) is able to rope just about anything…or anyone…in sight, while remaining a confirmed bachelor. However, he finds a pretty urban sophisticate (Arthur) a bit of a challenge. Screenplay by Robert Ardrey, from a story by Jo Swerling. Produced by Frank and Richard Ross. Portions filmed in Palmdale, California.

Song: *Swingin' at the Cotton Club* (Bob Bell) | Music by Roy Webb.

Released on August 19 | Box Office: $2,500,000 | (86 minutes/RCA Sound/video/DVD/Blu-Ray | Frank Ross Productions/RKO Radio

Thundering violence! The earth explodes as untamed men fight for power and a woman!

In Old Oklahoma/War of the Wildcats (1943) Directed by Albert S. Rogell.

John Wayne, Martha Scott, Albert Dekker, George 'Gabby' Hayes, Marjorie Rambeau, Dale Evans, Grant Withers, Sidney Blackmer, Paul Fix, Cecil Cunningham, Irving Bacon, Byron Foulger, Anne O'Neal, Richard Graham, Stanley Andrews, Edward Gargan, Tom London, Robert Warwick, Harry Woods, Roy Barcroft, Yakima Canutt, George Chandler, Mary Jane Croft, Myrna Dell, Kenne Duncan, Rhonda Fleming, Rebel Randall, Tom Steele, Will Wright, Charles Arnt, Charles Bates, Dick Botiller, Eddy Chandler, Wade Crosby, Pearl Early, Bud Geary, Charles Jordan, Arthur Loft, Harry Shannon, Karen X. Gaylord, LeRoy Mason, Shirley Jean Rickert, Slim Whitaker.

When citizens discover that she has written a 'sexy' book, school-teacher Scott is run out of town. On the train she meets a greedy oilman and a congenial cowboy (Wayne, as Daniel F. Somers). The two men soon fall into a conflict over oil lease rights on Indian land, as well as the attentions of Scott. Screenplay by Ethel Hill and Eleanore Griffin, from an original story by Thomson Burtis. Produced by Robert North. Portions filmed in these Arizona locations: Kaibab National Forest; Fredonia; and Colorado City. Portions filmed in these California locations: Modesto; Bakersfield; and Taft. Portions filmed in these Utah locations: Zion National Park and Kanab.

Song: *Red Wing* (Kerry Mills; Thurland Chattaway) (performed by Wayne) | Music by Walter Scharf (and uncredited Joseph Dubin, Mort Glickman and Marlin Skiles).

Academy Award Nominations
- (Sound Recording) Daniel J. Bloomberg.
- (Music-Scoring of a Dramatic or Comedy Picture) Walter Scharf.

Released on December 6 | Box Office: $2,500,000 | (102 minutes/RCA Sound/video/DVD/ Blu-Ray | Republic

Hard-muscled! Soft-hearted! The roughest, toughest picture of the year! The thrilling story of America's supermen!

The Fighting Seabees (1944) Directed by Edward Ludwig.

John Wayne, Susan Hayward, Dennis O'Keefe, William Frawley, Leonid Kinskey, J.M. Kerrigan, Grant Withers, Paul Fix, Ben Welden, William Forrest, Addison Richards, Jay Norris, Duncan Renaldo, Roy

Barcroft, Tom London, Adele Mara, LeRoy Mason, Charles Trowbridge, Kenne Duncan, Terry Frost, Tom Steele, Chief Thundercloud, Robert J. Wilke, Charles D. Brown, Ernest Golm, Herbert Heyes, Nora Lane, Harold Miller, Paul Parry, Jeffrey Sayre, Hal Taliaferro, Billy Wayne, Crane Whitley, Reed Howes, Bud Geary, Kit Guard, John James, Clarence Lung, Cyril Ring, Clarence Straight.

A rugged civilian foreman (John Wayne, as Lieutenant Commander Wedge Donovan) creates and commands World War Two's newest and toughest South Pacific fighting force, the Seabees: a combination of construction workers and fighting soldiers. Screenplay by Borden Chase and Aeneas MacKenzie, from a story by Chase; (uncredited writing contributions by Ethel Hill and Dale Van Every). Produced by Albert J. Cohen. Portions filmed at these California locations: Port Hueneme, Santa Barbara; Marine Corps Base Camp Pendleton, Oceanside; Iverson Ranch, Chatsworth; and San Diego. Portions also filmed at Camp Endicott, Davisville/North Kingston, Rhode Island.

Songs: *Song of the Seabees* (Peter DeRose; Sam M. Lewis), Where Do You Work-a, John? (Harry Warren; Mortimer Weinberg; Charley Marks), *Ireland Must Be Heaven, For My Mother Came from There* (Fred Fisher; Howard Johnson; Joseph McCarthy) | Music by Walter Scharf, Roy Webb (and uncredited Mort Glickman, Gil Grau, and Marlin Skiles).

Academy Award Nomination
- (Music-Scoring of a Dramatic or Comedy Picture) Walter Scharf, Roy Webb.

Released on January 27 | (100 minutes/RCA Sound/computer color version/video/DVD/ Blu-Ray | Republic

Romantic thriller of a lone wolf and his pistol packin' spitfire!

Tall in the Saddle (1944) Directed by Edwin L. Marin.

John Wayne, Ella Raines, Ward Bond, George 'Gabby' Hayes, Audrey Long, Elisabeth Risdon, Don [Donald] Douglas, Paul Fix, Russell Wade, Emory Parnell, Raymond Hatton, Harry Woods, Walter Baldwin, Cy Kendall, Frank Orth, Frank Puglia, Russell Simpson, Clem Bevans, George Chandler, Ben Johnson, Russell Hopton, Erville Alderson,

Wheaton Chambers, Robert McKenzie, Eddy Waller, Frank Darien, Sam McDaniel.

Rocklin (Wayne) travels to the ranch of a new employer, but before he gets there his new boss is murdered. Wayne investigates the killing, but finds little cooperation from the townspeople. He also uncovers a plot to steal the ranch away from the dead man's niece (Long). Screenplay by Michael Hogan and Paul P. Fix, from the novel by Gordon Ray Young. Produced by Robert Fellows. Fred Graham was Wayne's stunt double. Portions filmed in these Arizona locations: Sedona, Ironwood Forest National Monument, Picacho Peak State Park, Sonoran Desert. Portions filmed in these California locations: Agoura Ranch, Lake Sherwood.

Quotes: Miss Elizabeth Martin (Elisabeth Risdon): *"I saw you hit that poor man!"*, Rocklin (John Wayne): *"Yes, Ma'am, just as hard as I could."*

Music by Roy Webb.

Released on September 29 | Box Office: $2,000,000 | (87 minutes/RCA Sound/computer color version/video/laserdisc/DVD | RKO Radio

The brawling, colorful story of the queen of hearts and the ace of gamblers…with a shock climax such as the screen has never known!

Flame of Barbary Coast (1945) Directed by Joseph Kane.

John Wayne, Ann Dvorak, Joseph Schildkraut, William Frawley, Virginia Grey, Russell Hicks, Jack Norton, Paul Fix, Manart Kippen, Eve Lynne, Marc Lawrence, Butterfly McQueen, Rex Lease, Hank Bell, Al Murphy, Eddie Acuff, Tom London, Adele Mara, Emmett Vogan, Edmund Cobb, Kenne Duncan, Jack Mulhall, Bud Osborne, Hugh Prosser, Dorothy Christy, William Halligan, Gino Corrado, Lee Shumway, Eddie Parker, Edward Biby, Stuart Hamblen, Mahlon Hamilton, Michael Jeffers, Jack O'Shea.

A Montana rancher (Wayne, as Duke Fergus) goes to San Francisco to collect a debt and loses his shirt in a casino. Having fallen for the owner's fiancée, Wayne's luck takes a drastic turn on a winning streak and he builds a casino of his own across the street. The rivalry builds until the infamous earthquake of 1906 threatens everyone. Screenplay by Borden Chase, from a story by Prescott Chaplin. Choreography by Larry Ceballos. Produced by Joseph Kane.

Songs: *By the Light of the Silvery Moon* (Gus Edwards; Edward Madden), *Carrie* (Albert von Tilzer; Junie McCree), *Love, Here Is My Heart"* (Leo Silesu; Adrian Ross; Louis Delamarre), *Baby Blue Eyes, Have a Heart* (Jack Elliott), *That Man* (Is Always on My Mind)" (Harold Lewis; Bernie Grossman), *Cubanola Glide* (von Tilzer; Vincent Bryan), *Too Much Mustard* (Cecil Macklin), *A Hot Time in the Old Town* (Theodore A. Metz; Joseph Haydn), *King Chanticleer* (A. Seymour Brown; Nat Ayer), *Ta-Ra-Ra-Boom-De-Ay* (Henry J. Sayers) | Music by [R.] Dale Butts, Morton Scott (and uncredited Mort Glickman, Joseph Dubin).

Academy Award Nominations
- (Sound Recording) Daniel J. Bloomberg.
- (Music-Scoring of a Dramatic or Comedy Picture) [R.] Dale Butts, Morton Scott.

Released on May 28 | (91 minutes/RCA Sound/computer color version/video/DVD/Blu-Ray | Republic

True, timely, terrific…is this story of a Yankee colonel and his Philippine guerrillas.

Back to Bataan (1945) Directed by Edward Dmytryk.

John Wayne, Anthony Quinn, Beulah Bondi, Fely Franquelli, Richard Loo, Philip Ahn, J. Alex Havier, 'Ducky' Louie, Lawrence Tierney, Leonard Strong, Paul Fix, Abner Biberman, Vladimir Sokoloff, Kenneth MacDonald, John Miljan, Ray Teal, Robert Clarke, Benson Fong, Bill Williams, Erville Alderson, Leon Lontoc, Spencer Chan, Angelo Cruz, Harold Fong, Joseph Kim, Michael Mark, Carmen Padilla.

A courageous Army colonel (Wayne, as Joseph Madden) leads Filipino guerrillas to victory after organizing a resistance group against Philippine occupation by the Japanese during World War Two. Wayne would like to have Filipino Quinn as a dependable ally, but Quinn is heartbroken when he thinks his girlfriend is collaborating with the enemy. Screenplay by Ben Barzman and Richard H. Landau, from a story by Aeneas MacKenzie and William Gordon. Produced by Robert

Fellows. Portions filmed in these California locations: Tarzana Ranch, Thousand Oaks; Los Angeles County Arboretum and Botanic Garden.

Music by Roy Webb (and uncredited Max Steiner).

Released on May 31 | Box Office: $2,490,000 | (95 minutes/RCA Sound/computer color version/video/laserdisc/DVD | RKO Radio

Romance and excitement! Fighting bravely…living recklessly…loving tempestuously…here's the story of the men and women who stormed across the country to carve an empire out of the wilderness!

Dakota (1945) Directed by Joseph Kane.

John Wayne, Vera Hruba Ralston, Walter Brennan, Ward Bond, Ona Munson, Hugo Haas, Mike Mazurki, Olive Blakeney, Nicodemus [Nick] Stewart, Paul Fix, Grant Withers, Robert Livingston, Olin Howlin [Howland], Pierre Watkin, Robert H. Barrat, Jonathan Hale, Bobby [Robert] Blake, Paul Hurst, Eddy Waller, Sarah Padden, Jack LaRue, George Cleveland, Selmer Jackson, Claire Du Brey, Roy Barcroft, Kenne Duncan, Lorna Gray, William Haade, Tom London, Housley Stevenson, Linda Stirling, Dick Wessell, Rex Lease, LeRoy Mason, Victor Varconi, Dorothy Christy, Frances Gladwin, Cliff Lyons, Noble 'Kid' Chissell, Kansas Moehring, Art Miles.

A professional gambler (Wayne, as John Devlin) marries the daughter of a railroad tycoon. When the newlyweds try to buy up land for railroad expansion into Dakota, they find a couple of swindlers who are burning out the wheat farmers who are living there. Wayne decides to defend the families against the land-grabbers. Screenplay by Lawrence Hazard, from an adaptation by Howard Estabrook of Carl Foreman's original story. Choreography by Larry Ceballos. Produced by Joseph Kane. Portions filmed at these California locations: Vasquez Rocks Natural Area Park, Agua Dulce; Mammoth Lakes; Iverson Ranch, Chatsworth; and the San Joaquin Valley.

Quote: John Devlin (John Wayne): *"And speaking of politics, where we're going, there are only two parties: the quick and the dead."*

Song: *Coax Me* (Andrew B. Sterling; Harry von Tilzer) | Music by Walter Scharf (and uncredited R. Dale Butts, Joseph Dubin and Mort Glickman).

Released on December 25 | (82 minutes/RCA Sound/computer color version/video/laserdisc/DVD/Blu-Ray | Republic

Wayne and Ona Munson take the measure of each other in *Dakota*.

A tribute to those who did so much...with so little!

They Were Expendable (1945) Directed by John Ford (and uncredited Robert Montgomery).

Robert Montgomery, John Wayne, Donna Reed, Jack Holt, Ward Bond, Marshall Thompson, Paul Langton, Leon Ames, Arthur Walsh, Donald Curtis, Cameron Mitchell, Jeff York, Murray Alper, Harry Tenbrook, Jack Pennick, Alex Havier, Charles Trowbridge, Robert Barrat, Bruce Kellogg, Tim Murdock, Louis Jean Heydt, Russell Simpson, Vernon Steele, Tom Tyler, Pedro de Cordoba, Philip Ahn, Henry H. Daniels Jr., Blake Edwards, Kermit Maynard, Frank McGrath, Betty Blythe, William B. Davidson, Robert Emmett O'Connor, Jack Luden, George Magrill, John Carlyle, Sammy Stein, William Wilkerson, Emmett Vogan.

Frustrated with the Navy's reluctance to consider their small, fast patrol boats as true fighting craft, commanders Montgomery and Wayne (as Lt. [j.g.] Rusty Ryan) finally have a chance to prove their worth by protecting the Pacific Islands during the coming Japanese invasion. Screenplay by Frank Wead (and uncredited Jan Lustig), from the 1942 book by William L. White (additional uncredited writing contributions by Norman Corwin and George Froeschel). Produced by John Ford. Portions filmed at these Florida locations: Key Biscayne; Florida Keys; and Miami. Portions also filmed in Melville, Rhode Island.

Quote: Lt. Rusty Ryan (John Wayne): *"Listen, Brick, for years I've been taking your fatherly advice, and it's never been any good. So, from now on, I'm strictly a one-man band!"*

Song: *The Monkeys Have No Tails in Zamboanga* (Philippine melody; lyrics by G. Savoca) | Music by Herbert Stothart (and uncredited Alberto Colombo and Eric Zeisl).

Academy Award Nominations
- (Sound Recording) Douglas Shearer.
- (Special Effects) Arnold Gillespie, Donald Jahraus, R.A. MacDonald, Michael Steinore.

One of the 'Ten Best Films of 1945' as listed by The New York Times.

Released on December 31 | Box Office: $3,250,000 | (135 minutes/Western Electric Sound/ computer color version/video/laserdisc/DVD/Blu-Ray | Metro-Goldwyn-Mayer

Claudette on a Pullman without a ticket…he-man Wayne aboard without a care! Laugh-power setting for the screen's most sparkling gem of excitingly amorous adventure!

Without Reservations (1946) Directed by Mervyn LeRoy.

Claudette Colbert, John Wayne, Don DeFore, Anne Triola, Phil Brown, Frank Puglia, Thurston Hall, Dona Drake, Fernando Alvarado, Charles Arnt, Miss Louella Parsons, Jack Benny, Cary Grant, Mervyn LeRoy, Dolores Moran, Raymond Burr, Ruth Roman, Esther Howard, Sam McDaniel, Marvin Miller, Erskine Sanford, Minerva Urecal, Frank Wilcox, Ian Wolfe, John Crawford, Cy Kendall, John Kellogg, Bruce Lester, Houseley Stevenson, Will Wright, Lela Bliss, Charles Evans, Lisa Golm, Grayce Hampton, Harry Hayden, Junius Matthews, Lorin Raker, Charles Williams, Griff Barnett, William 'Billy' Benedict, William Challee, Dudley Dickerson.

The author of a best-selling novel and the real-life war hero (Wayne, as Captain 'Rusty' Thomas) she selects to star in the book's film adaptation begin to fall in love-despite the fact that he thinks her novel is a load of bull. Screenplay by Andrew Solt, from the novel *Thanks, God, I'll Take It from Here* by Jane Allen and Mae Livingston. Produced by Jesse L. Lasky [Jr.]. Portions filmed in Chatsworth and Beverly Hills, California.

Quote: Captain Rusty Thomas (John Wayne): *"Have you heard of some fellas who first came over to this country? You know what they found? They found a howling wilderness with summers too hot and winters freezing. Did they have insurance for their old age, for their crops, for their homes? They did not. They looked at the land and the forest and the rivers; they looked at their wives, their kids and their houses. Then they looked up at the sky and said, 'Thanks, God, we'll take it from here.' They were men!"*

Music by Roy Webb.

Released on May 13 | Box Office: $3,000,000 | 107 minutes/RCA Sound/video/DVD | Jesse L. Lasky Productions/ RKO Radio

Wayne and Claudette Colbert in the romantic comedy *Without Reservations*.

The dramatic story of a girl in a man's world who taught a killer the real meaning of love!

Angel and the Badman (1947) Directed by James Edward Grant.

John Wayne, Gail Russell, Harry Carey [Sr.], Bruce Cabot, Irene Rich, Lee Dixon, Stephen Grant, Tom Powers, Paul Hurst, Olin Howlin [Howland], John Halloran, Joan Barton, Craig Woods, Marshall Reed, Paul Fix, LeRoy Mason, Symona Boniface, Kenne Duncan, Hank Worden, Pat Flaherty, Rex Lease, Crane Whitley, Wade Crosby, Ed-

Wayne embraces Gail Russell, his co-star in *Angel and the Badman*.

die Parker, Rosemary Bertrand, Louis Faust, Tony Travers, Jack Stoney.

Notorious gunslinger Quirt Evans (Wayne) is wounded and given shelter by a Quaker family. Can his love for their angelic daughter (Russell) be enough to get him to change his ways, to keep him from killing the man who gunned down his foster father and avoid the sheriff? Screenplay by James Edward Grant. Produced by (uncredited John Wayne). Fred Graham was Wayne's stunt double. Portions filmed in these Arizona locations: Flagstaff; Schnebly Hill, Sedona; Bradshaw Ranch, Sedona; Boynton Canyon, Sedona; Courthouse Butte, Sedona; Red Rock Crossing, Sedona; Monument Valley; and Oak Creek Canyon.

Songs: *A Little Bit Different* (Kim Gannon; Walter Kent), *Darling Nellie Gray* (Benjamin Russell Hamby) | Music by Richard Hageman.

Quotes: Penelope Worth (Gail Russell): *"Quirt, please stay away from Laredo Stevens."*, Quirt Evans (John Wayne): *"He owes me money. And don't worry-I might come out on top."*, Penelope: *"That'd be even worse."* Quirt: *"Worse! Then it'd be worse if he goes down than if I go down?"*, Penelope: *"Of course, don't you see that..."*, Quirt: *"Oh, I know, I'd be a guy with a marked soul."*, Penelope: *"Don't make it sound so crude, Quirt. You see why...I couldn't love you."*, Quirt: *"Alright, I won't look up Laredo. It's better this way: every time he opens a door, every time he hears footsteps comin' around a corner...Laredo'll start sweatin', thinkin' it's me. His food won't sit well the rest of his life. (sees Penelope's annoyed and amused look) Well, alright; but if I'm gonna be holy, I gotta get some fun out of it!"*

Released on February 15 | (100 minutes/RCA Sound/computer color version/video/laserdisc/DVD/Blu-Ray) | John Wayne Productions/Patnal Productions/Republic

Adventure in the untamed Andes!

Tycoon (1947) Directed by Richard Wallace.

John Wayne, Laraine Day, Sir Cedric Hardwicke, Judith Anderson, James Gleason, Anthony Quinn, Grant Withers, Paul Fix, Fernando Alvarado, Harry Woods,Michael Harvey, Charles Trowbridge, Martin Garralaga, Trevor Bardette, Argentina Brunetti, Jan Sterling, Ann Codee, Frank Mills, Brick Sullivan, Nina Campana, Nacho Galindo, Julian Rivero, Alberto Morin, Eduardo Noriega, Joe Dominguez.

A wealthy American, who owns mines in the Andes, hires engineer Wayne (as Johnny Munroe) to build a railroad to them. The two men run into trouble when they strongly differ on the route for the line-and when Wayne gets involved with the boss' daughter. Screenplay by Borden Chase and John Twist, from the 1934 novel by C. [Charles] E. Scoggins. Produced by Stephen Ames. Portions filmed at these California locations: Alabama Hills, Lone Pine; Los Angeles County Arboretum & Botanic Garden, Arcadia.

Quote: Johnny Munroe (John Wayne): *"I'm gonna build your railroad, mister. And when I'm finished with it, you can take it and wrap it around your neck for a lavaliere!"*

Music by Leigh Harline.

Released on December 27 | Box Office: $2,500,000 | (128 minutes/RCA Sound/Technicolor/video/DVD | RKO Radio

Adventure thunders across the screen.

Fort Apache (1948) Directed by John Ford.

John Wayne, Henry Fonda, Shirley Temple, Pedro Armendariz, John Agar, Ward Bond, George O'Brien, Victor McLaglen, Anna Lee, Irene Rich, Dick Foran, Guy Kibbee, Grant Withers, Jack Pennick, Ray Hyke, Movita [Castaneda], Miguel Inclan, Mary Gordon, Philip Keiffer [Kieffer], Mae Marsh, Hank Worden, Frank Ferguson, Francis Ford, Frank McGrath, Fred Graham, William Forrest, Mickey Simpson, Brick Sullivan, Harry Tenbrook, Danny Borzage, Cliff Clark, Archie Twitchell.

Tyrannical cavalry officer Owen Thursday (Fonda) tries to gain military fame by killing Apache chief Cochise. Captain Kirby Yorke (Wayne) questions Thursday's tactics and is headed for a fateful clash when he goes against his convictions to disobey. Screenplay by Frank S. Nugent, suggested by the 1947 *Saturday Evening Post* magazine story *Massacre* by James Warner Bellah. Produced by John Ford and Merian C. Cooper. Portions filmed at these Utah locations: Arches National Park; Shafer Outlook; Goosenecks State Park, Mexican Hat; Dead Horse Point State Park; Goulding's Trading Post and Lodge, Monument Valley; Moab and Kanab. Portions filmed at the following Arizona locations: Monument Valley; Kayenia; Teec Nos Pos; Red Mesa and Mexican Water. Portions filmed at the following California locations: Corriganville-Ray Corrigan Ranch, Simi Valley; and Selznick International Studios, Culver City.

Quote: Captain Kirby Yorke (John Wayne): (about men lost in battle) *"They aren't forgotten because they haven't died. They're living-right out there* (points out the window) *and they'll keep on living as long as the regiment lives. The pay is thirteen dollars a month; their diet: beans and hay. Maybe horsemeat before this campaign is over. Fight over cards or rotgut whiskey, but share the last drop in their canteens. The faces may change…the names…but they're there; they're the regiment…the regular army…now and fifty years from now. They're better men than they used to be. Thursday did that. He made it a command to be proud of."*

Songs: *Sweet Genevieve* (Henry Tucker; George Cooper), *The Regular Army O* (David Braham; Edward Hart) | Music by Richard Hageman.

Writers Guild of America Award Nomination
- (Best Written American Western) Frank S. Nugent.

Locarno (Switzerland) International Film Festival Awards
- (Best Director) John Ford.
- (Best Cinematography-Black and White) Archie Stout.

#43 on the Western Writers of America's list of Top 100 Westerns.

Released on March 27 | Box Office: $3,000,000 | (127 minutes/Western Electric Recording/AFI 10 Top 10 Western Nominee/video/ laserdisc/DVD/Blu-Ray | Argosy/RKO Radio

Big as the men who faced this challenge! Bold as the women who loved them!

Red River (1949) Directed by Howard Hawks and Arthur Rosson.

John Wayne, Montgomery Clift, Walter Brennan, Joanne Dru, Colleen [Coleen] Gray, Harry Carey Sr., John Ireland, Noah Beery Jr., Harry Carey Jr., Chief Yowlatchie [Yowlachie], Paul Fix, Hank Worden, Mickey Kuhn, Ray Hyke, Hal Talliaferro [Taliaferro], Glenn Strange, William Self, Tom Tyler, Shelley Winters, Lane Chandler, Richard Farnsworth, Pierce Lyden, John Merton. 'Snub' Pollard, Harry Cording, Guy Wilkerson, Dan White, Davison Clark, Paul Fierro, Ivan Parry.

Thomas Dunson (Wayne) builds a cattle empire with his adopted son Matthew Garth (Clift) and begins a massive cattle drive north from Texas to Missouri. Along the trail, Dunson's rigid ways cause Matthew to usurp the herd and proceed to the more profitable cattle-buying railheads in Kansas. As a result, a raging Dunson swears vengeance and moves toward a showdown with his son. Screenplay by Borden Chase and Charles Schnee, from the 1946 *Saturday Evening Post* magazine story *Blazing Guns on the Chisholm Trail* by Chase. Produced by (uncredited Charles K. Feldman) and Howard Hawks. Portions filmed at these Arizona locations: Elgin; San Pedro River; Lil' Boquillas Ranch, Fairbank; Tucson; Whetstone Mountains; Old Tucson; Verde River; Sonoita; Empire Ranch; Santa Rita Mountains; Babocomari River; Kentucky Camp; Baboquivari Mountains; Canelo; Duquesne; Las Cienegas National Conservation Area; Mustang Mountains; Hacienda Corona de Guevavi, Nogales; Mule Mountains; Rain Valley; Hereford; and Biscuit Mountain. Portions filmed in Nogales, Sonora, Mexico and at the Samuel Goldwyn Studios, West Hollywood, California.

AFI Quote Nominee: Cherry Valance (John Ireland): *"There are only two things more beautiful than a good gun…a Swiss watch and a woman from anywhere."*

Academy Award Nominations
- (Writing-Motion Picture Story) Borden Chase.
- (Film Editing) Christian Nyby.

Music by Dimitri Tiomkin.

Released on September 17 | Box Office: $4,506,825 | 133 minutes/Western Electric Recording/ computer color version/National Film Registry 1990/ | AFI Greatest Nominee/AFI 10 Top 10 Western #5/video/laserdisc/DVD | Charles K. Feldman Group/Monterey/United Artists

3 Godfathers (1949) Directed by John Ford.

John Wayne, Pedro Armendariz, Harry Carey Jr., Ward Bond, Mae Marsh, Mildred Natwick, Jane Darwell, Guy Kibbee, Dorothy Ford, Ben Johnson, Charles Halton, Hank Worden, Jack Pennick, Fred Libby, Michael Dugan, Don Summers, Gertrude Astor, Francis Ford, Cliff Lyons, Eva Novak, Harry Tenbrook, Amelia Yelda, Jack Curtis, Richard Hageman, Jack Mower, Nora Bush, Ruth Clifford, Tex Driscoll, Jack Kenny, Charles Soldani.

A trio of fugitive bank robbers promise to care for a newborn whose mother they just buried. Though the child will hinder any chance of their easy escape, the outlaws travel onward with the child. Wayne leads the three as Robert Marmaduke Sangster Hightower. Screenplay by Laurence Stallings and Frank S. Nugent, from the 1913 novelette The Three Godfathers by Peter B. Kyne; (Robert Nathan made an uncredited writing contribution). Produced by (uncredited John Ford and Merian C. Cooper). Portions filmed at these California locations: Mojave Desert; Zabriskie Point, Death Valley National Park; Alabama Hills, Lone Pine; Carson & Colorado Railroad, Owens Valley; Keeler; and the RKO Encino Ranch. The film is dedicated "To the memory of Harry Carey (Sr.), bright star of the Western sky…"

Quotes: Robert Hightower (John Wayne): *"Little Robert…"*, William 'Abilene Kid' Kerney (Harry Carey Jr.): *"Robert William"*, Pedro 'Pete' Roca Fuerte (Pedro Armendariz): *"Robert William Pedro."*

Songs: *Beautiful River* (Shall We Gather at the River)" (Robert Lowry; Charles Ives), *Streets of Laredo* (Troy Hale), *The Holy City* (Michael Maybrick [Stephen Adams]; Frederick [Edward] Weatherly), *Bringing in the Sheaves* (Knowles Shaw; George A. Minor) | Music by Richard Hageman.

Released on January 13 | Box Office: $2,841,000 | (105 minutes/Western Electric Recording/ Technicolor/video/DVD | Argosy/Metro-Goldwyn-Mayer

Romance! Adventure!…As wild as the raging seas!

Wake of the Red Witch (1949) Directed by Edward Ludwig.

John Wayne, Gail Russell, Gig Young, Adele Mara, Luther Adler,

Eduard Franz, Grant Withers, Henry Daniell, Paul Fix, Dennis Hoey, Jeff Corey, Erskine Sanford, Duke Kahanamoku, Henry Brandon, Myron Healey, Rory Mallinson, John Pickard, Chuck Roberson, Harlan Warde, Fred Graham, Fred Libby, Frank Mills, James Nolan, John Wengraf, Mickey Simpson, David Clarke, Fernando Alvarado, Jose Alvarado, Harold Lishman, Grant Means, Carl Thompson, Harry J. Vejar, Al Kikume.

Wayne (as Captain Ralls) hits the high seas as a courageous sailor who matches wits with ruthless shipping magnate Adler over the love of beautiful Russell-and the treasure held aboard a scuttled ship. Screenplay by Harry Brown and Kenneth Gamet, from the 1946 novel by Garland Roark. Produced by (uncredited Herbert J. Yates) and Edmund Grainger. Portions filmed at these California locations: Los Angeles County Arboretum & Botanic Garden, Arcadia; Santa Catalina Island, Channel Islands; Rancho Santa Anita, Los Angeles County.

Music by Nathan Scott and (uncredited R. Dale Butts).

Released on March 1 | Box Office: $2,100,000 | 106 minutes/RCA Sound/computer color version/video/laserdisc/DVD/Blu-Ray | Republic

Rougher, tougher, more romantic than ever!

The Fighting Kentuckian (1949) Directed by George Waggner.

John Wayne, Vera Ralston, Philip Dorn, Oliver Hardy, Marie Windsor, John Howard, Hugo Haas, Grant Withers, Odette Myrtil, Paul Fix, Mae Marsh, Jack Pennick, Mickey Simpson, Fred Graham, Mabelle Koenig, Shy Waggner, Crystal White, Hank Worden, Chuck Roberson, David Sharpe, Tom Steel, Michael Ross, Franklyn Farnum, Gino Corrado, Fred Libby, Frank Mills, Steve Darrell, Richard Alexander, Sumner Getchell, Alberto Morin, Cliff Lyons, Sam Harris, Brick Sullivan, Dale Van Sickel, Henry Wills, Dave Anderson, Charles Andre, Ralph Bucko, Charles Cane.

After defeating the British at the Battle of New Orleans in 1814, frontiersman John Breen (Wayne) heads west to find adventure-and romance with a French beauty-in the unexplored land. He runs into swindlers out to grab land belonging to the French-American community. Screenplay by George Waggner. Produced by John Wayne. Portions filmed in Agoura, California. Chuck Roberson was also Wayne's stunt double.

Quotes: Beau Merritt (Paul Fix): (Holding up a glass) *"Have a shot?"*, John Breen (John Wayne): (Holding up his wounded arm) *"Just had one."*

Songs: *Let Me Down, Oh Hangman* (traditional; new lyrics by George Waggner), *Eight Hundred Miles to Go* (traditional; new lyrics by Waggner) (Performed by Wayne, Hardy, Pennick, others) | Music by George Antheil.

Released on September 15 | Box Office: $1,550,000 | (100 minutes/RCA Sound/computer color version/video/DVD/Blu-Ray | John Wayne Productions/Republic

A hundred unsung heroes against a thousand savages in war paint!

She Wore a Yellow Ribbon (1949) Directed by John Ford.

John Wayne, Joanne Dru, John Agar, Ben Johnson, Harry Carey Jr., Victor McLaglen, Mildred Natwick, George O'Brien, Arthur Shields, Michael Dugan, Chief John Big Tree, Fred Graham, George Sky Eagle, Tom Tyler, Noble Johnson, Paul Fix, Harry Woods, Francis Ford, Mickey Simpson, Jack Pennick, Frank McGrath, Fred Libby, Cliff Lyons, Rudy Bowman, Ray Hyke, Fred Kennedy, Don Summers. Narrated by Irving Pichel.

Captain Nathan Brittles (Wayne), just one week away from retirement, escorts the wife and niece of his commanding officer to Sudros Wells, where--unbeknownst to his c.o.-the Arapaho Indians are planning an attack. Screenplay by Frank [S.] Nugent and Laurence Stallings, from *The Saturday Evening Post* magazine stories *The Big Hunt* (1947) and *War Party* (1948) by James Warner Bellah. Produced by (uncredited John Ford, Merian C. Cooper and) Lowell Farrell. Portions filmed at the following Utah locations: Monument Valley; Moab; Mexican Hats, Goulding's Trading Post, Monument Valley; and Kanab Movie Fort. Portions filmed at the following Arizona locations: Kayenta; Red Mesa, Teec Nos Pos; and Mexican Water.

Quote: -Captain Nathan Brittles (John Wayne): *"Never apologize. It's a sign of weakness."*

Song: *O Bury Me Not on the Lone Prairie* (traditional; composer unknown) | Music by Richard Hageman.

Academy Award
- (Cinematography-Color) Winton C. Hoch.

Writers Guild of America Nomination (1950)
- (Best Written American Western-Screen) Frank S. Nugent, Laurence Stallings.

Released on October 22 | Box Office: $2,700,000 | (103 minutes/RCA Sound/Technicolor/video/laserdisc/DVD/Blu-Ray | Argosy/RKO Radio

A great human story…makes a mighty motion picture!

Sands of Iwo Jima (1949) Directed by Allan Dwan.

John Wayne, John Agar, Adele Mara, Forrest Tucker, Wally Cassell, James [Jim L.] Brown, Richard Webb, Arthur Franz, Julie Bishop, James Holden, Peter Coe, Richard Jaeckel, Bill [William] Murphy, George Tyne, Hal Fieberling [Baylor], John McGuire, Martin Milner, Leonard Gumley, William Self, Colonel D.M. Shoup USMC, Lieutenant Colonel H.P. Crowe USMC, Captain Harold G. Schrier USMC, Private First Class Rene A. Gagnon, Private First Class Ira H. Hayes, Pharmacist's Mate Third Class John H. Bradley, I. Stanford Jolley, Dickie Jones, Don Haggerty, William Hudson, Glen Vernon, Dick Wessel, Conrad Binyon, Dorothy Ford, Bruce Edwards, Fred Graham, David Clarke, Gil Herman, John Whitney.

Wayne's role of Sergeant John Stryker in *Sands of Iwo Jima* earned him an Academy Award nomination for Best Actor in 1949.

Strong-willed Marine Sgt. John M. Stryker (Wayne) shapes his men into an effective fighting unit for a perilous assault on a Japanese island during the last days of World War Two. Screenplay by Harry Brown and James Edward Grant, from a story by Brown. Produced by Edmund

Grainger. Portions filmed at these California locations: Marine Corps Base Camp Pendleton; Santa Catalina Island, Channel Islands; Janss Conejo Ranch, Thousand Oaks; Leo Carrillo State Beach, Malibu; and Universal Studios, Universal City.

Quote: Sgt. John Stryker (John Wayne): *"You gotta learn right and you gotta learn fast. And any man who doesn't want to cooperate, I'll make him wish he had never been born."*

Academy Award Nominations
- (Actor) John Wayne.
- (Writing-Motion Picture Story) Harry Brown.
- (Sound Recording) Daniel J. Bloomberg.
- (Film Editing) Richard L. Van Engel.

Photoplay Magazine Award
- (Most Popular Male Star) John Wayne.

Music by Victor Young.

Released on December 14 | Box Office: $4,000,000 | 110 minutes/RCA Sound/computer color version/AFI Greatest Nominee/AFI Thrills Nominee/AFI Cheers Nominee/video/laserdisc/DVD/Blu-Ray | Republic

The breathtaking saga of the United States cavalry!

Rio Grande (1950) Directed by John Ford.

John Wayne, Maureen O'Hara, Ben Johnson, Claude Jarman Jr., Harry Carey Jr., Chill Wills, J. Carrol Naish, Victor McLaglen, Grant Withers, The Sons of the Pioneers (Ken Curtis, Tommy Doss, Hugh Farr Karl Farr, Shug Fisher, Lloyd Perryman), Peter Ortiz, Steve Pendleton, Karolyn Grimes, Alberto Morin, Stan Jones, Fred Kennedy, Cliff Lyons, Chuck Roberson, Patrick Wayne, Lee Morgan, Jack Pennick, Barlow Simpson.

Wayne (as Lt. Col. Kirby Yorke) has a stormy relationship with his estranged wife and son as he prepares cavalrymen for a battle with Apache Indians during a campaign into Mexico. Screenplay by James Kevin McGuinness, from the September 27, 1947 *Saturday Evening Post* magazine story *Mission with No Record* by James Warner Bellah. Produced by (uncredited Merian C. Cooper and John Ford). Portions filmed at the following Utah locations: Colorado River, Moab; Professor Valley, Moab; Ida Gulch, Moab; Onion Creek Narrows, Moab; White's Ranch, Moab; and Mexican Hat. Portions filmed at these Arizona locations: Kayenta; Mexican Water; Teec Nos Pos; and Red Mesa.

Quote: Lt. Col. Kirby Yorke (John Wayne): *"I don't want you men to be fooled about what's coming up for you. Torture, at least that. The War Department promised me 180 men. They sent me eighteen. You are the eighteen…so each of you will have to do the work of ten men. If you fail, I'll have you spread-eagled on a wagon wheel. If you desert, you'll be found, tracked down and broken into bits. That is all."*

The cavalry western *Rio Grande*, starring Wayne and Maureen O'Hara, was directed by John Ford for Republic Pictures so that the studio would back a favored project of both Ford and Wayne: *The Quiet Man* (1952)

Songs: *My Gal Is Purple* (Stan Jones), *Footsore Cavalry* (Jones), *Yellow Stripes* (Jones), *Aha, San Antone* (Dale Evans), *Low Bridge* (*Fifteen Miles on the Erie Canal*) (Thomas A. Allen), *Down by the Glenside* (Peadar Kearney), *Cattle Call* (Tex Owens), *I'll Take You Home Again, Kathleen* (Thomas Payne Westendorf) | Music by Victor Young.

Writers Guild of America Award Nomination
• (Best Written American Western) James Kevin McGuinness.

Released on November 15 | Box Office: $2,250,000 | 105 minutes/RCA Sound/computer color version/AFI 10 Top 10 Western Nominee/video/ laserdisc/DVD/Blu-Ray | Argosy/Republic

Up from the floor of the sea to a high mark in excitement!

Operation Pacific (1951) Directed by George Waggner.

John Wayne, Patricia Neal, Ward Bond, Scott Forbes, Philip Carey, Paul Picerni, Bill [William] Campbell, Kathryn Givney, Martin Miller, Cliff Clark, Jack Pennick, Virginia Brissac, Vincent Fotre, Lewis Martin, Sam Edwards, Louis Mosconi, Christian Drake, James Flavin, Brett King, Harry Lauter, Michael St. Angel, Harlan Warde, John Baer, Gail Davis, Bess Flowers, Al Kikume, Mike Lally, Keith Larsen, Richard Loo, William Self, Milburn Stone, Carleton [S.] Young, Frank Sutton.

Lt. Commander Duke E. Gifford (Wayne) is a torpedo expert who must take command of a World War Two submarine while trying to rekindle the flame with his ex-wife-who happens to be a Navy nurse. Before they can resolve their problems, Wayne must get to the bottom of why many of the sub's torpedoes are misfiring. Screenplay by George Waggner. Produced by Louis F. Edelman.

Music by Max Steiner.

Released on January 27 | Box Office: $3,863,000 | (111 minutes/RCA Sound/computer color version/video/laserdisc/DVD | Warner Brothers

Second to westerns, Wayne was best known for his war pictures, such as *Flying Leathernecks*.

Air-devils of the sky!

Flying Leathernecks (1951) Directed by Nicholas Ray.

John Wayne, Robert Ryan, Don Taylor, Janis Carter, Jay C. Flippen, William Harrigan, James Bell, Barry Kelley, Maurice Jara, Adam Williams, James Dobson, Carleton [S.] Young, Steve Flagg [Michael St. Angel], Brett King, Gordon Gebert, Gail Davis, Mona Knox, Keith Larsen, Harry Lauter, Inez Cooper, Chuck Courtney, James Craven, Christian Drake, Sam Edwards, Hugh Sanders, Milburn Stone, Harlan Warde, Dick Wessel, John Mitchum, Fred Graham, Milton Kibbee, Jimmy Ogg, Elaine Roberts, Lynn Stalmaster, Hal Bokar, Douglas Henderson, Adam York, Ralph Cook, Michael Devery, Frank Fiumara, James Hickman, Tony Layng, Paul McGuire, Brit Norton, Leslie K. O'Pace, Patricia Prest, Noel Reyburn, Melville Robert, Don Rockland, Mavis Russell, Bernard Szold.

Wayne (as Major Daniel Xavier Kirby) is the rugged commander of a fighter squadron during the battle of Guadalcanal. As he tries to whip his young fliers into an effective unit, Wayne comes into conflict with his executive officer (Ryan), who finds it difficult to assign men on missions in which they may be killed. Screenplay by James Edward Grant (and uncredited Beirne Lay Jr.), from a story by Kenneth Gamet. Produced by Edmund Grainger. Portions filmed at these California locations: Marine Corps Base Camp Pendleton; and El Toro Marine Base, Lake Forest.

Quote: Major Daniel Xavier Kirby (John Wayne): *"When the command meets a commander for the first time, it's like a wedding. Nobody knows how it's going to turn out. Whether it'll be a happy golden anniversary or a divorce. We'll see."*

Music by Roy Webb.

Released on August 28 | Box Office: $2,600,000 | (102 minutes/RCA Sound/Technicolor/video/laserdisc/DVD | RKO Radio

He's a go-get-'em guy for the USA on a treason trail that leads half-a-world away!

Big Jim McLain (1952) Directed by Edward Ludwig.

John Wayne, Nancy Olson, James Arness, Alan Napier, Veda Ann Borg, Hans Conried, Hal Baylor, Gayne Whitman, Gordon Jones, Robert Keys, John Hubbard, Madame Soo Yong, Honolulu Chief of Police Dan Liu, Red [Vernon] McQueen, Sara[h] Padden, Kinko 'Lucky' Simunovich, Bishop Kinai Ikuma, Peter Brocco, Paul Fix (voice), William Forrest, Douglas Henderson, Edwin Layton, Jay Wilsey, Peter Whitney, Spencer Chan, Franklyn Farnum, Robert Fellows, Bess Flowers, Sam Harris, Joel Trapido, Sam 'Steamboat' Mokuaki, Charles 'Panama' Baptiste, Rennie Brooks, Akira Fukunaza, Ralph Honda. Narrated by Harry Morgan.

Two US investigators (Wayne, in the title role, and Arness) travel to Hawaii and begin breaking up a pro-Communist organization-but they find unexpected love for one of them and very real danger for both waiting. Screenplay by James Edward Grant, Richard English and Eric Taylor, from a short story by English and a story treatment by William

Wheeler (James Atlee Phillips made an uncredited writing contribution). Produced by Robert Fellows (and uncredited John Wayne). Portions filmed at these Hawaii locations: Moloka'I; Honolulu; Pearl Harbor; and Waikiki.

Quote: Jim McLain (John Wayne): *"Lot of wonderful things were written into our Constitution that were meant for honest decent citizens. I resent the fact that it can be used and abused by the very people who want to destroy it."*

Song: *Isle of Kuualoma* (Robert Willy Miller; Roc Hillman) | Music by Paul Dunlap, Arthur Lange, Emil Newman, (uncredited Hugo Friedhofer, Robert Willy Miller and Max Steiner).

Released on August 30 | Box Office: $2,600,000 | 90 minutes/RCA Sound/video/laserdisc/DVD | Wayne-Fellows Productions/Warner Brothers

Maureen O'Hara becomes Wayne's bride in *The Quiet Man*, but trouble with her brother must be settled before the couple finds happiness.

Action...excitement...romance...fill the screen!

The Quiet Man (1952) Directed by John Ford.

John Wayne, Maureen O'Hara, Barry Fitzgerald, Ward Bond, Victor McLaglen, Mildred Natwick, Francis Ford, Eileen Crowe, Hay Craig, Arthur Shields, Charles [B.] Fitzsimmons, James Lilburn [O'Hara], Sean McGlory [McClory], Jack McGowran [MacGowran], Joseph O'Dea, Eric Gorman, Kevin Lawless, Paddy O'Donnell, Ken Curtis, Mae Marsh, Brick Sullivan, Harry Tyler, Sam Harris, Noble 'Kid' Chissell, Douglas Evans, Patrick Wayne, Web Overlander, Harry Tenbrook, Jack Roper, Michael Wayne, Melinda Wayne, Toni Wayne, D.R.O. Hatswell, Tiny Jones. Narrated by Ward Bond.

A disgraced American boxer (Wayne, as Sean Thornton) returns to Ireland to reclaim his homestead and forget his dark past. However, he soon finds himself fighting for the love and respect of a feisty local beauty (Maureen O'Hara). Her distrustful and belligerent brother (McLaglen) provides conflict when he wishes the pair to stay apart. Screenplay by Frank S. Nugent, from the 1933 *Saturday Evening Post* magazine story by Maurice Walsh (John Ford made an uncredited writing contribution). Produced by (uncredited John Ford and Merian C. Cooper). Portions filmed at the following locations in Ireland: Cong; Ashford Castle, both in County Mayo; and the rest in County Galway-Connemara; Clifden; Galway City; Lettergesh Beach, Connemara; Maam; Ballyglunin, Taum; Oughterland; and Thoor Ballylee.

Quote: Sean Thornton (John Wayne): *"There'll be no locks or bolts between us, Mary Kate...except those in your own mercenary little heart!"*

Songs: *The Wild Colonial Boy* (traditional, composer unknown) (performed by Wayne, Curtis, Francis Ford, McLaglen, others), *The Young May Moon* (Thomas Moore), *The Humor Is on Me Now* (traditional, composer unknown), *Mush-Mush-Mush Tural-i-Addy* (traditional, composer unknown), *The Isle of Innisfree* (Dick Farrelly), *Galway Bay* (Arthur Colahan)

Academy Awards
- (Director) John Ford.
- (Cinematography-Color) Winton C. Hoch, Archie Stout.
- (Honorary) Merian C. Cooper, "For his many innovations and contributions to the art of motion pictures."

Academy Award Nominations
- (Picture) John Ford, Merian C. Cooper.
- (Supporting Actor) Victor McLaglen.
- (Writing-Screenplay) Frank S. Nugent.
- (Art Direction; Set Decoration-Color) Frank Hotaling; John McCarthy Jr., Charles Thompson.
- (Sound Recording) Daniel J. Bloomberg and the Republic Sound Department.

Directors Guild of America Award
- (Outstanding Directorial Achievement in Motion Pictures) John Ford (a plaque was also awarded in this category for assistant director Wingate Smith).

Golden Globe Nominations
- (Best Director) John Ford.
- (Best Original Score) Victor Young.

National Board of Review Award
- (Best Film) John Ford, Merian C. Cooper.

Venice Film Festival Awards
- (International) John Ford.
- (OCIC-International Catholic Organization for Cinema) John Ford.
- (Pasinetti) John Ford.

Venice Film Festival Award Nomination
- (Golden Lion) John Ford.

Writers Guild of America Award
- (Best Written American Comedy-Screen [1953]) Frank S. Nugent.

Released on September 14 | Box Office: $3,800,000 | 129 minutes/RCA Sound/Technicolor/AFI Greatest Films Nominee/AFI Passions 76/National Film Registry 2013/Online Film & Television Association Hall of Fame 2021/video/laserdisc/DVD/Blu-Ray | Argosy/Republic

That all-man 'Quiet Man' has a new kind of dame to tame!

Trouble Along the Way (1953) Directed by Michael Curtiz.

John Wayne, Donna Reed, Charles Coburn, Tom Tully, Sherry Jackson, Marie Windsor, Tom Helmore, Dabbs Greer, Leif Erickson, Douglas Spencer, Lester Matthews, Chuck Connors, James Dean, Frank Ferguson, James Flavin, Howard Petrie, Fred Graham, Joan Freeman, Robert Keys, Larry Merrill, Ted Eckelberry, William H. O'Brien, Vici Raaf, Ned Glass, Merv Griffin (voice), Martin Milner, Olan Soule, Gayne Whitman, Bill Radovich, Anitra Stevens, Charles Watts, Jeri Weil, Murray Alper, Phil Chambers, Mike Lally.

Wayne (as Steve Williams), threatened with losing custody of his daughter, takes a job as a Catholic college's football coach and is charged with making the team a paying concern so the school can remain open. His zealous recruitment methods indeed build a successful team-but they also land him in a whole new kettle of hot water. Screen-

Wayne put aside his cowboy duds and military uniforms to play a college football coach in *Trouble Along the Way*; Donna Reed is with him.

play by Melville Shavelson and Jack Rose, from a story by Douglas Morrow and Robert Hardy Andrews (uncredited script revisions were made by James Edward Grant). Produced by Melville Shavelson. Portions filmed at these California locations: Pomona College, Claremont; Loyola Marymount University and High School, Los Angeles; and Cathedral Chapel School, Los Angeles. Portions filmed at these New York City locations: Polo Grounds, Manhattan; and the Lower East Side, Manhattan.

Quote: Steve Williams (John Wayne): *"What do you know about love? I think love is watching your child go off to school for the first time alone…sitting beside a sick kid's bed waiting for the doctor, praying it isn't polio…or that cold chill you get when you hear the screech of brakes, and you know your kid's outside on the street someplace…and a lot of other things you can't get out of books, 'cause nobody knows how to write 'em down."*

Songs: *St. Anthony's Alma Mater Hymn* (Max Steiner; Sammy Cahn), *Auld Lang Syne* (Traditional, composer unknown), *Mother Machree* (Chauncey Olcott; Ernest Ball; Rida Johnson Young) | Music by Max Steiner.

Released on April 4 | Box Office: $2,450,000 | 110 minutes/RCA Sound/video/laserdisc/DVD | Warner Brothers-First National

Island in the Sky (1953) Directed by William A. Wellman.

John Wayne, Lloyd Nolan, Walter Abel, James Arness, Andy Devine, Allyn Joslyn, James [Jimmy] Lydon, Harry Carey Jr., Hal Baylor, Sean McClory, Wally Cassell, Gordon Jones, Frank Fenton, Robert Keys, Sumner Getchell, Regis Toomey, Paul Fix, Jim Dugan, George Chandler, Louis [Jean] Heydt, Bob Steele, Darryl Hickman, Touch [Mike] Connors, Carl ['Alfalfa'] Switzer, Cass Gidley, Guy [Herbert] Anderson, Tony [Anthony] DeMario, Tom Irish, Michael Wellman, Tim Wellman, Phyllis Winger, Ann Doran, Fess Parker, Dawn Bender, John Indrisano. Narrated by William A. Wellman.

The crew of a downed DC-3 must survive in the unforgiving Canadian wilderness with few rations and very little hope as a rescue squadron is dispatched to find them. All parties realize that locating the stranded men is, at best, a long shot. Wayne is Captain Dooley, leader of the

Island in the Sky: James Lydon, Hal Baylor and Wayne await rescue when their plane goes down in the frozen wilderness of Canada.

grounded crew. Screenplay by Ernest K. Gann, from his story that was later written into his 1961 novel *Fate Is the Hunter*. Produced by Robert Fellows and John Wayne. Portions filmed at Donner Lake, Truckee, California and at these Arizona locations: White Mountains, including Hawley Lake and Mount Baldy.

Quote: Captain Dooley (John Wayne): *"I'll shoot the first one of ya to leave camp. I'll aim for your legs. I may miss and hit ya in the back of the head. Either way serves ya right."*

Songs: *Island in the Sky* (Emil Newman; Hugo Friedhofer; Johnny Lehmann), *Blue Waters* (Emil Newman; Irving Newman) | Music by Emil Newman (uncredited Hugo Friedhofer and Arthur Lange).

Released on September 5 | Box Office: $2,750,000 | (109 minutes/WarnerPhonic-RCA Sound/ video/DVD | Wayne-Fellows Productions/Warner Brothers

Heat of the plains in his veins...the gunfighter's stain on his name, and now a woman's life in his hands!

Hondo (1953) Directed by John Farrow (and uncredited John Ford).

John Wayne, Geraldine Page, Ward Bond, Michael Pate, James Arness, Rodolfo Acosta, Leo Gordon, Tom Irish, Lee Aaker, Paul Fix, Rayford Barnes, Chuck Roberson, Frank McGrath, Morry Ogden, Pal [Lassie] (a dog).

After losing his horse in a battle with Apaches, cavalry scout Hondo Lane (Wayne) takes refuge on a ranch run by a woman and her son. Realizing that her husband is never going to return-because Hondo killed him in self-defense-he takes the responsibility of watching out for the widow and the boy when the Apache go on the warpath. Screenplay by James Edward Grant, from the 1952 *Collier's* magazine story *The Gift of Cochise* by Louis L'Amour. Produced by Robert Fellows (and John Wayne). Portions filmed at these Arizona locations: Patagonia; Fredonia; and Sasabe. Portions filmed at these Utah locations: Delle; Lonerock; Skull Valley; Tooele County; and Snow Canyon State Park, Ivins. Portions filmed at these Mexico locations: Camargo, Chihuahua; El Sasabe, Sonora; and the Church of San Francisco de Asis, San Francisco de Conchos, Chihuahua.

Quote: Hondo Lane (John Wayne): *"Everybody gets dead. It was his turn."*

Academy Award Nomination

- (Supporting Actress) Geraldine Page.

Music by Hugo Friedhofer and Emil Newman.

Released on November 27 | Box Office: $4,100,000 | (84 minutes/RCA Sound/WarnerColor/3-D/video/DVD | Wayne-Fellows Productions/Warner Brothers

The powerful best seller becomes the screen sensation of the year!

The High and the Mighty (1954) Directed by William A. Wellman.

John Wayne, Claire Trevor, Laraine Day, Robert Stack, Jan Sterling, Phil Harris, Robert Newton, David Brian, Paul Kelly, Sidney Blackmer, Julie Bishop, [Pedro] Gonzales Gonzales, John Howard, Wally Brown, William Campbell, Ann Doran, John Qualen, Paul Fix, George Chandler, Joy Kim, Michael Wellman, Douglas Fowley, Regis Toomey, Carl ['Alfalfa'] Switzer, Robert Keys, William DeWolf Hopper, William Schallert, Julie Mitchum, Doe Avedon, Karen Sharpe, John Smith, Dorothy Ford, Douglas Kennedy, Walter Reed, Philip Van Zandt, Scotty Beckett, Robert Easton, William Hudson, John Indrisano.

A disparate group of passengers are trapped aboard an apparently doomed aircraft that experiences engine problems. Co-pilot Wayne (as Dan Roman), considered washed up, endeavors to land the plane safely as the passengers reassess their varied lives. Screenplay by Ernest K. Gann, from his 1953 novel. Produced by (uncredited Robert Fellows and John Wayne). Wayne's whistling was dubbed by Muzzy Marcellino. Filmed at Samuel Goldwyn Studios, with other portions filmed at the following California locations: San Francisco Municipal Airport; Oakland Municipal Airport; and Glendale Grand Central Air Terminal. Portions filmed at these Hawaii locations: Royal Hawaiian Hotel, Honolulu, Oahu; and Waikiki Beach, Honolulu, Oahu.

Quote: Dan Roman (John Wayne): *"We're takin' this bird all the way to Frisco."*

Songs: *The High and the Mighty* (Dimitri Tiomkin; Ned Washington), *Ramblin' Wreck from Georgia Tech* (Traditional, composer unknown)

(whistled by Wayne/Marcellino) | Music by Dimitri Tiomkin (and un-credited John Qualen).

Academy Award
- (Music-Scoring of a Dramatic or Comedy Picture) Dimitri Tiomkin.

Academy Award Nominations
- (Supporting Actress) Jan Sterling.
- (Supporting Actress) Claire Trevor.
- (Direction) William A. Wellman.
- (Film Editing) Ralph Dawson.
- (Music-Song) *The High and the Mighty*, Dimitri Tiomkin, Ned Washington.

Directors Guild of America Award Nomination
- (Outstanding Directorial Achievement in Motion Pictures) William A. Wellman.

Golden Globe Awards
- (Best Supporting Actress) Jan Sterling.
- (Most Promising Newcomer-Female) Karen Sharpe.

Golden Laurel Awards
- (Top Male Dramatic Performance) John Wayne.
- (Top Female Character Performance) Claire Trevor.

Released on July 3 | Box Office: $8,500,000 | (147 minutes/RCA Sound 4-Track Stereo/Warner-Color/CinemaScope/AFI Thrills Nominee/Video/DVD | Wayne-Fellows Productions/Warner Brothers

The elusive sea captain and his blonde woman in an explosive, suspense-packed story of high daring on the high seas!

The Sea Chase (1955) Directed by John Farrow.

John Wayne, Lana Turner, David Farrar, Lyle Bettger, Tab Hunter, James Arness, Dick [Richard] Davalos, John Qualen, Paul Fix, Lowell Gilmore, Luis Van Rooten, Alan Hale [Jr.], Wilton Graff, Peter Whitney, Claude Akin[s], John Doucette, Alan Lee, A. Cameron Grant, John O'Malley, Fred Stromsoe, Adam Williams, Bruce Lester, Tudor Owen, Gil Perkins, Charles Wagenheim, Harold Dyrenforth, Nacho Galindo,

Stuart Holmes, John Indrisano, Richard Lupino, Hank Mann. Narrated by David Farrar.

German captain Karl Ehrlich (Wayne) must feign his allegiance to Hitler in the early days of World War Two, as he skippers a freighter that has the enemy fleet on its tail and a seductive spy on board. Screenplay by James Warner Bellah and John Twist, from the 1948 novel by Andrew Geer. Produced by John Farrow. Portions filmed in Hawaii.

Quote: Captain Karl Ehrlich (John Wayne): *"Don't confuse sincerity of purpose with success."*

Music by Roy Webb.

Released on June 4 | Box Office: $6,000,000 | (117 minutes/RCA Sound/WarnerColor/Cinema-Scope/video/laserdisc/DVD/Blu-Ray | Warner Brothers

Movie poster for *Blood Alley*.

Two people with their backs to the ancient wall of China!

Blood Alley (1955) Directed by William A. Wellman (and uncredited John Wayne).

John Wayne, Lauren Bacall, Paul Fix, Joy Kim, Berry Kroger [Kroeger], Mike Mazurki, Anita Ekberg, Lowell Gilmore, Victor Sen Yung, James Hong, Spencer Chan, Danny Chang, George Chan, W.T. Chang, Henry Nakamura, Chester Gan, Suey Chan, David Chow, Paul King, Esther Ling Yee, Edwin Luke, Owen Song, Walter Soo Hoo.

The infamous Formosa Straits waterway escape route has 300 Communist Chinese soldiers at one end—and an American Merchant Marine captain (Wayne, as Tom Wilder) fleeing from a prison camp at the other. If that wasn't tough enough, Wayne has to make good his escape while guiding a steamer boat full of local villagers seeking refuge in Hong Kong. Screenplay by A. S. [Albert Sidney] Fleischman, from his 1955 novel. Produced by (uncredited John Wayne). Portions filmed at these California locations: Stockton; Belvedere Island; Colusa County; San Francisco; San Joaquin-Sacramento River Delta; and San Raphael.

Golden Globe Award
  • (Most Promising Newcomer-Female) Anita Ekberg.

Music by Roy Webb.

Released on October 1 | Box Office: $2,200,000 | 115 minutes/WarnerPhonic-RCA Sound/WarnerColor/CinemaScope/video/laserdisc/DVD/Blu-Ray | Batjac/Warner Brothers

Spectacular as its barbaric passions and savage conquests!

The Conqueror (1956) Directed by Dick Powell.

John Wayne, Susan Hayward, Pedro Armendariz, Agnes Moorehead, Thomas Gomez, John Hoyt, William Conrad, Ted de Corsia, Leslie Bradley, Lee Van Cleef, Peter Mamakos, Leo Gordon, Richard Loo, Barrie Chase, George E. Stone, Lane Bradford, Weaver Levy, Charles Horvath, Ken Terrell, Phil Arnold, Fred Graham, Gregg Barton, David Hoffman, Jarma Lewis, Torben Meyer, John Daheim, Norman S. Powell, Michael Wayne, Patrick Wayne.

Mongol warlord Temujin, a.k.a. Genghis Khan (John Wayne) battles river tribes and tries to tame the beautiful Tartar woman (Hayward) whom he captured in a raid. Temujin is later taken captive by the Tartars, but escapes to hunt the traitor who put him in enemy hands. Screenplay by Oscar Millard. Choreography by Robert Sidney. Produced by Dick Powell (and uncredited Howard Hughes). Portions filmed at Universal Studios and Warner Canyon in California. Portions filmed at these Utah locations: Escalante Desert, St. George; Hurricane; and Snow Canyon State Park, Ivins.

Quote: Temujin (John Wayne): *"I feel this Tartar woman is for me, and my blood says "Take her!""*

Song: *The Conqueror* (Victor Young; Edward Heyman) | Music by Victor Young.

Released on March 28 | Box Office: $9,000,000 | (111 minutes/Western Electric Recording/Technicolor/CinemaScope/video/DVD | RKO Radio

He had to find her…he had to find her…

The Searchers (1956) Directed by John Ford.

John Wayne, Jeffrey Hunter, Vera Miles, Ward Bond, Natalie Wood, John Qualen, Olive Carey, Henry Brandon, Ken Curtis, Harry Carey Jr., Antonio Moreno, Hank Worden, Beulah Archuletta, Walter Coy, Dorothy Jordan, Pippa Scott, Pat [Patrick] Wayne, Lana Wood, Gertrude Astor, Mae Marsh, Peter Mamakos, Jack Pennick, Chuck Roberson, Cliff Lyons, Chief Thundercloud, Frank McGrath, Terry Wilson, Nacho Galindo, Chuck Hayward, Carmen D'Antonio, Robert Lyden, William Steele.

Ethan Edwards (Wayne), a former Confederate soldier and loner, returns several years after the Civil War only to have his brother and sister-in-law murdered by Comanches. Driven by his hatred for the culprits, Wayne goes on an obsessive hunt for his kidnapped niece. Screenplay by Frank S. Nugent, from the 1954 novel by Alan LeMay. Produced by Merian C. Cooper. Portions filmed at these Arizona locations: Monument Valley; Kayenta; Teec Nos Pos; Mexican Water; and Red Mesa. Portions filmed at these California locations: Bronson Caves, Bronson Canyon, Griffith Park, Los Angeles; RKO-Pathe Studios, Culver City; and Aqua Dulce, Santa Clarita. Portions filmed at these Colorado locations: Aspen and Gunnison. Portions filmed at these Utah locations: Monument Valley; Goosenecks State Park, Mexican Hat. Other filming locations were Edmonton, Alberta, Canada; and Cut Bank, Montana.

Quotes: Ethan Edwards (John Wayne): *"What you saw wasn't Lucy."*, Brad Jorgensen (Harry Carey Jr.): *"But it was, I tell you!"*, Ethan: *"What you saw was a buck wearin' Lucy's dress. I found Lucy back in the canyon. Wrapped her in my coat, buried her with my own hands. I thought it best to keep it from ya."*, Brad: *"Did they…? Was she…?"*, Ethan: *"What do you want me to do? Draw you a picture? Spell it out? Don't ever ask me! Long as you live, don't ever ask me more!"*, Ethan: *"Let's go home, Debbie."* (AFI Quote nominee)

Songs: *The Searchers* (Stan Jones), *Lorena* (J.P. Webster; Henry D.L. Webster), *Shall We Gather at the River* (Robert Lowry), *Skip to My Lou* (Traditional, composer unknown) | Music by Max Steiner.

Golden Globe Award
- (Most Promising Newcomer-Male) Patrick Wayne.

Directors Guild of America Award Nomination
- (Outstanding Directorial Achievement in Motion Pictures) John Ford.

Released on May 26 | Box Office: $4,800,000 | (119 minutes/RCA Sound/Technicolor/VistaVision/National Film Registry 1989/AFI's Greatest Movies 12 (revised from 96)/AFI Heroes Nominee/AFI's 10 Top 10 Westerns 1/Video/laserdisc/DVD | C.V. Whitney Pictures/Warner Brothers

The life-inspired story of reckless, fun-loving, romantic 'Spig' Wead, squadron commander.

The Wings of Eagles (1957) Directed by John Ford.

John Wayne, Dan Dailey, Maureen O'Hara, Ward Bond, Ken Curtis, Edmund Lowe, Kenneth Tobey, James Todd, Barry Kelley, Sig Ruman, Henry O'Neill, Willis Bouchey, Dorothy Jordan, William Henry, Olive Carey, Veda Ann Borg, Louis Jean Heydt, Mae Marsh, Tige Andrews, Jody McCrea, Evelyn Rudie, Charles Trowbridge, James Flavin, William Tracy, Harlan Warde, Franklyn Farnum, May McAvoy, Jack Pennick, Fred Graham, Sam Harris, Tom Steele, Chuck Roberson, Cliff Lyons, Matt Moore, Dale Van Sickel, Terry Wilson, Danny Borzage, William Forrest, Mimi Gibson, Peter Ortiz, Ralph Volkie, Ruth Clifford, Stuart Holmes, Harry Strang, Blue Washington.

Biographical picture that unfolds the story of Commander Frank 'Spig' Wead's days as a pioneer aviator, screenwriter and a man of war who helped the US Navy in getting an aerial division to support its military vessels; Wayne portrays Wead. Screenplay by Frank Fenton and William Wister Haines, based on the life and writings of Commander Frank W. 'Spig' Wead. Produced by Charles Schnee. Chuck Roberson was John Wayne's stunt double. Portions filmed at the Naval Air Station, Pensacola, Florida; and the United States Navy Building, Washington, DC.

Quotes: Min Wead (Maureen O'Hara) (as she and Frank are cuddling-the phone rings): *"Let it ring."*, Frank W. 'Spig' Wead (John Wayne): *"Why not, it's probably just Washington. Oh, I forgot-you know you're in the arms of a new lieutenant commander in the United States Navy."*, Min: *"Star-Spangled Spig."*, Frank: *"And a squad leader."*, Min: *"All I know is I'm in the arms of a fellow named 'Spig' that I'm nuts about. Hey! How about getting back to your necking with a little more enthusiasm.",* Frank: *"Right!"*

Song: *Toot, Toot, Tootsie* (*Goodbye*) (Dan Russo; Ernie Erdman; Gus Kahn) | Music by Jeff Alexander.

Released on February 22. | Box Office: $3,650,000 | 110 minutes/Westrex Recording, Perspecta Stereo/Metrocolor/video/DVD | Metro-Goldwyn-Mayer

Wayne finds himself imprisoned when he tangles with a female Russian spy in *Jet Pilot*.

Exploding with all the power of the jet age...with all the passion of a daring love story!

Jet Pilot (1957) Directed by Josef von Sternberg (and uncredited Jules Furthman, Philip Cochran, Edward Killy, Byron Haskin, and Howard Hughes).

John Wayne, Janet Leigh, Jay C. Flippen, Paul Fix, Richard Rober, Roland Winters, Hans Conried, Ivan Triesault, Kenneth Tobey, Joyce Compton, Paul Frees, Denver Pyle, Carleton [S.] Young, James Brown, Gene Evans, Harry Lauter, Mamie Van Doren, William Bryant, Rick Vallin, Don Haggerty, Lamont Johnson, Gregg Barton, Gene Roth, Fred Graham, Mason Alan Dinehart, Bill Erwin, Mike Lally, Wendell Niles, Nelson Leigh, John Bishop, Perdita Chandler, Smoki Whitfield.

Wayne (as Colonel Jim Shannon) agrees to help lovely Soviet Leigh defect to the US, but she is really a Russian spy planning to lure the smitten Wayne to the USSR. Screenplay by Jules Furthman, who also produced; presented by Howard Hughes. Portions filmed at these California locations: Edwards Air Force Base; George Air Force Base, Victorville; March Air Force Base, Riverside; Palm Springs; and Republic Studios, North Hollywood. Filming also took place in Gilbert, Arizona. The movie was completed in 1950, but tinkering and reshooting by

Howard Hughes kept the picture out of release for seven years.

Music by Bronislau Kaper.

Released on October 1 | (112 minutes/RCA Sound/Technicolor/RKO-Scope/video/DVD | RKO Radio/Universal-International

A hundred times he challenged the blazing desert only to find that man's greatest adventure was still woman!

Legend of the Lost (1957) Directed by Henry Hathaway.

John Wayne, Sophia Loren, Rossano Brazzi, Kurt Kasznar, Sonia Moser, Angela Portaluri, Ibrahim El Hadish.

A treasure hunter (Brazzi) and his guide (Wayne, as Joe January) are on a quest for riches in the Sahara Desert. Their partnership is rent by a wanton woman (Loren), who joins their party and begins to fall for both men. Screenplay by Ben Hecht and Robert Presnell Jr. Produced by Robert Haggiag and Henry Hathaway. Portions filmed at these Libya locations: Leptis Magna; Zliten; Libyan Desert; Ptole Mais, Cyrenaica; Great Sand Sea; Rebiana Sand Sea; Gilf Kebir; and Calanshio Sand Sea. Portions also filmed at Cinecitta Studios, Rome, Italy.

Quotes: Paul Bonnard (Rossano Brazzi) (after learning the truth about his father): *"He lied!"*, Joe January (John Wayne): *"Come on, he's paid his bills."*, Paul: *"An adulterer! A murderer!"*, Joe: *"It can happen to any man, Paul-good or bad. Woman throws a harpoon into ya, and ya go where she pulls."*

Music by A.F. [Angelo Francesco] Lavagnino.

Released on December 17 | Box Office: $2,200,000 | (109 minutes/RCA Sound/Technicolor/Technirama/video/DVD | Batjac/Dear Film/United Artists

What happens to the mouse when the cheesecake bites back?

I Married a Woman (1958) Directed by Hal Kanter.

George Gobel, Diana Dors, Adolphe Menjou, Jessie Royce Landis, Nita Talbot, William Redfield, Steve [Stephen] Dunne, John McGiver, Steve Pendleton, John Wayne, Angie Dickinson, Stanley Adams, Cheerio Meredith, Don C. Harvey, Jack Mulhall, 'Snub' Pollard, Sam Harris, Bess Flowers, Lou Lubin, Charles Tannen, Jack Pepper, Suzanne Alexander, Suzanne Ames, Paul Bradley, James Gonzalez, Gloria Moreland.

Marshall 'Mickey' Briggs (Gobel) launched a successful advertising campaign for a beer company that involved statuesque beauty Janice Blake (Dors). Briggs won Janice's affections and married her, but Marshall's boss wants him to come up with another winning ad scheme–which causes Marshall to spend too much time at the office. This leads to suspicions that Marshall may be cheating on his lovely wife. Wayne (as Leonard) appears in a movie that Gobel and Dors go to see. Screenplay by Goodman Ace. Produced by William Bloom. Completed in 1956, this film was shelved for two years.

Quotes: Screen Wife (Angie Dickinson): *"Oh, Leonard, I'm so happy it frightens me."*, Leonard (John Wayne): *"Frightens you? Nonsense!"*, Wife: *"Even after five years, it seems as if we're still on our honeymoon."*, Leonard: *"Our honeymoon will go on forever, and forever, and forever."*, Wife: *"Yes, darling, forever."*, Leonard: *"And forever, and forever."*

Music by Cyril [J.] Mockridge.

Released on May 14 | 84 minutes/RCA Sound/Technicolor sequence/RKO-Scope/video/laserdisc | Gomalco/RKO Radio/Universal-International

The Geisha girl they sent to love and destroy the barbarian from the West.

The Barbarian and the Geisha (1958) Directed by John Huston.

John Wayne, Eiko Ando, Sam Jaffe, So Yamamura, James Robbins, Norman Earl Thomson, Kodayu Ichikawa, Tokujiro Iketaniuchi, Fuji Kasai, Ryuzo Demura, Takeshi Kumagai, Fuyukichi Maki, Morita, Hiroshi Yamato.

In 1856, Townsend Harris (Wayne) is sent to Japan to set up the American consulate there. His welcome is not friendly and the Japanese send a beautiful Geisha to distract Wayne from his duties. She instead falls in love with him and becomes his protector at a fateful moment. Screenplay by Charles Grayson, from a story by Ellis St. Joseph (with uncredited writing contributions by Nigel Balchin, James Edward Grant and Alfred Haye. Produced by (uncredited Darryl F. Zanuck) and Eugene Frenke. Portions filmed at these Japan locations: Nijojo Castle, Kyoto; Lake Biwa, Shiga; Todai-ji Shrine, Nara; Kawani; and Eiga Film Studios, Tokyo.

Quotes: Henry Heusken (Sam Jaffe): *"You're in good hands now."*, Townsend Harris (John Wayne): *"Yes, indeed."*, Okichi (Eiko Ando): *"Also, 'yes, indeed'?"*, Harris: *"Yes, indeed!"*

Music by Hugo Friedhofer.

Released on September 30 | 105 minutes/Westrex Recording/DeLuxe Color/CinemaScope/video/DVD/Blu-Ray | 20th Century-Fox

The big guy with the battered hat...and the ragged woman-wrecked castoff called Dude...and the rockin' baby-faced gun-fisted kid...and time was running out through bullet holes.

Rio Bravo (1959) Directed by Howard Hawks.

John Wayne, Dean Martin, Ricky Nelson, Angie Dickinson, Walter Brennan, Ward Bond, John Russell, Pedro Gonzalez-Gonzalez, Estelita Rodriguez, Claude Akins, Robert Donner, Myron Healey, Bing Russell, Nesdon Booth, Bob Steele, Yakima Canutt, Fred Graham, Riley Hill, Chuck Roberson, Ted White, Walter Barnes, George Bruggeman, Jose Cuchillo, James B. Leong.

Small-town sheriff Wayne (as John T. Chance) takes into custody a man responsible for killing an innocent in a bar fight. The murderer's brother, a local wealthy landowner, sends his men to get his sibling out of jail-leaving the town in the middle of a huge battle. Screenplay by Jules Furthman and Leigh Brackett, from a short story by B.H. McCampbell. Produced by Howard Hawks. Portions filmed at these Arizona locations: Old Tucson; Sonoran Desert; Ironwood Forest National Monument; Picacho Peak State Park; and the Sierrita Mountains. Harry Carey Jr. and Malcolm Atterbury originally had roles in the film, but their scenes were deleted from the final release print.

Quotes: Burt (James B. Leong) (referring to three dead hired gunman): *"Oh, Senor Chance, what do you wish me to do with these three dead men?"*, John T. Chance (John Wayne): *"Well, you're the undertaker,*

Burt-bury 'em. Another one down by the bridge. Send in your bill and the county will pay you.", -Burt: "No need for that. Each one of them had two new fifty-dollar gold pieces in his pocket.", Chance (pensively): "Price is going up."

Songs: *Rio Bravo* (Dimitri Tiomkin; Paul Francis Webster), *My Rifle, My Pony and Me* (Tiomkin; Webster), *Get Along Home, Cindy* (composer unknown) | Music by Dimitri Tiomkin.

Directors Guild of America Award Nomination
- (Outstanding Directorial Achievement in Motion Pictures) Howard Hawks.

Golden Globe Award
- (Most Promising Newcomer-Female) Angie Dickinson.

Golden Globe Award Nomination
- (Most Promising Newcomer-Male) Ricky Nelson.

Golden Laurel Award Nominations
- (Top Action Drama) Howard Hawks.
- (Top Action Performance) Dean Martin.

Released on April 4 | Box Office: $5,750,000 | (141 minutes/RCA Sound/Technicolor/AFI Top 10 Westerns Nominee/National Film Registry 2014/video/laserdisc/DVD | Armada Productions/Warner Brothers

...Rides where only the great ones go!

The Horse Soldiers (1959) Directed by John Ford.

John Wayne, William Holden, Constance Towers, Judson Pratt, Hoot Gibson, Ken Curtis, Willis Bouchey, Bing Russell, O.Z. Whitehead, Hank Worden, Chuck Hayward, Denver Pyle, Strother Martin, Basil Ruysdael, Carleton [S.] Young, William Leslie, William Henry, Walter Reed, Anna Lee, William Forrest, Ron Hagerthy, Russell Simpson, Althea Gibson, Jack Pennick, Stan Jones, Richard H. Cutting, Charles Seel, Gertrude Astor, Fred Graham, Sam Harris, Wilbur Mack, John Ford, Jan Stine, William Wellman Jr.

Civil War western in which a Union Cavalry unit is sent behind Confederate lines to destroy a key supply depot. Wayne is Colonel John Marlowe, who has to take with him a female Southern spy (Towers)

to keep her from divulging their sabotage plans; he also deals with a soldier-doctor (Holden) possessing a pacifistic streak. Screenplay by John Lee Mahin and Martin Rackin, from the 1956 novel by Harold Sinclair, in turn based on an actual incident. Produced by (uncredited Walter Mirisch), Martin Rackin and John Lee Mahin. Portions filmed at these California locations: The Lot, West Hollywood; and Janss Conejo Ranch, Thousand Oaks. Portions filmed at these Louisiana locations: Oakland Plantation, Natchitoches; and Alexandria. Portions filmed at these Mississippi locations: Jefferson Military College, Washington; Natchez; and the Homochitto River.

Quotes: Miss Hannah Hunter (Constance Towers) (under fire from military cadets): *"What are you going to do now, Mister Colonel Marlowe?"*, Colonel John Marlowe (John Wayne): *"With all due respect, Ma'am, I'm gonna get the hell outta here."*

Songs: *I Left My Love* (Stan Jones), *The Bonnie Blue Flag* (Traditional Irish melody; lyrics by Harry McCarthy), *Lorena* (J.P. Webster; Henry D.L. Webster) | Music by David Buttolph.

Directors Guild of America Award Nomination
- (Outstanding Directorial Achievement in Motion Pictures) John Ford.

Released on June 26 | Box Office: $3,800,000 | (119 minutes/Westrex Recording/DeLuxe Color/ video/Laserdisc/DVD | Mahin-Rackin/Mirisch Corporation/United Artists

They stood firing until they could stand no longer…156 men against a raging army of 7,000!

The Alamo (1960) Directed by John Wayne.

John Wayne, Richard Widmark, Laurence Harvey, Frankie Avalon, Patrick Wayne, Linda Cristal, Joan O'Brien, Chill Wills, Joseph Calleia, Ken Curtis, Carlos Arruza, Jester Hairston, Veda Ann Borg, John Dierkes, Denver Pyle, Aissa Wayne, Hank Worden, Bill [William] Henry, Bill Daniel, Wesley Lau, Chuck Roberson, Guinn [Big Boy] Williams, Olive Carey, Ruben Padilla, Richard Boone, Big John Hamilton, Rosita Fernandez, Fred Graham, Cliff Lyons, Boyd 'Red' Morgan, Pilar Wayne, Toni Wayne, Julian Trevino, Carol Baxter, LeJean Eldridge, Tom Hennesy, Cy Malis.

In 1836, Davy Crockett (John Wayne) and Jim Bowie (Widmark) join a hastily-assembled Texan army to rebel against Mexican rule. General Sam Houston (Boone) buys time as the Mexican forces make its way across Texas by ordering Colonel William Travis (Harvey) to join the small band of Texans to protect a mission in San Antonio from enemy General Santa Ana and his army. Screenplay by James Edward Grant based on a true historical incident. Produced by John Wayne. Portions filmed in Mexico and at Alamo Village, Brackettville, Texas.

Quote: Davy Crockett (John Wayne): *"Republic, I like the sound of the word. It means people can live free, talk free, go or come, buy or sell, be drunk or sober, however they choose."*

Songs: *The Green Leaves of Summer* (Dimitri Tiomkin; Paul Francis Webster) (Academy Award Nominee), *Tennessee Babe* (Tiomkin; Webster), *Here's to the Ladies* (Tiomkin; Webster), *Ballad of the Alamo* (Tiomkin; Webster)

Academy Award
  • (Sound) Gordon E. Sawyer, Fred Hynes.

Academy Award Nominations

  • (Picture) John Wayne.
  • (Supporting Actor) Chill Wills.
  • (Cinematography-Color) William H. Clothier.
  • (Film Editing) Stuart Gilmore.
  • (Music-Scoring of a Dramatic or Comedy Picture) Dimitri Tiomkin.

Golden Globe Award
  • (Best Original Score) Dimitri Tiomkin.

Golden Laurel Awards
  • (Top Action Drama) John Wayne.
  • (Top Action Performance) John Wayne.
  • (Top Musical Score) Dimitri Tiomkin.

Golden Laurel Award Nomination
  • (Top Male Supporting Performance) Chill Wills.

Western Heritage Bronze Wrangler Award
  • (Theatrical Motion Picture) James Edward Grant (writer), Laurence Harvey, Richard Widmark, John Wayne.

Released on October 26 | Box Office: $20,000,000 | #1 on the National Board of Review's Top Ten Films | 161 minutes/Westrex Recording, 3-Channel Stereo/Technicolor/Todd A-O/video/ laserdisc/DVD | The Alamo Company/Batjac/United Artists

It's fun-filled adventure all the way from Seattle to Nome!

North to Alaska (1960) Directed by Henry Hathaway.

John Wayne, Stewart Granger, Ernie Kovacs, Fabian, Capucine, Mickey Shaughnessy, Karl Swenson, Joe Sawyer, Kathleen Freeman, John Qualen, Stanley Adams, Stephen Courtleigh, Lilyan Chauvin, Douglas Dick, Frank Faylen, Esther Dale, Richard Deacon, Oscar Beregi Jr., James Griffith, Vic Tayback, Fred Graham, Alan Carney, Rayford Barnes, Franklyn Farnum, Sam Harris, Joey Faye, Richard Collier, Marcel Hillaire, Paul Maxey, Tudor Owen, Milton Selzer, Charles Seel, Roy Jenson, Narda Onyx, Ruth Perrott, Arlene Harris, Kermit Maynard, Boyd 'Red' Morgan, Ollie O' Toole, Peter Bourne, Max Mellinger, Dale Van Sickel.

In 1901, gold prospectors Sam McCord (Wayne) and George Pratt (Granger) have struck it rich in Nome, Alaska. During a trip to gather supplies and equipment, Wayne agrees to fetch George's fiancée from Seattle. When Wayne arrives, he discovers the woman is already married and decides to bring back a girl named Angel (Capucine) as a substitute. However, Angel has already fallen in love with Wayne. Screenplay by Martin Rackin, John Lee Mahin and Claude Binyon, from the 1939 play *Birthday Gift* by Laszlo Fodor and an idea by John H. Kafka; (Ben Hecht and Wendell Mayes made uncredited writing contributions). Choreography by Josephine Earl. Produced by Henry Hathaway, (uncredited Charles K. Feldman and John Lee Mahin). Portions filmed in Yukon, Canada; and at these California locations: Hot Creek, Inyo National Forest; Big Bear Lake and Valley, San Bernardino National Forest; Mammoth Lakes; Point Mugu; Alabama Hills, Lone Pine. Fred Graham was Wayne's stunt double.

Quote: Sam McCord (John Wayne): *"Ahh, women! I never met one yet that was half as reliable as a horse!"*

Songs: *If You Knew* (Russell Faith; Robert P. Marcucci; Peter DeAngelis), *North to Alaska* (Mike Phillips) | Music by Lionel Newman, (uncredited Cyril J. Mockridge and Irving Gertz).

Golden Laurel Award
- (Sleeper of the Year) Charles K. Feldman, Henry Hathaway, John Lee Mahin.

Writers Guild of America Award Nomination
- (Screen-Best Written American Comedy) Martin Rackin, John Lee Mahin, Claude Binyon.

Released on November 10 | Box Office: $10,000,000 | 122 minutes/Westrex Recording, 4-track Stereo/DeLuxe Color/CinemaScope/video/laserdisc/DVD/Blu-Ray | 20th Century-Fox

Big Jake the adventurer…Paul Regret the gambler…Picar the gypsy beauty…three with a past…destined to cross and clash…in a kingdom of killers

The Comancheros (1961) Directed by Michael Curtiz (and uncredited John Wayne).

John Wayne, Stuart Whitman, Ina Balin, Nehemiah Persoff, Lee Marvin, Michael Ansara, Pat [Patrick] Wayne, Bruce Cabot, Joan O'Brien, Jack Elam, Edgar Buchanan, Henry Daniell, Richard Devon, Guinn 'Big Boy' Williams, Bob Steele, Leigh Snowden, Gregg Palmer, Roger Mobley, Alan Carney, George J. Lewis, John Dierkes, Booth Colman, Jon Lormer, Dennis Cole, William Fawcett, Anne Barton, Eric Feldary, Iphigenie Castiglioni, Jackie Cubat, Gabriel Curtis, Ilana Dowding, Tom Hennesy, Cliff Lyons, Henry Wills, Aissa Wayne.

Tough Texas Ranger Jake Cutter (Wayne) pursues an outlaw gang selling guns to the Indians, as well as a murder suspect who unexpectedly becomes an ally. Screenplay by James Edward Grant and Clair Huffaker, from the 1952 novel by Paul I. Wellman. Choreography by Hal [Harold] Belfer. Produced by George Sherman. Portions filmed at these Arizona locations: Red Rock Crossing, Sedona; Mexican Water; Fredonia; Colorado City; Paiute Wilderness Area; Moccasin Mountains. Portions filmed at these Utah locations: Dead Horse Point State Park; Castle Valley, Moab; Fisher Towers, Moab; Professor Valley, Moab; King's Bottom; La Sal Mountains; Colorado River.

Quotes: Captain Jake Cutter (John Wayne): *"You think I'm simple mind-*

ed.", Paul Regret (Stuart Whitman): *"Yes, I think you're simple mind-ed.",* Cutter: *"Well, don't make a point of saying it too often...and once more would be too often!"*

Songs: *The Comancheros* (Tillman [B.] Franks), *Red Wing* (Kerry Mills; Thurland Chattaway) (performed by Wayne and Marvin) | Music by El-mer Bernstein.

Golden Laurel Award
- (Top Action Performance) John Wayne.

Golden Laurel Award Nominations
- (Top Action Drama) George Sherman.
- (Top Male Supporting Performance) Lee Marvin.
- (Top Action Performance) Stuart Whitman.

Western Heritage Bronze Wrangler Award
- (Theatrical Motion Picture) George Sherman, James Edward Grant, Clair Huffaker, Michael Curtiz, John Wayne, Stuart Whitman, Ina Balin.

Released on November 1 | 107 minutes/Westrex Recording, 4-track Stereo/DeLuxe Color/CinemaScope/video/laserdisc/DVD/Blu-Ray | 20th Century-Fox

Together for the first time-James Stewart-John Wayne-in the master-piece of four-time Academy Award winner John Ford.

The Man Who Shot Liberty Valance (1962) Directed by John Ford.

John Wayne, James Stewart, Vera Miles, Lee Marvin, Edmond O'Brien, Andy Devine, Ken Murray, John Carradine, Jeanette Nolan, John Qualen, Willis Bouchey, Carleton [S.] Young, Woody Strode, Denver Pyle, Strother Martin, Lee Van Cleef, Robert F. Simon, O.Z. Whitehead, Paul Birch, Joseph Hoover, Anna Lee, William Henry, Gertrude Astor, Jack Pennick, Earle Hodgins, Shug Fisher, Eva Novak, Ethan Laidlaw, 'Snub' Pollard, Sam Harris, Charles Seel, Chuck Roberson, Buddy Roosevelt, Ted Mapes, Rudy Sooter, Tom Hennesy, Jacqueline Malouf.

Respected politician Ransom Stoddard (Stewart) returns to a small frontier town for the funeral of Tom Doniphon (Wayne), a man who years earlier had unselfishly set him on the path to success. Stoddard thinks back to the time he was a greenhorn lawyer attempting to civilize the town, but was challenged at every turn by dangerous outlaw Liberty Valance (Marvin). This led to an intense showdown and Doniphon's secret. Screenplay by James Warner Bellah and Willis Goldbeck, from the 1953 short story by Dorothy M. Johnson. Produced by Willis Goldbeck (and uncredited John Ford). Portions filmed at these California locations: Janss Conejo Ranch, Thousand Oaks; and Jamestown.

Quotes: Tom Doniphon (John Wayne): *"Whoa, take 'er easy there, Pilgrim."*, Maxwell Scott (Carleton [S.] Young): *"This is the West, sir. When the legend becomes fact, print the legend."*-AFI Quotes Nominee.

Academy Award Nomination
- (Costume Design-Black and White) Edith Head.

Golden Laurel Award
- (Top Action Performance) John Wayne.

Golden Laurel Award Nomination
- (Top Action Drama) Willis Goldbeck.
- (Top Action Performance) Lee Marvin.

Western Heritage Bronze Wrangler Award
- (Theatrical Motion Picture) Willis Goldbeck, John Ford, James Warner Bellah, John Wayne, James Stewart, Vera Miles, Lee Marvin, Edmond O'Brien.

Tom Doniphon (John Wayne) was an AFI Hero Nominee.

Music by Cyril J. Mockridge.

Released on April 22 | Box Office: $8,000,000 | (123 minutes/Westrex Recording/National Film Registry 2007/AFI Top 10 Western Nominee/ video/laserdisc/DVD | John Ford Productions/ Paramount

Hatari means fun! Hatari means adventure! Hatari means thrills!

Hatari! (1962) Directed by Howard Hawks.

John Wayne, Hardy Kruger, Elsa Martinelli, Red Buttons, Gerard Blain, Bruce Cabot, Michele Girardon, Valentin de Vargas, Eduard Franz, Cathy Lewis, Sam Harris, Jon Chevron, Eric Rungren, Henry Scott, Emmett Smith, Jack Williams.

Wayne (as Sean Mercer) and his band of big-game wranglers face danger (what the film's title means in Swahili) in the jungles of eastern Africa as they capture wild animals for zoos around the world. Romantic tension develops between Wayne and Martinelli, a Swiss animal photographer who arrives at the compound and triggers Wayne's memories of a failed engagement. Screenplay by Leigh Brackett, from a story by Harry Kurnitz. Produced by Howard Hawks. Portions filmed at these Tanzania locations: Arusha National Park; Mount Meru; Serengeti National Park; Tanganyika National Park; Meru; Ngorongoro Crater and Conservation Area, Arusha; Naberara; Ruvu River; Lake Manyara; Momella Wildlife Lodge. Chuck Roberson was Wayne's stunt double.

Quotes: Dallas (Elsa Martinelli): *"You have been drinking a little, hm?"*, Sean Mercer (John Wayne): *"No, Ma'am. I've been drinking a lot."*

Songs: *Just for Tonight* (Hoagy Carmichael; Johnny Mercer), *Baby Elephant Walk* (Henry Mancini), *Old Folks at Home* (*Swanee River*) (Stephen Foster) | Music by Henry Mancini (AFI Film Score Nominee).

Academy Award Nomination
- (Cinematography-Color) Russell Harlan.

Golden Laurel Award Nomination
- (Top Action Drama) Howard Hawks.

Released on June 19 | Box Office: $12,923,077 | 159 minutes/Westrex Recording/Technicolor/ video/laserdisc/DVD/Blu-Ray | Malabar/Paramount

This is the day that changed the world...when history held its breath.

The Longest Day (1962) Directed by Ken Annakin, Andrew Marton, Bernhard Wicki (and uncredited Darryl F. Zanuck).

Don Adams, Eddie Albert, Paul Anka, Arletty, Patrick Barr, Jean-Louis Barrault, Yves Barsacq, Richard Beymer, Hans Christian Blech, [Andre] Bourvil, Lyndon Brook, Richard Burton, Wolfgang Buttner, Red Buttons, Pauline Carton, Jean Champion, Bryan Coleman, Gary Collins, Sean Connery, John Crawford, Mark Damon, Ray Danton, Richard Dawson, Eugene Deckers, Leslie de Laspee, Irina Demich [Demick], Colin Drake, Fred Dur, Fabian, Mel Ferrer, Frank Finlay, Henry Fonda, Steve Forrest, Harry Fowler, Bernard Fox, Robert Freitag, Bernard Fresson, Gert Frobe, Leo Genn, Walter Gotell, Henry Grace (dubbed by Allen Swift), John Gregson, Clement Harari, Paul Hartmann, Ruth Hausmeister, Jack Hedley, Peter Helm, Michael Hinz, Werner Hinz, Walter Horsbrugh, Donald Houston, Jeff [Jeffrey] Hunter, Karl John, Curt [Curd] Jergens, Til Kiwe, Alexander Knox, Mickey Knox, Simon Lack, Peter Lawford, Fernand Ledoux, Joseph Lowe, Wolfgang Lukschy, Victor Maddern, Howard Marion-Crawford, Christian Marquand, Dewey Martin, Roddy McDowall, Michael Medwin, John Meillon, Kurt Meisel, Sal Mineo, Robert Mitchum, Tony Mordente, Kenneth More, Louis Mounier, Richard Munch, Bill Nagy, Edmond O'Brien, Rainer Penkert, Leslie Phillips, Sian Phillips, Maurice Poli, Wolfgang Preiss, Ron Randell, Harmut Reck, Trevor Reid, Heinz Reincke, Madeleine Renaud, Georges Riviere, John Robinson, Norman Rossington, Paul Edwin Roth, Robert Ryan, Tommy Sands, Dietmar Schonherr, Ernst Schroder, George Segal, Jean Servais, Hans Sohnker, Heinz Spitzner, Bob Steele, Rod Steiger, Nicholas Stuart, Alice Tissot, Richard Todd, Tom Tryon, Peter Van Eyck, Vicco von Bulow, Robert Wagner, Richard Wattis, Stuart Whitman, Georges Wilson, John Wayne.

The story of the D-Day landings at Normandy during World War Two. As top-secret preparations for the invasion are being made and carried out, Allied maneuvers are undertaken to mislead the Germans. The British mount a glider assault on Pegasus Bridge and the French Resistance carries off sabotage operations. Wayne plays Lieutenant Colonel Benjamin Vandervoort. Screenplay by Cornelius Ryan, from his 1959 novel; additional sequences written by Romain Gary, James Jones, David Pursall and Jack Seddon. Produced by Darryl F. Zanuck. Portions filmed in Cyprus and at these locations in France: La Pointe du Hoc, Calvados; Chateau de Chantilly, Oise; Ile de Re, Charente-Maritime; Sainte-Mere-Eglise, Manche; Benouville, Calvados; Plage de Saleccia, Saint-Florent Haute-Corse; Rivedoux-Plage, Ile de Re, Charente-Maritime; La Rochelle, Charente-Maritime; Ouistreham, Calvados; Fox Boulogne Studios, Boulogne-Billancourt, Hauts-de-Seine; Plage de Lotu, Saint-Florent, Haute-Corse; Orne; Port-en-Bessin-Huppain, Calvados.

Quotes: Lt. Col. Benjamin Vandervoort (John Wayne): *"I don't think I have to remind you that this war has been going on for almost five years.*

Over half of Europe has been overrun and occupied. We're comparative new-comers. England's going through a blitz with a knife at her throat since 1940. I'm quite sure that they, too, are impatient and itching to go. Do I make myself clear?", Captain Harding (Steve Forrest): *"Yes, sir. Quite clear."*, Vandervoort: *"Three million men penned up on this island all over England in staging areas like this. We're on the threshold of the most crucial day of our times. Three million men out there, keyed up, just waiting for that big step-off. We aren't exactly alone. Notify the men, full packs and equipment, 1400 hours."*, Harding: *"Yes, sir."*

Song: *The Longest Day* (Paul Anka) | Music by Maurice Jarre.

Academy Awards

- (Cinematography-Black and White) Jean Bourgoin, Walter Wottitz.
  (Special Effects) Robert MacDonald, Jacques Maumont.

Academy Award Nominations

- (Picture) Darryl F. Zanuck.
- (Art Decoration-Set Decoration-Black and White) Ted Haworth, Leon Barsacq, Vincent Korda; Gabriel Bechir.
- (Film Editing) Samuel E. Beetley.

American Cinema Editors Award

- (Best Edited Feature Film) Samuel E. Beetley.

David di Donatello Award

- (Best Foreign Production) Darryl F. Zanuck.

Directors Guild of America Award Nomination

- (Outstanding Directorial Achievement in Motion Pictures) Ken Annakin, Andrew Marton, Bernhard Wicki.

Golden Globe Award

- (Best Cinematography-Black and White) Henri Persin; Walter Wottitz, Jean Bourgoin.

Golden Globe Award Nomination

- (Best Motion Picture-Drama) Darryl F. Zanuck.

Golden Laurel Award

- (Top Action Drama) Darryl F. Zanuck.

Golden Laurel Award Nomination

- (Top Action Performance) Robert Mitchum.

National Board of Review Award

• (Best Film) Darryl F. Zanuck.

Released on October 4 | Box Office: $50,100,000 | (180 minutes/Westrex Recording, 4-track Stereo/CinemaScope/computer color version/AFI Greatest Films Nominee/AFI Thrills Nominee/video/laserdisc/DVD | 20th Century-Fox

The epic journey of four generations of Americans who carved a country with their bare hands.

How the West Was Won (1962) Directed by John Ford, Henry Hathaway, George Marshall (and uncredited Richard Thorpe).

Carroll Baker, Lee J. Cobb, Henry Fonda, Carolyn Jones, Karl Malden, Gregory Peck, George Peppard, Robert Preston, Debbie Reynolds, James Stewart, Eli Wallach, John Wayne, Richard Widmark, Brigid Bazlen, Walter Brennan, David Brian, Andy Devine, Raymond Massey, Agnes Moorehead, Henry [Harry] Morgan, Thelma Ritter, Mickey Shaughnessy, Russ Tamblyn, Jay C. Flippen, Ken Curtis, Tudor Owen, John Anderson, John Larch, Stanley Livingston, Jack Pennick, Willis Bouchey, William Henry, Claude Akins, Karl Swenson, Walter Reed, Lee Van Cleef, Dub Taylor, Joe Sawyer, Bing Russell, Harry Dean Stanton, James Griffith, Christopher Dark, Clinton Sundberg, Jack Lambert, J. Edward McKinley, Cliff Osmond, Walter Burke, Roy Jenson, Rodolfo Acosta, Kem Dibbs, Harvey Parry, Gene Roth, Chuck Roberson, Boyd 'Red' Morgan, Mark Allen, Kim Charney, Charlie Briggs, Craig Duncan, Barry Harvey, Claude Johnson, Ken Terrell, William Wellman Jr., Carleton [S.] Young, Jamie Ross, Bryan Russell. Narrated by Spencer Tracy.

When a man and his wife move their children and grandchildren from New York to the West in hopes of finding a better life during the California Gold Rush, they struggle against the violent Civil War, roaming outlaws and other hardships. Wayne plays General William Tecumseh Sherman in 'The Civil War' segment. Screenplay by James R. Webb, suggested by a *Life* magazine series (John Gay made an uncredited writing contribution). Produced by Bernard Smith. Chuck Roberson was Wayne's stunt double. Portions filmed at these Arizona locations: Verde River Railroad Bridge, Perkinsville; Oatman; Canyon deChelly National Monument; Tonto National Forest; Tucson; Superstition Mountains; Superior; Monument Valley; Mammoth; Old Tucson; Sonoran Desert; Dudleyville; Winkelman; Magma Arizona Railroad, Superior. Portions filmed at these California locations: Alabama Hills, Lone Pine; Pinnacles National Park; Lone Pine Campground; Inyo National Forest; Sierra Nevada Mountains; Simi Valley; Whitney Portal Road, Lone Pine Creek Canyon; Corriganville-Ray Corrigan Ranch, Simi Valley; San Francisco; Bishop; Hal Roach Studios, Culver City; Convict Lake; Scotia. Portions filmed at these Colorado locations: Silverton; Denver & Rio Grande Western Railroad, Durango; Uncompahgre National Forest; Montrose; Rocky Mountains. Portions filmed at these Illinois locations: Cave-In-Rock State Park; Battery Rock, Shawnee National Forest. Portions filmed at these Kentucky locations: Cumberland River; Paducah; Ohio River. Portions filmed at these Oregon locations: Grants Pass; Eugene. Portions filmed at these South Dakota locations: Badlands National Park; Custer State Park; Rapid City; Black Hills. Portions filmed at these Utah locations: Monument Valley; Duck Creek Village, Kanab; Cedar Mountain.

Songs: *How the West Was Won* (Alfred Newman; Ken Darby), *Home in the Meadow* (traditional 16th century melody *Greensleeves* adapted by Robert Emmett Dolan; lyrics by Sammy Cahn), *Raise a Ruckus* (melody adapted by Dolan; lyrics by Johnny Mercer), *Wait for the Hoedown* (melody adapted by Dolan; lyrics by Mercer), *What Was Your Name in the States?* (music by Dolan; lyrics adapted by Mercer), *I'm Bound for the Promised Land* (Ken Darby; Dolan), *Shenandoah* (traditional, composer unknown), *(Fifteen Miles) On the Erie Canal* (traditional, composer unknown), *Rock of Ages* (Thomas Hastings; Augustus Montague Toplady), *Nine Hundred Miles from Home* (Alfred Newman; Ken Darby), *When Johnny Comes Marching Home* (Louis Lambert), *Battle Hymn of the Republic* (William Steffe; Julia Ward Howe), *Come Share My Life* (Newman), *On the Banks of Sacramento* (Newman; Darby), *Endless Prairie* (Darby; Dolan), *Poor Wayfarin' Stranger* (traditional, composer unknown), *First Kiss* (Newman), *Careless Love* (H.D. Handy; Martha Koenig; Spencer Williams), *A Railroader's Bride I'll Be* (Newman), *No Goodbye* (Newman), *Miss Bailey's Ghost* (Newman) | Music by Alfred Newman and Ken Darby.

Academy Awards

- (Writing-Story and Screenplay-Written Directly for the Screen) James R. Webb.
- (Sound) Franklin E. Milton.
- (Film Editing) Harold F. Kress.

Academy Award Nominations

- (Picture) Bernard Smith.
- (Cinematography-Color) William H. Daniels, Milton Krasner, Charles Lang Jr., Joseph La Shelle.
- (Art Direction-Set Decoration-Color) George W. Davis, William Ferrari, Addison Hehr, Henry Grace, Don Greenwood Jr., Jack Mills.
  (Costume Design-Color) Walter Plunkett.
- (Music-Score, Substantially Original) Alfred Newman, Ken Darby.

American Cinema Editors Award

- (Best Edited Feature Film) Harold F. Kress.

Golden Laurel Award

- (Special) Bernard Smith.

Motion Picture Sound Editors Award

- (Best Sound Editing-Feature Film) Franklin Milton.

National Board of Review Award

- (Top Ten Film) Bernard Smith.

Photoplay Magazine Award

- (Gold Medal) Bernard Smith.

Western Heritage Bronze Wrangler Award

- (Theatrical Motion Picture) Henry Hathaway, John Ford, George Marshall, James R. Webb.

Released on November 1 (United Kingdom), February 20, 1963 (US) | Box Office: $50,000,000 | 155 minutes/Westrex Recording, 4-track Stereo, Cinerama 7-track/Metrocolor, Technicolor/ Cinerama, Ultra Panavision 70/National Film Registry 1997/AFI Scores 25/AFI Cheers Nominee/AFI Top Ten Western Nominee/AFI Top Ten Epic Nominee/Video/laserdisc/DVD/Blu-ray | Cinerama/Metro-Goldwyn-Mayer

Gangway...for this year's big adventure!

Donovan's Reef (1963) Directed by John Ford.

John Wayne, Lee Marvin, Elizabeth Allen, Jack Warden, Cesar Romero, Dick Foran, Dorothy Lamour, Marcel Dalio, Mike Mazurki, Jacqueline Malouf, Cherylene Lee, Tim Stafford [Jeffrey Byron], Edgar Buchanan, Jon Fong, John Qualen, Patrick Wayne, John Alderson, Charles Seel, Mae Marsh, Ralph Volkie, Yvonne Peattie, Chuck Roberson, Cliff Lyons, Sam Harris, Clyde Cook, Frank Baker, Carmen Estrabeau, Aissa Wayne.

Wayne (as Michael Patrick 'Guns' Donovan), Marvin and Warden are former navy men who live a leisurely life on an idyllic Pacific island where they had fought during World War Two. However, Wayne finds his boozing and brawling ways could be coming to an end when he falls for Warden's estranged daughter (Allen). She has arrived on the island to determine if her father is worthy of collecting a sizeable family inheritance. Screenplay by James Edward Grant and Frank S. Nugent, from a story by Edmund Beloin (and uncredited James A. Michener). Produced by John Ford. Portions filmed at these Kaua'i, Hawaii locations: Waimea Canyon; Hanamaulu Bay; Ahukini Pier.

Quote: Michael Patrick 'Guns' Donovan (John Wayne): (oft-repeated line) *"Pax?"*

Music by Cyril [J.] Mockridge.

Released on June 12 (Philadelphia, Pennsylvania) | Box Office: $6,600,000 | (109 minutes/Westrex Recording/Technicolor/video/laserdisc/DVD | John Ford Productions/Paramount

He likes his whiskey hard…his women soft…and his West all to himself!

McLintock! (1963) Directed by Andrew V. McLaglen.

John Wayne, Maureen O'Hara, Patrick Wayne, Stefanie Powers, Jack Kruschen, Chill Wills, Yvonne De Carlo, Jerry Van Dyke, Edgar Buchanan, Bruce Cabot, Perry Lopez, Strother Martin, Gordon Jones, Robert Lowery, Hank Worden, Michael Pate, Edward Faulkner, Mari Blanchard, Leo Gordon, Chuck Roberson, Bob Steele, Aissa Wayne, 'Big' John Hamilton, H.W. Gim, Pedro Gonzales-Gonzales Jr., Frank Hagney, Hal Needham, Kari Noven, Mary Patterson, John Stanley, Charles Horvath, Cliff Lyons, Dean Smith.

Cattle baron George Washington McLintock (John Wayne) must

Edgar Buchanan makes his opinion known to Wayne in *McLintock!*

deal with the return of his estranged wife (O'Hara), a deteriorating relationship with his daughter and the changing ways of the West. Screenplay by James Edward Grant. Produced by Michael Wayne. Portions filmed at these Arizona locations: Old Tucson; San Rafael Ranch House-San Rafael State Natural Area and State Park, Patagonia; Lochiel; Fairbank; Harshaw; Ruby; Las Cienegas National Conservation Area; Klondyke; Chiricahua National Monument; Sonoita; Nogales; Sonoran Desert; Duquesne; San Raphael Valley; and San Xavier.

Quote: George Washington McLintock (John Wayne): *"I know, I know. I'm gonna use good judgement. I haven't lost my temper in forty years, but Pilgrim you caused a lotta trouble this morning, might have got somebody killed…and somebody oughta belt you in the mouth, but I won't, I won't…..the hell I won't!"* (belts Jones [Leo Gordon] in the mouth).

Songs: *Love in the Country* (Frank DeVol; By Dunham), *Just Right for Me* (Dunham), *Cake Walk* (Dunham), *When We Dance* (Dunham) | Music by [Frank] DeVol.

Golden Laurel Awards
  • (Top Action Drama) Michael Wayne.
  • (Top Action Performance) John Wayne.

Released on November 13 | Box Office: $14,500,000 | (127 minutes/Westrex Recording/Technicolor/Panavision/video/laserdisc/DVD | Batjac/United Artists

All Wayne…and a world wide…

Circus World (1964) Directed by Henry Hathaway.

John Wayne, Claudia Cardinale, Rita Hayworth, Lloyd Nolan, Richard Conte, John Smith, Katharyna, Katherine Kath, Wanda Rotha, Maggie Macgrath [Rennie], Miles Malleson, Jose Maria Cafarell, Kay

Walsh, Francois Calepides, Robert Cunningham, Hans Dante[s], George Tyne, Synda Scott, Catherine Ellison.

Showman Matt Masters (Wayne) travels Europe with his Wild West circus while in search of his former love (Hayworth) and faces peril-including a spectacular fire which engulfs the show. Screenplay by Ben Hecht, Julian Halevy [Zimet] and James Edward Grant, from a story by Philip Yordan (acting as a front for blacklisted Bernard Gordon) and Nicholas Ray. Produced by Samuel Bronston. Portions filmed at these locations in Spain: Paseo Colon, Barcalona, Catalonia; Banks of the Tagus River, Toledo; Vicalvaro; Chinchon; Aranjuez; El Ritiro Park, Madrid; Samuel Bronston Studios, Madrid; Gran Teatro der Liceo. Barcelona; Circo Price, a.k.a. Price Circus Theatre, Madrid; and Toledo, Castilla-La Mancha. Bob Terhune was Wayne's stunt double.

Songs: *Circus World* (Dimitri Tiomkin; Ned Washington) (Golden Globe Award Winner), *Kingdom Coming* (Henry Clay Work), *Oh! Susanna* (Stephen Foster), *Buffalo Gals* (William Cool White), *Yankee Doodle* (traditional, composer unknown), *Turkey in the Straw* (traditional, composer unknown), *Frankie and Johnny* (traditional, composer unknown), *Sweet Betsy from Pike* (traditional, composer unknown), *Over the Waves* (Juventino Rosas), *The Thunderer* (John Philip Sousa), *Camptown Races* (Foster), *The Dying Cowboy* (*Oh, Bury Me Not on the Lone Prairie*) (traditional, composer unknown), *A Hot Time in the Old Town* (Theodore A. Metz), *Viennese Medley* (Johann Strauss) | Music by Dimitri Tiomkin.

Golden Globe Award Nomination
- (Best Actress-Drama) Rita Hayworth.

Golden Laurel Award Nomination
- (Action Performance) John Wayne.

Released on June 25 | Box Office: $1,600,000 | (135 minutes/Westrex Recording/Technicolor, Eastman Color/Super Technirama 70, Cinerama/video/laserdisc | Samuel Bronston Productions/ Paramount

A richly rewarding entertainment experience for the entire family.

The Greatest Story Ever Told (1965) Directed by George Stevens, (uncredited David Lean and Jean Negulesco).

Max von Sydow, Michael Anderson Jr., Carroll Baker, Ina Balin, Pat Boone, Victor Buono, Richard Conte, Joanna Dunham, Jose Ferrer, Van Heflin, Charlton Heston, Martin Landau, Angela Lansbury, Janet Margolin, David McCallum, Roddy McDowall, Dorothy McGuire, Sal Mineo, Nehemiah Persoff, Donald Pleasance, Sidney Poitier, Claude Rains, Gary Raymond, Telly Savalas, Joseph Schildkraut, Paul Stewart, John Wayne, Shelley Winters, Ed Wynn, John Abbott, Rodolfo Acosta, Michael Ansara, Robert Blake, Burt Brinckerhoff, Robert Busch, John Considine, Philip Coolidge, John Crawford, Frank de Kova [DeKova], Cyril Delevanti, Jamie Farr, David Hedison, Russell Johnson, Mark Lenard, Robert Loggia, John Lupton, Peter Mann, Tom Reese, Marian Seldes, David Sheiner, Frank Silvera, Joseph Sirola, Abraham Sofaer, Harold J. Stone, Chet Stratton, Michael Tolan, Ron Whelan, Jay C. Flippen, Celia Lovsky, Richard Bakalyan, John Pickard, Mickey Simpson, Gene Roth, Kay Hammond, Johnny Seven, Nesdon Booth, Dorothy Neumann, Joseph V. Perry, Peggy Webber, Marc Cavell, Gil Perkins, Dal Jenkins.

The epic and awe-inspiring look at the life of Jesus Christ (von Sydow), from his ignoble birth through his teachings to his crucifixion and resurrection. Wayne plays the Centurion at Jesus' crucifixion. Screenplay by James Lee Barrett and George Stevens, from source writings of the 1947-56 radio series by Henry Denker and the 1949 book by Fulton Oursler, in creative association with Carl Sandburg. Produced by George Stevens. Bob Terhune was Wayne's stunt double. Portions filmed at these Arizona locations: Page; Crazy Canyon, Page; Glen Canyon. Portions filmed at these California locations: Death Valley National Park; Metro-Goldwyn-Mayer Studios, Culver City; Desilu Studios, Culver City. Portions filmed in Illinois. Portions filmed in Nevada at Pyramid Lake Paiute Tribe Reservation. Portions filmed at these Utah locations: Arches National Park; Canyonland's National Park; Dead Horse Point State Park; Green River Overlook, Canyonland's National Park; Lake Powell; Moab; Kanab; Ken's Lake; Glen Canyon.

Quote: The Centurion (John Wayne): *Truly, this man was the Son of God.*

Songs: *Hallelujah Chorus* from *The Messiah* (George Frederic Handel), *Requiem* (Giuseppi Verdi), *Adagio for Strings* (Samuel Barber) | Music by Alfred Newman, Ovadia Tuvia (and uncredited Hugo Friedhofer, Lyn Murray and Fred Steiner).

Academy Award Nominations
- (Cinematography-Color) William C. Mellor, Loyal Griggs.
- (Art Direction-Set Decoration-Color) Richard Day, William Creber and David Hall; Ray Moyer, Fred MacLean and Norman Rockett.
- (Costume Design-Color) Vittorio Nino Novarese, Marjorie Best.
- (Special Visual Effects) J. McMillan Johnson.
- (Music Score-Substantially Original) Alfred Newman.

National Board of Review Award
- (Top Ten Films) George Stevens.

Released on February 15 | Box Office: $15,500,000 | 190 minutes/Westrex Recording, 3-channel Stereo/Technicolor/Ultra Panavision 70/AFI Scores Nominee/AFI Cheers Nominee/AFI 10 Top 10 Epic Nominee/video/laserdisc/DVD/Blu-Ray | George Stevens Productions/United Artists

Stripped of everything-they lived and loved and fought as if there were no tomorrow.

In Harm's Way (1965) Directed by Otto Preminger.

John Wayne, Kirk Douglas, Patricia Neal, Tom Tryon, Paula Prentiss, Brandon De Wilde, Jill Haworth, Dana Andrews, Stanley Holloway, Burgess Meredith, Franchot Tone, Patrick O'Neal, Carroll O'Connor, Slim Pickens, James Mitchum, George Kennedy, Bruce Cabot, Barbara Bouchet, Tod Andrews, Larry Hagman, Stewart Moss, Richard Le Pore, Chet Stratton, Soo Yong, Dort Clark, Phil Mattingly, Henry Fonda, Hugh O'Brien, Christopher George, Hal Needham, Jerry Goldsmith, Fritz Ford, Yankee Chang.

After the Japanese attack on Pearl Harbor, veteran officer Rockwell 'Rock' Torrey (Wayne) deals with the loss of his command and the return of his estranged son. Torrey's longtime friend, Paul Eddington (Douglas), faces his own personal and professional demons. They both receive an opportunity for redemption with a mission to capture a strategically-located island. Screenplay by Wendell Mayes, from the 1962 novel *Harm's Way* by James Bassett. Produced by Otto Preminger. Portions filmed at these California locations: San Diego and San Francisco.

Portions filmed at these Hawaii locations: Ford Island, Pearl Harbor, Oahu; Hell's Half Acre District, Honolulu, Oahu; and Kaneohe Marine Corps Air Station.

Quote: Rockwell 'Rock' Torrey (John Wayne): (toast) *"To our country, the Navy, and the best things they stand for."*

Academy Award Nomination
- (Cinematography-Black and White) Loyal Griggs.

British Academy of Film and Television Arts (BAFTA) Award
- (Best Foreign Actress) Patricia Neal.

Music by Jerry Goldsmith (and uncredited Michael Hennagin).

Released on April 6 | Box Office: $4,500,000 | 165 minutes/Westrex Recording/Panavision/video/DVD | Sigma/Paramount

From the four winds they came, the four brothers, their eyes smoking and their fingers itching...

The Sons of Katie Elder (1965) Directed by Henry Hathaway.

John Wayne, Dean Martin, Martha Hyer, Michael Anderson Jr.,

Wayne and Dean Martin were brothers seeking the killers of their father and the swindlers who cheated their mother in *The Sons of Katie Elder*.

Earl Holliman, Jeremy Slate, James Gregory, Paul Fix, George Kennedy, Dennis Hopper, Sheldon Allman, John Litel, John Doucette, James Westerfield, Rhys Williams, John Qualen, Rodolfo Acosta, Strother Martin, Percy Helton, Karl Swenson, Chuck Roberson, Henry Wills, Loren Janes, Boyd 'Red' Morgan, Jerry Gatlin, Joe Yrigoyan, Harvey Grant, Jack Williams.

Four troublemaking brothers (Wayne, Martin, Holliman and Anderson Jr.) return home for their mother's funeral and attempt to get their ranch back from the town's gunsmith-who swindled it away from their mother and murdered their father. Wayne plays the oldest brother, John Elder. Screenplay by William H. Wright, Allan Weiss and Harry Essex, from a story by Talbot Jennings. Produced by Hal B. Wallis. Portions filmed at Hereford, Arizona; and the Denver & Rio Grande Western Railroad in Durango, Colorado. Portions also filmed at these Mexico locations: Churubusco Studios, Mexico City, Distrito Federal; Chupaderos, Durango; Casa Blanca, Durango; Navojoa, Sonora; Mayo River, Sonora; and Alamos, Sonora. Chuck Roberson was Wayne's stunt double.

Quotes: Bud Elder (Michael Anderson Jr.): *"I'm going with you. I can draw pretty fast. We can be famous-like the Dalton Brothers!"*, John Elder (John Wayne): *"They're famous-but they're just a little bit dead."*

Western Heritage Bronze Wrangler Award
- (Theatrical Motion Picture) Hal B. Wallis, Henry Hathaway, Earl Holliman, Martha Hyer, Dean Martin, Jeremy Slate, Michael Anderson Jr.

Music by Elmer Bernstein.

Released on June 24 | Box Office: $23,000,000 | 122 minutes/Technicolor/Panavision/video/laserdisc/DVD | Wallis-Hazen Productions/Paramount

Outnumbered-unarmed-unprepared-they stunned the world with their incredible victory!

Cast a Giant Shadow (1966) Directed by Melville Shavelson.

Kirk Douglas, Senta Berger, Angie Dickinson, James Donald, Stathis Giallelis, Luther Adler, Topol, Ruth White, Gordon Jackson, Michael Hordern, Allan Cuthbertson, Jeremy Kemp, Sean Barrett, Michael

Shillo, Rina Ganor, Roland Bartrop, Robert Gardett, Michael Balston, Claude Aliotti, Samra Dedes, Michael [Micha] Shagrir, Frank Lattimore [Latimore], Ken Buckle, Rodd Dana, Robert Ross, Arthur Hansel, Don [Dan] Sturkie, Hillel Rave, Shlomo Hermon, Frank Sinatra, Yul Brynner, John Wayne, Michael Douglas, Geoffrey Palmer.

Colonel David 'Mickey' Marcus (Douglas) fights to help establish the state of Israel in 1948. He builds the first Israeli army from an untrained mob and develops them into a fighting defense force. Wayne plays General Mike Randolph. Screenplay by Melville Shavelson, from the book by Ted Berkman. Produced by Melville Shavelson. Portions filmed in Israel and at Cinecitta Studios, Rome, Lazio, Italy.

Quote: General Mike Randolph (John Wayne): *"Give this insubordinate son-of-a-bitch every truck and every blanket in the Third Army. And I don't care who you have to steal them from!"*

Music by Elmer Bernstein.

Released on March 30 | Box Office: $3,500,000 | (142 minutes/Westrex Recording/Technicolor/Panavision/video/laserdisc/DVD | Batjac/Llenroc/The Mirisch Corporation/United Artists

A Nation Builds Under Fire (1967) Directed by Harry Middleton.

Hubert H. Humphrey, Mark Nelson, Shelley Blunt, Ken Sanders, Dale Kemery, John Keeler, Peter Dawkins, Mike Rolla, Gene Savaggio. Narrated by John Wayne.

Wayne details how the United States helped South Vietnam modernize and defend their country while under invasion by communist forces in North Vietnam. Written by Harry Middleton. Produced by Ben Stelson.

40 minutes/color | Armed Forces Information and Education/US Department of Defense

When these two men ride-the legend of the west was born!

The War Wagon (1967) Directed by Burt Kennedy.

John Wayne, Kirk Douglas, Howard Keel, Robert Walker [Jr.], Keenan Wynn, Bruce Cabot, Joanna Barnes, Valora Noland, Bruce Dern, Gene Evans, Terry Wilson, Don Collier, Sheb Wooley, Ann Mc-

Crea, Emilio Fernandez, Frank McGrath, Chuck Roberson, Red Morgan, Hal Needham, Marco Antonio, Perla Walters [Walter], Cliff Lyons, Chuck Hayward, Tom Hennesy, Margarite Luna, Miko Mayama, Midori, Jose Trinidad Villa.

When a revenge-seeking ex-convict (Wayne, as Taw Jackson) discovers that his archenemy is driving an armored stagecoach full of gold, he assembles a colorful crew and sets out to rob it. Screenplay by Clair Huffaker from his 1957 novel Badman. Produced by Marvin Schwartz (and uncredited Michael Wayne). Portions filmed at these Mexico locations: Durango; Sierra de Organos, Sombrerete, Zacatecas; Bacerac, Sonora; Pilares de Nacozari, Sonora; San Miguelito, Sonora; Bavispe River, Sonora; Sierra del Tigre, Sonora.

Quotes: (After shooting down two gunmen) Lomax (Kirk Douglas): *"Mine hit the ground first."*, Taw Jackson (John Wayne): *"Mine was taller."*

Song: *Ballad of the War Wagon* (Dimitri Tiomkin; Ned Washington) | Music by Dimitri Tiomkin.

Western Heritage Bronze Wrangler Award
• (Theatrical Motion Picture) Burt Kennedy.

Released on May 24 | Box Office: $9,528,000 | (101 minutes/Westrex Recording/Technicolor/Panavision/video/laserdisc/DVD/Blu-Ray | Marvin Schwartz Productions/Batjac/Universal

Range war! A lawless time when no man dares turn his back...even to a friend!

El Dorado (1967) Directed by Howard Hawks.

John Wayne, Robert Mitchum, James Caan, Charlene Holt, Paul Fix, Arthur Hunnicutt, Michele Carey, R.G. Armstrong, Edward Asner, Christopher George, Marina Chane, Robert Donner, John Gabriel, Johnny Crawford, Robert Rothwell, Adam Roarke, Victoria George, Jim Davis, Anne Newman [Bacal], Diane Strom, Olaf Wieghorst,Don Collier, Chuck Courtney, William Henry, Chuck Horne, Joe King, John Mitchum, Anthony Rogers, Dean Smith, Rosa Turich, Charlita, Linda Dangcil, Nacho Galindo, Robert 'Buzz' Henry, Riley Hill, Rodolfo Hoyos Jr., Chuck Roberson.

Alcoholic but gutsy Sheriff J.P. Harrah (Robert Mitchum) finds himself in relentless battle against cattle barons and crooked businessmen. When his old pal Cole Thornton (Wayne)-an aging gunslinger mixed up in a range war-rides into town, Cole whips J.P. into shape. With the help of crotchety deputy Bull (Hunnicutt) and a kid called Mississippi (Caan), the foursome endeavor to clean up the town. Screenplay by Leigh Brackett, from the 1960 novel The Stars in Their Courses by Harry Brown. Produced by Howard Hawks. Portions filmed in Kanab, Utah, and at these Arizona locations: Old Tucson; Tucson; Sonoran Desert; Sierrita Mountains; Fairbank; San Pedro River; Canelo; Picacho Peak State Park; St. David; Santa Cruz River; Fredonia; Tucson Mountains; Ironwood Forest National Monument; and San Xavier.

Quotes:Sheriff J.P. Harrah (Robert Mitchum): *"What the hell are you doin' here?"*, Cole Thornton (John Wayne): *"I'm lookin' at a tin star with a…drunk pinned on it!"*

Song: *El Dorado* (Nelson Riddle; John Gabriel) | Music by Nelson Riddle.

San Sebastian International Film Festival Golden Seashell Award
  • (Best Film) Howard Hawks.

Released on June 7 | Box Office: $5,950,000 | (126 minutes/Technicolor/video/laserdisc/DVD/ Blu-Ray | Laurel Productions/Paramount

They had to be the toughest fighting force on Earth-and the man who led them had to be just a little bit tougher!

The Green Berets (1968) Directed by John Wayne, Ray Kellogg (and uncredited Mervyn LeRoy).

John Wayne, David Janssen, Jim Hutton, Aldo Ray, Raymond St. Jacques, Bruce Cabot, Jack Soo, George Takei, Patrick Wayne, Luke Askew, Irene Tsu, Edward Faulkner, Jason Evers, Mike Henry, Craig Jue, Chuck Roberson, Eddy Donno, Rudy Robbins, Richard 'Cactus' Pryor, James Seay, Jess Barker, Walker Edmiston, Cliff Lyons, Charles Bail, Bill Shannon, Hayward Soo Hoo, Tom Hennesy, Paul Genge, Frank Koomen, David Lowe, William Olds, Ernie F. Orsatti, Laird Stuart.

A tough-as-nails colonel (Wayne, as Mike Kirby) leads his special forces troops through the treacherous jungles of Vietnam to face a deadly enemy and kidnap a North Vietnamese general. Screenplay by James Lee Barrett, from the 1965 novel by Robin Moore. Produced by Michael Wayne. Portions filmed at Hurlburt Field, Florida; Fort McClellan, Alabama; and at these Georgia locations: Fort Benning and Columbus.

Quotes: Colonel Mike Kirby (John Wayne): *"What is there not to like? Who is she?"*, Colonel Morgan (Bruce Cabot): *"Her name is Lin. Her father was chief of the Han Phou Province."*, Colonel Cai (Jack Soo): *"Until he refused to cooperate with the Viet Cong."*, Kirby: *"So they killed him."*, Cai: *"They murdered him and her little brother in the most hideous way."*, Kirby: *"That's their style."*, Colonel Mike Kirby (John Wayne): *"Out here, due process is a bullet."* (AFI Quote Nominee)

Songs: *The River Seine* (*La Seine*) (Guy LaFarge; Flavien Monod; Geoffrey Parsons), *Ballad of the Green Berets* (Robin Moore; Barry Sandler) | Music by Miklos Rozsa.

Golden Laurel Award Nominations
  • (Action Drama) Michael Wayne.
  • (Action Performance) John Wayne.

Released on June 19 | Box Office: $32,000,000 | (141 minutes/Technicolor/Panavision/Rated [G]/video/laserdisc/DVD/Blu-Ray | Batjac/Warner Brothers-Seven Arts

They've got the hottest, meanest jobs on Earth! This is the true story of the men who fight oil field infernos around the globe…and the woman who go through hell night after night!

The Hellfighters (1968) Directed by Andrew V. McLaglen.

John Wayne, Katharine Ross, Jim Hutton, Vera Miles, Jay C. Flippen, Bruce Cabot, Edward Faulkner, Barbara Stuart, Edmund Hashim, Valentin De Vargas, Frances Fong, Alberto Morin, Alan Caillou, Laraine Stephens, John Alderson, Lal Chand Mehra, Rudy Diaz, Bebe Louie, Chris Chandler, William Hardy, Howard Finch, [Richard] 'Cactus' Pryor, Big John Hamilton, Elizabeth Germaine, Pedro Gonzalez Gonzalez, John Stephenson, Edward Colmans, Chuck Roberson, Ethelreda Leopold.

Fire expert Chance Buckman (Wayne) leads a company of men

risking their lives battling oil well blazes around the world. After he is injured and hospitalized, Wayne's estranged daughter pays him a visit-only to fall in love with his closest colleague. Screenplay by Clair Huffaker, based on the exploits or Red Adair and his Wild Well Control Company. Produced by Robert Arthur. Portions filmed at these Wyoming locations: Snodgrass Ranch, Casper; Gillette; Jackson Airport, Jackson Hole. Portions filmed at these Texas locations: Conroe; William P. Hobby Airport, Houston; and Baytown.

Quotes: Chance Buckman (John Wayne): (Referring to the fact that Greg brings a different girl to each fire) *"What did you use for openers this time, the old headache gag? Why, you poor man, perhaps if I rubbed your neck?"*, Greg Parker (Jim Hutton): *"True-every word, true. But it works."*, Chance: *"Can't say I blame you. A fellow as ugly as you are probably couldn't get to first base without a fire."*

Music by Leonard Rosenman.

Released on November 27 | Box Office: $3,750,000 | (121 minutes/Westrex Recording/Technicolor/Panavision/Rated [R]/video/DVD/Blu-Ray | Universal

The strangest trio to ever track a killer.

True Grit (1969) Directed by Henry Hathaway.

John Wayne, Glen Campbell, Kim Darby, Jeremy Slate, Robert Duvall, Dennis Hopper, Alfred Ryder, Strother Martin, Jeff Corey, Ron Soble, John Fielder, James Westerfield, John Doucette, Donald Woods, Edith Atwater, Carlos Rivas, Isabel Boniface, H.W. Gim, John Pickard, Elizabeth Harrower, Ken Renard, Jay Ripley, Kenneth Becker, Jay Silverheels, Hank Worden, Myron Healey, Stuart Randall, Wilford Brimley, Guy Wilkerson, Boyd 'Red' Morgan, James McEachin, Connie Sawyer, Vincent St. Cyr, Ginger Cat (a cat).

One-eyed, boozing US Marshal Rooster Cogburn (Wayne) is hired by a young girl to find her father's killer. Cogburn is soon saddled with unwanted help when she insists on coming along and a Texas Ranger joins them in their search. Screenplay by Marguerite Roberts, from the 1968 novel by Charles Portis. Produced by Hal B. Wallis (and uncredited Joseph H. Hazen). Jim Burk was Wayne's stunt double. Portions filmed at these California locations: Hot Creek, Inyo National Forest;

Sherwin Summit, Inyo National Forest; and Bishop. Portions filmed at these Colorado locations: Buckskin Joe Frontier Town & Railway, Canon City; Owl Creek Pass, Ridgeway; Montrose; Durango; Ouray; Gunnison; and Hastings Mesa, Placerville.

Quotes: (Rooster Cogburn faces four outlaws) Ned Pepper (Robert Duvall): *"What's your intention? Do you think one on four is a dogfall?"*, Rooster Cogburn (John Wayne): *"I mean to kill you in one minute, Ned. Or see you hanged in Fort Smith at Judge Parker's convenience. Which'll it be?"*, Pepper: *"I call that bold talk for a one-eyed fat man."*, Rooster: (reels back) *"Fill your hand, you son of a bitch!"*, Rooster (cocks his gun): *"Mr. Rat…I have a writ here says you're to stop eating Chen Lee's cornmeal forthwith. Now it's a rat writ, writ for a rat, and this is lawful service of same. See? Doesn't pay any attention to me."* (shoots the rat), Chen Lee (H.W. Gim): (runs into the room) *"Outside is place for shooting!"*, Rooster: *"I'm serving some papers."*

Song: *True Grit* (Elmer Bernstein; Don Black) | Music by Elmer Bernstein.

Wayne played crusty older lawman Rooster Cogburn in *True Grit* and won the Academy Award for Best Actor. Kim Darby is at right.

Academy Award

- (Actor) John Wayne.

Academy Award Nomination

- (Music-Song) *True Grit*, Elmer Bernstein, Don Black.

Golden Globe Award

- (Best Actor-Drama) John Wayne.

British Academy of Film and Television Arts Award Nomination

- (Most Promising Newcomer to Leading Film Roles) Kim Darby.

Golden Globe Award Nominations

- (Most Promising Newcomer-Male) Glen Campbell.
- (Best Original Song) *True Grit*, Elmer Bernstein, Don Black.

Golden Laurel Awards

- (General Entertainment) Hal B. Wallis.
- (Action Performance) John Wayne.

Golden Laurel Award Nominations

- (Male New Face) Glen Campbell.
- (Female New Face) Kim Darby.

National Board of Review Award

- (Top Ten Film) Hal B. Wallis.

Western Heritage Bronze Wrangler Award

- (Theatrical Motion Picture) Hal B. Wallis, Henry Hathaway, Marguerite Roberts, Glen Campbell, Kim Darby, John Wayne.

Writers Guild of America Award Nomination

- (Screen-Best Drama Adapted from Another Medium) Marguerite Roberts.

Released on June 11 | Box Office: $31,100,000 | (128 minutes/Technicolor/Rated [G]/video/laserdisc/DVD/Blue-Ray | Hal Wallis Productions/Paramount

Across 2000 miles of savage wasteland…they lived a thundering adventure that rocked two nations!

The Undefeated (1969) Directed by Andrew V. McLaglen.

John Wayne, Rock Hudson, Tony [Antonio] Aguilar, Roman Gabriel, Marian McCargo, Lee Meriwether, Merlin Olsen, Melissa Newman, Bruce Cabot, [Jan] Michael Vincent, Ben Johnson, Edward Faulkner, Harry Carey Jr., Paul Fix, Royal Dano, Richard Mulligan, Carlos Rivas, John Agar, Guy Raymond, Don Collier, Big John Hamilton, Dub Taylor, Henry Beckman, Victor Junco, Robert Donner, Pedro Armendariz Jr., James Dobson, Rudy Diaz, Richard Angarola, James McEachin, Gregg Palmer, Juan Garcia, Kiel Martin, Bob Gravage, Chuck Roberson, Hal Needham, John Hudkins, 'Chico' Hernandez, Barbara Faulkner, Barbara Faulkner Jr., Jan Faulkner, Leslie Faulkner.

Two formal colonels, one Confederate (Hudson), the other Union (Wayne, as John Henry Thomas) become allies after Hudson and his displaced Southerners fall afoul of Mexican revolutionaries in Mexico. Together, they fight off bandits. Screenplay by James Lee Barrett, from a story by Stanley L. Hough, in turn based on a novel by Lewis B. Patten. Produced by Robert L. Jacks. Portions filmed in Baton Rouge, Louisiana and at these Mexico locations: Durango; Bavispe River, Sonora; Sierra de Organos, Sombrerete, Zacatecas; Sierra de los Ajos, Bavispe, Sonora; Huasabas, Sonora; Nacori Chico, Sonora; La Presa de la Angostura, Sonora; San Pedro de la Cueva, Sonora; and Bacadehuachi, Sonora.

Quotes: Ann Langdon (Marian McCargo): *"You went out there to talk, why did you have to shoot the man?"*, Colonel John Henry Thomas (John Wayne): *"Conversation kinda dried up, Ma'am."*

Music by Hugo Montenegro | Released on October 4 | Box Office: $8,000,000 | (119 minutes/ Westrex Recording/DeLuxe Color/Panavision/video/laserdisc/DVD | 20th Century-Fox

The legend-John Wayne is Chisum.

Chisum (1970) Directed by Andrew V. McLaglen.

John Wayne, Forrest Tucker, Christopher George, Ben Johnson, Glenn Corbett, Andrew Prine, Bruce Cabot, Patric Knowles, Richard Jaeckel, Lynda Day [George], Geoffrey Deuel, Pamela McMyler, John Agar, Lloyd Battista, Robert Donner, Ray Teal, Edward Faulkner, Ron Soble, John Mitchum, Glenn Langan, Alan Baxter, Alberto Morin, Bill [William] Bryant, Pedro Armendariz Jr., Christopher Mitchum, John Pickard, Abraham Sofaer, Gregg Palmer, Hank Worden, Pedro Gonzalez Gonzalez, Jim Burk, Eddy Donno, Bob Morgan, John Kelly, Cliff Lyons, Chuck Roberson, Henry Wills. Narrated by William Conrad.

John Chisum (Wayne) is a tough cattle baron who has to defend his ranch from Lawrence Murphy (Tucker). Wayne and fellow rancher Knowles try to handle things legally, but Tucker owns the law. Conflicts occur and soon Wayne and Knowles' men, including gunslinger Deuel, are in a land and cattle war. Screenplay by Andrew J. Fenady, from his short story *Chisum and the Lincoln County Cattle War*. Produced by Michael A. Wayne and Andrew J. Fenady. Filmed at 20th Century-Fox Ranch, Calabasas, California, and the Eaves Movie Ranch, Santa Fe, New Mexico. Portions filmed at these Arizona locations: Sonoita; San Pedro River. Portions filmed at these Mexico locations: Rancho Marley, Durango; Yecora, Sonora; Rio Bavispe; Huachinera, Sonora; Bacerac, Sonora; Janos, Chihuahua; Paral, Chihuahua; and Granados, Sonora.

Quotes: James Pepper (Ben Johnson): *"You know, there's an old saying, Miss Sally. There's no law west of Dodge and no God west of the Pecos. Right, Mr. Chisum?"*, John Chisum (John Wayne): *"Wrong, Mr. Pepper. Because no matter where people go, sooner or later there's the law. And sooner or later they find God's already been there."*

Songs: *Turn Me Around* (Dominic Frontiere; Norman Gimbel), *Ballad of John Chisum* (Frontiere; Andrew J. Fenady) | Music by Dominic Frontiere.

Golden Laurel Award
- (Best Action Performance) John Wayne.

Released on June 24 | Box Office: $6,000,000 | 111 minutes/Technicolor/Panavision/video/laserdisc/DVD/Blu-Ray | Batjac/Warner Brothers

Give 'em hell, John.

Rio Lobo (1970) Directed by Howard Hawks.

John Wayne, Jorge Rivero, Jennifer O'Neill, Jack Elam, Christopher Mitchum, Victor French, Susana Dosamantes, Sherry Lansing, David Huddleston, Mike Henry, Bill Williams, Jim Davis, Dean Smith, Robert Donner, George Plimpton, Edward Faulkner, Peter Jason, Chuck Courtney, Robert Rothwell, Don 'Red' Barry, Gregg Palmer, Hank Worden,

Bob Steele, Chuck Roberson, Boyd 'Red' Morgan, Chuck Hayward, Ethan Wayne, John Hudkins, Tommy Tedesco, Conrad Hool, Lance Hool.

Two former Confederate soldiers team up with an ex-Union officer (Wayne, as Cord McNally) to settle some old scores with a bootlegger, a crooked sheriff and the traitor who caused Wayne's unit to be defeated-as well as being responsible for the loss of a close friend. Screenplay by Burton Wohl and Leigh Brackett, from a story by Wohl. Produced by Howard Hawks. Chuck Roberson was Wayne's stunt double. Portions filmed at these Arizona locations: Old Tucson; Tucson; Sierrita Mountains; Picacho Peak State Park; Sonoran Desert; Tucson Mountains; Ironwood Forest National Monument; Ruby; Arivaca; and Tumacacor. Portions filmed at these Mexico locations: Cuernavaca, Morelos; Bavispe, Sonora; and Bacerac, Sonora.

Quotes: Sheriff 'Blue Tom' Hendricks (Mike Henry): *I should've taken you this morning!*, Cord McNally (John Wayne): *You shoulda tried!*

Music by Jerry Goldsmith.

Released on December 16 | Box Office: $4,250,000 | (114 minutes/Technicolor/Rated [G]/video/laserdisc/DVD/Blu-Ray | Batjac/Malabar/Cinema Center/National General

No Substitute for Victory (1971) Directed by (uncredited Robert F. Slatzer).

John Wayne, Albert C. Wedemeyer, Paul D. Harkins, Barry Sadler, Ulysses S. Grant Sharp Jr., Martha Raye, Peter Stark, Tom Hayden, Ezra Taft Benson, Lowell Thomas, William C. Westmoreland. Narrated by Mark [W.] Clark and Sam Yorty.

Wayne hosts this documentary feature in support of America's participation in the Vietnam War. Includes archive footage of Nikolai [V.I.] Lenin, Adolf Hitler, Neville Chamberlain, Joseph Stalin, Douglas MacArthur, Mao Zedong, Enlai Zhou, Chiang Kai-Shek, Ho Chi Minh, Nikita Khruschev, Nguyen Ngoctho, Winston Churchill, Franklin D. Roosevelt.

Released on February 1 | (80 minutes/color/video/DVD) | Alaska Pictures

Big Jake...a legend of a man. A man who fought his way through hell to save a grandson he had never seen!

Big Jake (1971) Directed by George Sherman (and uncredited John Wayne).

John Wayne, Richard Boone, Maureen O'Hara, Patrick Wayne, Chris [Christopher] Mitchum, Bobby Vinton, Bruce Cabot, Glenn Corbett, Harry Carey Jr., John Doucette, Jim Davis, John Agar, Gregg Palmer, Jim Burk, Robert Warner, Dean Smith, John Ethan Wayne, Virginia Capers, William [Bill] Walker, Jerry Gatlin, Don Epperson, Everett Creach, Jeff Wingfield, Hank Worden, Bernard Fox, John McLiam, Roy Jenson, Chuck Roberson, Lisa Todd, Jerry Summers, Tom Hennesy, Maria Rocio. Narrated by George Fenneman.

Wealthy, wandering, gun-slinging businessman Big Jake McCandles (John Wayne) has not been home in a decade. He is summoned by his estranged wife (O'Hara) when their grandson is kidnapped by a ruthless killer (Boone) and his gang. Wayne makes plans to rescue his grandson and is joined by his two sons-along with an Indian scout and a dog with no name. The party also takes along s strongbox that contains the boy's ransom…but paying off the kidnappers is not Big Jake's intention. Story and screenplay by Harry Julian Fink and Rita M. Fink. Produced by (uncredited John Wayne) and Michael A. Wayne. Chuck Roberson was Wayne's stunt double. Portions filmed at these Mexico locations: El Saltito Waterfall, Nombre de Dios, Durango; Rancho Marley, Durango; Sierra de Organos, Sombrerete, Zacatecas; La Punta, Durango; El Arenal, Durango; Las Huertas, Durango; Lerdo de Tejaca, Durango; El Pueblito, Durango; Rio Sonora, Sonora; and Mesa Tres Rios, Sonora.

Quotes: Big Jake McCandles (John Wayne): *"What do you do when cockroaches get in the woodwork?"* James McCandles (Patrick Wayne): *"Smoke 'em out?"*, Jake: *"That's right."*, Michael McCandles (Christopher Mitchum): *"Why not wait for them to make the first move?"*, Jake: *"Because waiting is good for them and bad for us. You get impatient, nervy, careless and maybe dead."*

Image Award Nomination
• (Outstanding Actress in a Motion Picture) Virginia Capers.

Music by Elmer Bernstein | Released on May 26 | Box Office: $7,500,000 | 110 minutes/Technicolor/Panavision/Rated [PG]/video/laserdisc/DVD/Blu-Ray | Batjac/Cinema Center/National General

Directed by John Ford (1971, 2006) Directed by Peter Bogdanovich.

John Ford, Peter Bogdanovich, John Wayne, James Stewart, Henry Fonda, Katharine Hepburn, Harry Carey Jr., Martin Scorsese. Narrated by Orson Welles.

Documentary about the noted Oscar-winning film maker who was instrumental in making Wayne a star and advancing the careers of Fonda, Maureen O'Hara, Jeffrey Hunter; and is regarded as the foremost director of American movie westerns. Includes archive footage of Ward Bond, Harry Carey [Sr.], Jeffrey Hunter and Richard Widmark. In 2006 a re-edited version was released with additional interviews featuring Harry Carey Jr., Clint Eastwood, Maureen O'Hara, Martin Scorsese, Steven Spielberg, Walter Hill and a recording of a conversation between Ford and Katherine Hepburn. Written by Peter Bogdanovich. Produced by Tom Brown, Frank Marshall, James R. Silkie and George Stevens Jr. Portions filmed at the Center for Advanced Film Studies, American Film Institute, Los Angeles, California; and Monument Valley, Utah.

Music by Gaylord Carter.

Initial 1971 release: Sept 6 | Initial release version: 99 minutes; re-edited version 110 minutes/ Technicolor/DVD | American Film Institute/California Arts Commission

All they wanted was their chance to be men...and he gave it to them.

The Cowboys (1972) Directed by Mark Rydell.

John Wayne, Roscoe Lee Browne, Bruce Dern, Colleen Dewhurst, Alfred Barker Jr., Nicholas Beauvy, Steve Benedict, Robert Carradine, Norman Howell Jr., Stephen [R.] Hudis, Sean Kelly, A Martinez, Clay O'Brien, Sam O'Brien, Mike Pyeatt, Slim Pickens, Lonny Chapman, Charles Tyner, Sarah Cunningham, Allyn Ann McLerie, Maggie Costain, Matt Clark, Jerry Gatlin, Walter Scott, Dick [Richard] Farnsworth, Wallace Brooks, Charise Cullen, Colette [Collette] Poeppel, Norman Howell [Sr.], Rita Hudis, Margaret Kelly, Larry Randles, Larry Finley, Jim Burk, Fred Brookfield, Tap Canutt, Chuck Courtney, Gary Epper, Tony Epper, Kent Hays, J.R. Randall, Henry Wills, Joe Yrigoyen, Ralph Volkie, Ivan Brutsche.

When a rancher's regular hands leave him to search for gold, he hires a group of youngsters for a 400-mile cattle drive. After the rancher

(Wayne as Wil Anderson) meets with a cruel fate, the boys have the chance to prove themselves by bringing in the herd. Screenplay by Irving Ravetch, Harriet Frank Jr., and William Dale Jennings, from Jennings' 1971 novel. Produced by Mark Rydell and Tim Zinnemann. Chuck Roberson was Wayne's stunt double. Portions filmed at these Arizona locations: Empire Ranch, Sonoita; Coconino National Forest; Elgin; and Hereford. Portions filmed at these Colorado locations: Castle Rock; Buckskin Joe Frontier Town & Railway, Canon City; Durango; and Pagosa Springs. Portions filmed at these New Mexico locations: Chama; Galisteo; Bonanza Creek Ranch, Santa Fe; San Cristobal Ranch, Lamy; and Eaves Movie Ranch, Santa Fe.

Quotes: Cimarron (A Martinez): *"They didn't even dig him a decent grave."*, Wil Anderson (John Wayne): *"Well, it's not how you're buried, it's how you're remembered."*

Western Heritage Bronze Wrangler Award
- (Theatrical Motion Picture) Tim Zinnemann, Mark Rydell, Harriet Frank Jr., William Dale Jennings, Irving Ravetch, Charles Tyner, Lonny Chapman, Roscoe Lee Browne, Colleen Dewhurst, Bruce Dern.

Music by John Williams.

Released on January 13 | Box Office: $19,250,211 | (128 minutes/Technicolor/Panavision/Rated [PG]/AFI Film Scores Nominee/AFI Cheers Nominee/video/laserdisc/DVD/Blu-Ray | Sanford Productions/Warner Brothers

When his doctor suggested a rest…how did it come out arrest?

Cancel My Reservation (1972) Directed by Paul Bogart.

Bob Hope, Eva Marie Saint, Ralph Bellamy, Forrest Tucker, Anne Archer, Keenan Wynn, Henry Darrow, Chief Dan George, Doodles Weaver, Betty Ann Carr, Herb Vigran, Pat Morita, Gordon Oliver, Isabella Hoopes, Buster Shavers, Tracy Bogart, Trudy Bordoff, Richard Yniguez, Priscilla Garcia, Robert Dahdah, Paul Bogart, Johnny Carson, Bing Crosby, John Wayne, Flip Wilson.

Talk show host Dan Bartlett (Hope) is sent on a rest vacation. When he and his wife (Saint) arrive in Arizona, it takes no time at all for hapless Bartlett to become implicated in a murder-which he has to solve to prove his innocence. Comedy with Wayne making a cameo appearance as himself. Screenplay by Arthur Marx and Robert Fisher, from the novel The Broken Gun by Louis L'Amour. Produced by Bob Hope and Gordon Oliver. Filmed at Samuel Goldwyn Studios, West Hollywood, California; New York City and the following Arizona locations: Southwestern Studios, Carefree; Phoenix; Verde River; Carl Harvgard Mansion; Superstition Wilderness & Mountains; Sonoran Desert; Apache Junction;and Blue Point.

Song: *"Cancel My Reservation"* (Dominic Frontiere; Bobby Hart) | Music by Dominic Frontiere

Released on September 21 | 99 minutes/Technicolor/Rated [G]/video/DVD | Naho Enterprises/ Warner Brothers

Cursed gold, a vanished train and a thief's widow. He'd do better walking into Hell!

The Train Robbers (1973) Directed by Burt Kennedy.

John Wayne, Ann-Margret, Rod Taylor, Ben Johnson, Christopher George, Bobby Vinton, Jerry Gatlin, Ricardo Montalban, Ralph Volkie.

A trio of Civil War veterans (including Wayne as Lane) are hired by a young train robber's widow to travel into Mexico and track down a half-million dollars in gold for a $50,000 reward. Little do they know an unseen enemy is following their every move. Screenplay by Burt Kennedy. Produced by (uncredited John Wayne and) Michael Wayne. Portions filmed in Yuma, Arizona and the following locations in Mexico: Bavispe, Sonora; Parral, Chihuahua; Pinacate and Grand Desert of Altar, Sonora; Cumpas, Sonora; Otinapa, Durango; Nacozari de Garcia, Sonora; La Goma, Durango; Sierra de Organos, Sombrerete, Zacatecas; San Miguel de Horcasitas, Sonora; Bavispe River, Sonora; Sierra de los Ajos, Bavispe, Sonora; Huachinera, Sonora; and Bacerac, Sonora.

Quote: Lane (John Wayne): *"You're a man, you're stuck with it. You'll find yourself standing your ground and fightin' when you oughtta run, speakin' out when you oughtta keep your mouth shut, doin' things that seem wrong to a lot of people but you'll do them all the same. You're gonna spend the rest of your life getting up one more time when you're knocked down, so you better start getting' used to it."*

Music by Dominic Frontiere.

Released on February 7 | Box Office: $2,600,000 | (92 minutes/Technicolor/Panavision/Rated [PG]/video/laserdisc/DVD/Blu-Ray | Batjac/Warner Brothers

Break the law and he's the last man you want to see. And the last man you ever will.

Cahill: United States Marshal (1973) Directed by Andrew V. McLaglen.

John Wayne, George Kennedy, Gary Grimes, Neville Brand, Clay O'Brien, Marie Windsor, Morgan Paull, Dan Vadis, Royal Dano, Scott Walker, Denver Pyle, Jackie Coogan, Rayford Barnes, Dan Kemp, Harry Carey Jr., Walter Barnes, Paul Fix, Pepper Martin, Vance Davis, Ken [Kenneth] Wolger, Hank Worden, James Nusser, Murray MacLeod, Hunter von Leer, Ralph Volkie, Chuck Roberson, Joseph Culliton.

Tough marshal J.D. Cahill (Wayne) faces a moral dilemma when his rebellious sons seek to make their own names by robbing a bank-and becoming fugitives from the law. Screenplay by Harry Julian Fink and Rita M. Fink, from a story by Barney Slater. Produced by (uncredited John Wayne and) Michael Wayne. Chuck Roberson was Wayne's stunt double. Portions filmed in Calderon, California, and the following Arizona locations: Elgin; Canelo; San Rafael Valley & State Natural Area. Portions also filmed in these Mexico locations: Moctezuma, Sonora; Durango; Chihuahua; Sierra al sur de Moctezuma, Sonora; Fronteras, Sonora; Yaqui River, Sonora; Bavispe River, Sonora; Sahuaripa, Sonora; Sierra Madre Occidental, Sonora.

Quote:J.D. Cahill (John Wayne): *"You call the tune and you pay the piper. Meaning...you don't like the treatment, don't rob the banks."*

Song: *A Man Gets to Thinkin'* (Elmer Bernstein; Don Black) | Music by Elmer Bernstein.

Released on July 11 | Box Office: $3,100,000 | (103 minutes/Technicolor/Panavision/Rated [PG]/video/laserdisc/DVD/Blu-Ray | Batjac/Warner Brothers

He's a busted cop, his gun is unlicensed, his methods are unlawful and his story is incredible.

McQ (1974) Directed by John Sturges.

John Wayne, Eddie Albert, Diana Muldaur, Colleen Dewhurst, Clu Gulager, David Huddleston, Jim Watkins [Julian Christopher], Al Lettieri, Julie Adams, Roger E. Mosley, William Bryant, Richard Kelton, Joe Tornatore, Dick Friel, Richard Eastham, Fred Waugh, Kim Sanford, Hal Needham, Chuck Roberson, Larry Buck, Jack Evans, Arthur Mason, June Foray (voice).

Seattle police lieutenant Lon McQ (Wayne), anxious to get at the bottom of the murders which claimed two cops (one of whom was his best friend), resigns from the police force to go after the drug dealers he thinks are responsible. Screenplay by Lawrence Roman. Produced by Michael Wayne, Jules Levy and Arthur Gardner. Portions filmed in these Washington State locations: Quinault Indian Reservation; Olympic Peninsula, Aberdeen; and Seattle.

Quotes: Captain Edward Kosterman (Eddie Albert): *"Lon, I know you. I'm not gonna stand for you making up your own rules. You're not going to pull that Mickey Peters thing again!"*, Lon McQ (John Wayne): *"Peters was a hood and everybody knew it!"*, Kosterman: *"Yeah, and you weren't satisfied with throwing him up on the roof! You had to go up there and throw him back down! Six months in the hospital! Four lawyers screaming about his civil rights!"*, McQ: *"Well, it kept him off the streets, didn't it?"*, McQ (after being rescued from a car crash in which his vehicle was trapped between two semi-trucks) *"I'm up to my butt in gas."*

Music by Elmer Bernstein.

Released on January 4 | Box Office: $4,000,000 | 116 minutes/Technicolor/Panavision/Rated [PG]/video/laserdisc/DVD/Blu-Ray | Batjac/Levy-Gardner Productions/Warner Brothers

Big Jim Brannigan takes on London-Chicago style!

Brannigan (1975) Directed by Douglas Hickox.

John Wayne, Richard Attenborough, Judy Geeson, Mel Ferrer, John Vernon, Daniel Pilon, John Stride, James Booth, Arthur Batanides,

Movie poster for *Brannigan*.

Ralph Meeker, Barry Dennen, Lesley Ann Down, Pauline Delany [Delaney], Del Henney, Brian Glover, Stewart Bevan, Janette Lesse, Anthony Booth, Tony Robinson, Don Henderson, Kathryn Leigh Scott, Enid Jaynes, Michael Crane, Steve Kelly, Charles Pemberton.

An Irish cop (Wayne, as Jim Brannigan) from Chicago goes to London in search of an American racketeer who fled the United States to avoid a grand jury. However, the gangster and his hitmen plan a deadly ambush for the tough detective. Screenplay by Christopher Trumbo, Michael Butler, William P. McGivern and William Norton, from a story by Trumbo and Butler. Produced by Michael Wayne, Jules Levy and Arthur Gardner. Portions filmed at O'Hare International Airport, Chicago, Illinois; Shepperton Studios, Surrey, England; and at the following London, England locations: Rac Club; The Lamb Tavern; Beckton Gasworks; Garrick Club; Piccadilly Circus; 61-80 York Mansions; Dorchester Hotel; Hyde Park; St. Pancras International Railway Station; St. Thomas' Hospital; Tower Bridge; West India Quay, Canaray Wharf; steps at Waterloo Place; Lime Street; Bishops Gate Without; Park Lane; Maida Vale; Covent Garden; Hounslow; Battersea; Broadgate; Lambeth; Heathrow Airport; Mayfair; Paddington; Pall Mall; Soho; and Douglas House.

Quotes: Detective Sergeant Jennifer Thatcher (Judy Geeson): *"My father flew with the RAF. He said there were only three things wrong with the Yanks: 'oversexed, overpaid and over here'."*, Jim Brannigan (John Wayne): *"I really walked into that one-and deserved it. I'm sorry."*, Jennifer: *"Might we start again, sir?"*, Brannigan: *"Why? We're doing fine."*

Song: *"Let the Sunshine In"* (Galt MacDermot; Gerome Ragni; James Rado) | Music by Dominic Frontiere.

Released on March 21 | (111 minutes/DeLuxe Color/Panavision/Rated [PG}/video/DVD/Blu-Ray | Wellborn Ltd./Levy-Gardner-Laven/United Artists

The man of 'True Grit' is back and look who's got him!

Rooster Cogburn (1975) Directed by Stuart Millar.

John Wayne, Katharine Hepburn, Anthony Zerbe, Richard Jordan, John McIntire, Paul Koslo, Jack Colvin, Jon Lormer, Richard Romancito, Lane Smith, Warren Vanders, Jerry Gatlin, Strother Martin, Tommy Lee, Andrew Prine, Chuck Hayward, Mickey Gilbert, Gary McLarty, John Howard Hamilton, General Sterling Price (a cat).

Gun-toting, whiskey-guzzling Marshal Rooster Cogburn (Wayne), alongside prim and proper missionary Eula Goodnight (Hepburn), make an unlikely team as they set out to catch the outlaw gang responsible for the murder of Hepburn's father. Written by Martin Julien [Martha Hyer], suggested by the character 'Rooster Cogburn' from the novel True Grit by Charles Portis. Produced by Hal B. Wallis. Chuck Roberson was Wayne's stunt double. Portions filmed at these Oregon locations: Rogue River; Grants Pass; Smith Rock State Park; and Deschutes National Forest.

Quotes: Eula Goodnight (Katharine Hepburn): *"Just to whom do you think you are talking, Mr. Marshal?"*, Rooster Cogburn (John Wayne): *"You is to whom I am talking, Ma'am."*, Eula: *"It's true that you are larger than me...but only physically."*, Rooster: *"In this case, my dear lady, that is enough."*, Eula: *"Do you mean to tell me that you are prepared to use brute force?"*, Rooster: *"That is exactly what I mean."*, Eula: (pauses) *"Oh."*

Music by Laurence Rosenthal.

Released on October 17 | Box Office: $17,600,000 | 107 minutes/Westrex Recording/Technicolor/Panavision/Rated [PG]/video/laserdisc/DVD/Blu-Ray | Hal Wallis Productions/Universal

Chesty: A Tribute to a Legend (1976) Directed by John Ford.

John Ford, Lewis B. Puller. Narrated by John Wayne.

Documentary about the US Marines' most decorated officer, General Lewis B. 'Chesty' Puller, whose military career included engagements in Haiti, Nicaragua, Guadalcanal, New Guinea and Korea. Written by Jay Simms. Produced by James Ellsworth. Portions filmed at the US Military Academy, West Point, New York; Old Tucson, Arizona, and the following Virginia locations: Virginia Military Institute, Lexington; Washington and Lee University, Lexington; Stonewall Jackson Tomb, Lexington; Saluda; and Arlington. Filmed in 1970, but remained unreleased for six years.

Music by Jack Marshall | Released on April 4 | (47 minutes/color | James Ellsworth Productions/ Dyna-Plex

He got to face a gunfight once more to live up to his legend once more-to win just one more time.

The Shootist (1976) Directed by Don Siegel.

John Wayne, Lauren Bacall, Ron Howard, James Stewart, Richard Boone, Hugh O'Brien, Bill McKinney, Harry Morgan, John Carradine, Sheree North, Richard [Rick] Lenz, Scatman Crothers, Gregg Palmer, Alfred Dennis, Dick Winslow, Melody Thomas [Scott], Kathleen O'Malley, Jonathan Goldsmith, James Nolan, Ralph Volkie, Charles G. Martin. Archive footage of Johnny Crawford, Christopher George, Leo Gordon, Ricky Nelson and Bob Steele.

After being diagnosed with terminal cancer, aging legendary gunfighter John Bernard Books (Wayne) decides to get his affairs in line and places an order for his tombstone. He also spends time boarding with a widow and her impressionable son, before catching a trolley to face three deadly gunmen in his final shoot-out. Screenplay by Miles Hood Swarthout and Scott Hale, from the 1975 novel by Glendon Swarthout. Produced by M.J. Frankovich and William Self. Portions filmed at Warner Brothers Burbank Studios, Paramount Studios, and at these Carson City, Nevada, locations: Krebs-Peterson House; and Washoe Lake State Park. To 'illustrate' the career of Wayne's character, J.B. Books, film clips from former Wayne films were used: **Red River** (1948), **Hondo** (1953), **Rio Bravo** (1959) and **El Dorado** (1967).

Quote: John Bernard Books (John Wayne): *"I won't be wronged, I won't be insulted, and I won't be laid a hand on. I don't do these things to other people, and I require the same from them."*

Song: *Willow, Tit Willow* (Arthur Sullivan; W.S. Gilbert) (performed by Wayne and Bacall) | Music by Elmer Bernstein.

Academy Award Nomination
- (Art Direction-Set Decoration) Robert F. Boyle; Arthur Jeph Parker.

British Academy of Film and Television Arts Award Nomination
- (Best Actress) Lauren Bacall.

Golden Globe Award Nomination
- (Best Actor in a Supporting Role-Motion Picture) Ron Howard.

National Board of Review Award
- (Top Ten Film) M.J. Frankovich, William Self.

Writers Guild of America Award Nomination
- (Screen-Best Drama Adapted from Another Medium) Miles Hood Swarthout, Scott Hale.

Released on July 16 | Box Office: $13,400,000 | (99 minutes/Technicolor/Panavision/Rated [PG]/AFI 10 Top 10 Western Nominee/video/ laserdisc/DVD | Dino De Laurentiis Corporation/A Siegel Film/Paramount

Short Subjects

The Draw-Back (1927) Directed by Norman Taurog.

Johnny Arthur, Kathryn McGuire, Wallace Lupino, Al Thompson, John Wayne.

Not-so-smart Arthur goes to college, only to be victimized by bullies and mistaken for a nimble athlete by the dean's wife. He is put on the football team just in time for the big game. Comedy with Wayne as an opposing player in a confrontation at the goal post. Entry in the ***Tuxedo Comedies*** series.

Released on April 10 | 2 reels/silent/DVD | Goodwill Productions/Educational

Seeing Stars (1927) Directed by Stephen Roberts.

George Davis, Molly Malone, Jack Lloyd, Phil Dunham, Jack Miller, Ray Turner, John Wayne, Pal the Dog.

Comedy about a pair of buddies who want to meet some movie stars, but get sidetracked by a lively bar. Wayne is seen as 'Tall Boy'. Entry in the *Mermaid Comedies* series. Produced by Jack White.

Released on October 16 | 2 reels/silent | Educational

A Home-Made Man (1928) Directed by Norman Taurog.

Lloyd Hamilton, Lucille Hutton, Kewpie Morgan, John Wayne.

Soda jerk Hamilton makes a mess of his job at a lunch counter, and things get worse when he is switched to working in the adjoining gymnasium. Wayne can be seen sitting on a stool. Scenario by Norman Taurog.

Produced by Lloyd Hamilton | Released on July 17 | 15 minutes/silent | Educational

The Voice of Hollywood No. 13 (*Second Series*) (1932) Directed by Mark D'Agostino.

Allen 'Farina' Hoskins, John Wayne, George Bancroft, El Brendel, Jackie Cooper, Gary Cooper, Lupe Velez, Thelma Todd.

Wayne is emcee opposite guest host Farina (of *Our Gang* fame), as radio station STAR provides entertainment from a list of film notables. Produced by Louis Lewyn. Filmed at the Tec-Art Studios in Hollywood.

Released on January 17 | 12 minutes | Tiffany

Running Hollywood (1932) Directed by Charles Lamont.

Arthur Lake, Charles Murray, George Sidney, Noah Beery [Sr.], Benny Rubin, Ralph Ince, Guinn 'Big Boy' Williams, John T. Murray, Eddie Kane, Kit Guard, Bud Flanagan [Dennis O'Keefe], Kane Richmond, Ronald R. Rondell, Florence Lake, Ben Turpin, Monte Collins, Gertrude Astor, Sally Blane, Mary Carr, Leo Carrillo, Louise Fazenda, Claude Gillingwater [Sr.], Sessue Hayakawa, 'Little Billy' Rhodes, Vivian Oakland, Charles 'Buddy' Rogers, Virginia Sale, John Wayne,

Marion Byron, Ginger Rogers, George E. Stone, Nancy Dover [Judith Barrett], Claude Gillingwater Jr.

Arthur Lake is a police chief pursuing a thief, who stole a valuable pearl at a party. Wayne appears as himself. Screenplay by Harry Sauber, from a story by William Halligan. Produced by Bryan Foy. Entry in the ***Thalians Club Comedy*** series.

Released on January 27 | (18 ½ minutes/Western Electric Sound | Foy Productions Ltd./Thalians Club/Universal

A Hollywood Handicap (1932) Directed by Charles Lamont.

Marion Byron, Anita Stewart, Bert Wheeler, Dorothy Christy, John Wayne, Dickie Moore, James Murray, Jack Duffy, Tully Marshall, Harold Goodwin, Ivan Lebedeff, John Harron, Vernon Dent, David Rollins, Mary Kornman, Dorothy Ates, Monte Collins, Lincoln Stedman, Tom McGuire, Eddie Borden, Billy Bletcher, Virginia Sale, Florence Roberts, Estelle Bradley, Ann Brody, James Burke, Ralph Brooks, Anita Garvin, Billy Taft, Billy Gilbert, Horace McCoy, Don Alvarado.

Some film funny people, character actors and former silent players congregate in this entry in the ***Thalians Club Comedy*** series. John Wayne appears as a singing cowboy (dubbed). Screenplay by Elwood Ullman. Produced by Bryan Foy.

Released on August 10 | 18 minutes/Western Electric Sound | Foy Productions Ltd./Thalians Club/Universal

Screen Snapshots Series 19, No. 8: Cowboy Jubilee (1940) Directed by Ralph Staub.

Gene Autry, Roy Rogers, John Wayne, The Meglin Kiddies. Narrated by Hobart Cavanaugh.

Popular western stars (including Wayne) are seen on and off camera. Written by Ralph Staub. Produced by (uncredited Harriet Parsons and) Ralph Staub.

Music by Mischa Bakaleinikoff.

Released on July 7. | 10 minutes | Columbia

Meet the Stars #9: Stars Past and Present (1941) Directed by Harriet Parsons.

Brenda Joyce, William T. Orr, Ilona Massey, Jane Russell, Cesar Romero, Patricia Morison, Mary Martin, Wally Westmore, Walter Abel, Gene Autry, Binnie Barnes, Richard Bennett, Jack Buetel, Smiley Burnette, Mae Busch, Judy Canova, Chester Conklin, Minta Durfee, Sally Eilers, William Farnum, Eddie Gribbon, George 'Gabby' Hayes, Edgar Kennedy, The Keystone Kops, Mary Lee, Walter McGrail, Ann Miller, Jack Mulhall, Charlie Murray Sr., Eddie Quillan, Charles Ray, Wesley Ruggles, Mack Sennett, Eddie Sutherland, John Wayne. Narrated by Harriet Parsons.

Joyce, Orr, Massey and Russell cavort at an outdoor pool. Romero and Morison play a game of ten-pins. Makeup man Westmore glamorizes Martin. Republic Studios dedicates its new sound stages to the memory of Mabel Normand (seen in archive footage). Wayne appears as himself. Produced by Harriet Parsons.

Released on July 24 | 9 minutes/RCA Sound | Republic

Memo for Joe (1944) Directed by Richard Fleischer.

Quentin Reynolds, Joe E. Brown, Gary Cooper, Marlene Dietrich, Bob Hope, Frances Langford, John Wayne.

Hollywood stars participate in a charity campaign put on by the American Community Chest, which also aids the Allied war effort. Entry in the ***Victory Reel*** series. Written by Quentin Reynolds.

Released on August 10 | 10 minutes/color | National War Fund/US Public Relations Department of Community Chests & Councils/RKO Radio

Screen Snapshots: Hollywood Rodeo (Series 28, No. 8) (1949) Directed by Ralph Staub.

Gene Autry, Montie Montana, Jane Russell, Ralph Staub, John Wayne.

Staub goes to the annual Hollywood Rodeo held at Los Angeles Memorial Coliseum, where Autry comments and introduces some attendees, including Wayne and Russell. Written and produced by Ralph Staub.

Music by Mischa Bakaleinikoff.

Released on November 17 | (10 minutes | Columbia

Screen Snapshots: Hollywood's Famous Feet (*Series 29, No. 7*) (1950) Directed by Ralph Staub.

Gene Autry, Edgar Bergen & 'Charlie McCarthy', Sid Grauman, Ken Murray, Donna Reed, John Wayne. Narrated by Al Jolson.

The story of Grauman's Chinese Theater and its courtyard of footprints and signatures of the stars. Wayne is one of the top names in Hollywood viewing the proceedings. Includes archive footage of the Four Marx Brothers, Tom Mix, the Ritz Brothers, Shirley Ross and film director John M. Stahl. Written and produced by Ralph Staub.

Music by Mischa Bakaleinikoff.

Released on July 26 | 8 minutes | Columbia

Screen Snapshots: Reno's Silver Spur Awards (*Series 30, No. 2*) (1951) Directed by Ralph Staub.

Don Wilson, Harry Carey Jr., Bill [William] Elliott, John Ford, John Wayne.

Wilson, hosting the awards presentation, centers on the film **Rio Grande** and its participants: director Ford and cast members Wayne and Carey. Written and produced by Ralph Staub.

Music by Mischa Bakaleinikoff.

Released on January 25 | 9 minutes | Columbia

The Screen Director (1951) Directed by (uncredited Richard L. Bare).

Ray Heindorf, Gordon MacRae, Lewis Martin, John Pickard, Brick Sullivan, Jack Wise, Jack Mower, Bess Flowers, Creighton Hale, Harold

Miller, Richard L. Bare, Frank Capra, Phyllis Coates, Michael Curtiz, John Ford, Burt Lancaster, Leo McCarey, John Wayne, William Wyler, Roy Del Ruth, Gordon MacRae, Ruth Roman, Jane Wyman, Ray Heindorf. Narrated by Art Gilmore.

This featurette shows the responsibilities of a movie director. Wayne appears in a sequence of staged footage. Includes archive footage of Paul Douglas, John Huston, Elia Kazan, Vivien Leigh, Ida Lupino, Joseph L. Mankiewicz and Tennessee Williams. Twentieth entry in *The Movies and You* series. Written by (uncredited Richard L. Bare). Produced by Gordon Hollingshead.

Released on March 13 | (9 minutes/RCA Sound/video/DVD | Academy of Motion Picture Arts and Sciences/Warner Brothers

Screen Snapshots: Hollywood Awards (Series 30, No. 6) (1951) Directed by Ralph Staub.

Ronald Reagan, Broderick Crawford, John Derek, Farley Granger, Mercedes McCambridge, Gregory Peck, Robert Rossen, David Wayne, John Wayne, Jane Wyman, Loretta Young. Narrated by Ralph Staub.

At the annual Photoplay magazine Gold Medal Awards dinner, toastmaster Reagan presents awards to the stars, including John Wayne. Written and produced by Ralph Staub.

Music by Mischa Bakaleinikoff.

Released on May 17 | (10 minutes | Columbia

Miracle in Motion (1952)

Narrated by John Wayne.

A fund-raising featurette for the benefit of the United Cerebral Palsy Foundation.

(3 minutes/RCA Sound) | Republic

Screen Snapshots: The Great Al Jolson (1955) Directed by Ralph Staub.

Ralph Staub, L. Wolfe Gilbert, Sidney Clare, M.K. Jerome, Sammy Fain, Harry Ruby, Jean Schwartz, Benny Davis, Isham Jones, Jimmy McHugh, Gene Autry, The Marx Brothers, Ken Murray, John Wayne.

Some of America's notable composers pay tribute to Al Jolson, who popularized many of their songs. Other screen personalities (including Wayne) also appear. Includes archive footage of Jolson, Sid Grauman, Tom Mix and The Ritz Brothers. Written and produced by Ralph Staub.

Released on October 20 | 10 minutes | Columbia

John Wayne for Christmas Seals (1955)

John Wayne, William Wellman.

While on a movie set, Wayne urges theater audiences to purchase Christmas Seals and help fight tuberculosis.

1 ½ minutes | National Tuberculosis Association/Warner Brothers

Screen Snapshots: Salute to Hollywood (1958) Directed by Ralph Staub.

John Wayne, Jayne Mansfield, Charlton Heston, Zsa Zsa Gabor, Dinah Shore, George Montgomery, Rhonda Fleming, Virginia Mayo, Ann Miller, Agnes Moorehead, Ronald Reagan. Narrated by Ralph Staub.

Film stars (including Wayne) are greeted as they arrive at a party hosted by *The Saturday Evening Post* magazine. Written and produced by Ralph Staub.

Released on January 2 | 11 minutes/Eastmancolor | Columbia

World's Heavyweight Championship Fight: Floyd Patterson Heavyweight Champion of the World versus Ingemar Johansson Heavyweight Champion of Europe (1959) Directed by E.J. Spiro.

Floyd Patterson, Ingemar Johansson, Howard Cosell, Ruby Goldstein, William Holden, John Wayne. Narrated by Chris Schenkel.

In this documentary featurette, the title prizefight bout is chronicled.

Wayne is seen among the spectators. Produced by E.J. Spiro. Filmed at Yankee Stadium, Bronx, New York City.

17 minutes | TelePrompTer/United Artists

The Challenge of Ideas (1961)

Hanson Baldwin, Lowell Thomas. Narrated by Helen Hayes, Frank McGee, Edward R. Murrow, John Wayne.

The polarization of the Western Allies versus the Soviet Bloc prompts strict vigilance and actions on part of the United States and freedom-loving countries to guard against totalitarian takeover.

Released in August | 30 minutes/DVD | US Information Agency/US Department of Defense

Choice (1964)

John Wayne.

Wayne speaks in support of Presidential candidate Senator Barry Goldwater. Archive footage of Goldwater is seen.

29 minutes

The Victory Squad (1966) Directed by Kurt Simon.

John Wayne, Ronald Reagan.

Wayne hosts this campaign film for Reagan, a candidate for Governor of California. Produced by Kurt Simon.

Released in October | 11 minutes/color | Kurt Simon Productions

The Moviemakers (1968) Directed by Elliot Geisinger.

John Wayne, David Janssen, Jim Hutton, Aldo Ray, Bruce Cabot, Winton C. Hoch, Jack Soo, Raymond St. Jacques, George Takai, Irene Tsu.

A look at the production of Wayne's film *The Green Berets* (1968).

Written by Jay Anson. Produced by Ronald Saland.

7 minutes/color/DVD | Robbins Nest Productions/Professional Film Services

John Wayne and "Chisum" (1970) Directed by Elliot Geisinger and Ronald Saland.

John Wayne, Forrest Tucker, Pamela McMyler, Abraham Sofaer, John Pickard, Andrew V. McLaglen, William H.Clothier.

Documentary about the making of Wayne's film ***Chisum***. Written by Jay Anson.

Music by Dominic Frontiere.

9 minutes/color/DVD | Professional Films/Warner Brothers

This Little Bullet (1977) Directed by Wes Keys.

Narrated by John Wayne and Jack Ellison.

Gun safety is the subject of this featurette as Wayne describes the deadly consequences when firearms are not handled properly. Written by Bob Hernbrode.

Released on January 7 | 19 minutes/color | US Department of Defense, Information and Education Division/Arizona Game and Fish Department

Home for the Seabees (1977) Directed by Bobby Hatley.

Carl Irwin, John Wayne.

Documentary featurette with Wayne describing the work being done for the Seabee Museum at Naval Base Ventura, Port Hueneme, California, by the US Naval Construction Battalions. Written by John Frederick. Produced by Harry Flynn. Portions filmed at these California locations: Naval Base Ventura County; National Construction Battalion Center, Port Hueneme; and Golden Gate National Recreation Area, San Francisco.

Released on August 5 | 19 minutes/color

Radio Appearances

Kraft Music Hall (NBC) April 13, 1939.

Stars: Bing Crosby, Bob Burns. Vocalists: The Music Maids. Announcer: Ken Carpenter. The John Scott Trotter Orchestra.

Guests: movie player John Wayne; film director Leo McCarey; and Vronsky & Babin, piano duet team. Bing sings Hang Your Heart on a Hickory Limb; Sailboat of Dreams; It Must Be True; Sly Old Gentleman and his 'Memory Song' of 1930: I Get Along Without You Very Well. With interruptions from Bob, Bing talks over movie topics with Wayne, best known for his accurate gunplay in westerns, and McCarey, Academy Award winner. Vronsky & Babin are heard in a group of piano selections. The orchestra plays Dancing Tambourine.

In Chicago Tonight (WGN-MBS) *The Long Voyage Home* November 21, 1940.

Radio adaptation of John Wayne's 1940 motion picture.

John Qualen, Arthur Shields.

Three Sheets to the Wind (NBC) (Series) February 15 to July 5, 1942.

A female British spy and an American operator posing as a drunken passenger pursue the killer of several people in London when he boards an ocean liner.

Cast:
Joan Lockwood...................................Helga Moray
Dan O'Brien .... John Wayne
Narrator... Tay Garnet
Also............................Sharon Douglas, Lee Bonnell

Melody Roundup (AFRS) Program #1. August 28, 1942.

Host: Andy Devine.

Country and western music with guests Judy Canova and John Wayne.

Note: AFRS stands for the Armed Forces Radio Service.

Melody Roundup (AFRS) Program #2. September 4, 1942.

Host: Andy Devine.

Judy Canova and John Wayne return for a second week.

The Lady Esther Screen Guild Players (CBS) *Pittsburgh* April 12, 1943.

Announcer: Truman Bradley. The Wilbur Hatch Orchestra.

Radio adaptation of Wayne's 1942 motion picture. When an industrialist devotes more time to his steel business than to his wife, the door is open for his rival to move in. Narrated by Frank Craven. Adapted from the story by Tom Reed and George Owen; and the screenplay by Reed, Kenneth Gamet and John Twist.

Josie 'Hunky' Winters: Marlene Dietrich. John 'Cash' Evans: Randolph Scott. Charles Markham/Charles Ellis: John Wayne. Barbara Stanwyck speaks on behalf of the Second War Loan bond campaign.

Soldiers with Wings (WGN-MBS) May 5, 1943.

Broadcast from Santa Ana Air Force Training Center. Wartime show promoting the United States Army Air Force. Guests: Members of the crew of the raiding plane Jack the Ripper; Constance Bennett and John Wayne appear in an original drama.

Barbara Stanwyck speaks on behalf of the Second War Loan bond campaign.

This Is Hollywood (CBS) *Angel and the Badman* April 5, 1947.

Host: Hedda Hopper. Announcer: Bernard Dudley. The Adolphe Deutsch Orchestra.

Adaptation of John Wayne's 1947 film. Written for radio by Bill Hampton. Directed by Frank Woodruff. Jane Wyatt.

Screen Director's Guild Assignment (NBC) *Stagecoach* January 9, 1949.

Guest Director: John Ford.

Radio adaptation of John Wayne's 1939 motion picture. Written for radio by Milton Geiger, from the story and screenplay by Ernest Haycox.

John Wayne, Claire Trevor, Ward Bond.

Lux Radio Theater (CBS) *Red River* March 7, 1949.

Host: William Keighley. Announcer: John Milton Kennedy. The Louis Silvers Orchestra.

Adaptation of John Wayne's 1948 film. During the first cattle drive along the Chisholm Trail, Tom Dunson (Wayne) and his ward, Matt Garth (Jeff Chandler), show the stalwart character and brave daring necessary to head up the drive-until they come into conflict over their ultimate destination: Missouri, where payment is sure, or the new railheads in Kansas…which promise a highly profitable reward. Written for radio by S.H. Barnett, from the screenplay by Borden Chase and Charles Schnee and *The Saturday Evening Post* magazine story, "The Chisholm Trail" by Borden Chase. Directed by Frederic MacKaye.

Tess Millay: Joanne Dru. Groot: Walter Brennan. Cherry: Bernard [Barney] Phillips. Teeler: Jeff Corey. Melville: Bill [William] Johnstone. Mexican/Donegal: Alan Reed. Meecker: Herbert Butterfield. Also: Jimmy Ogg, Willard Waterman, Lillian Buyeff, Lou Krugman, Jay Novello, Ed Max, Eddie Marr. Dorothy Lovett plays 'Libby Collins' in the Lux Soap commercials.

Truth or Consequences (NBC) May 7, 1949.

Host: Ralph Edwards. Announcer: Harlow Wilcox. Organist: Buddy Cole.

Ralph puts a 'hot seat' in the audience. Ralph, disguised as a vacuum-cleaner salesman, visits housewife Mrs. John Mihld and proceeds to litter the living room with dirt and sawdust in order to demonstrate his vacuum-cleaner-which does not work; Mrs. Mihld's reaction is censored in spots. In the studio, Ralph presents Mrs. Mihld with a prize after she solves a word puzzle. John Wayne does a dramatic playlet with blind Norma Sharrett, who wished to meet a real movie star. Ralph sends Norma to the Guiding Eye School where she will be presented with her own Guiding Eye dog. Buddy Barnick wins a Nash automobile that matches a key he is carrying. A 'mother banquet' is held. Directed by Al Paschall.

Screen Director's Playhouse (NBC) *Fort Apache* August 5, 1949.

Announcer: Jimmy Wallington. Guest Director: John Ford. The Henry Russell Orchestra.

A cavalry veteran (John Wayne) clashes with his new commanding officer. The soldier questions the commander's tactics and is headed for ruin when he goes against his convictions to disobey. What is more important-a just outcome or obeying orders? Ward Bond, Paul McVey, Lou Merrill, Tony Barrett.

Time for Defense (ABC) January 17, 1950.

A report on the electronic jet trainer. John Wayne appears in a scene from his film, ***Sands of Iwo Jima***.

Louella Parsons Show (ABC) January 5, 1951.

Host: Louella Parsons.

Hollywood news and gossip. Burgess Meredith has been secretly married. The divorce of Elizabeth Taylor and Nicky Hilton moves ahead. Louella pans the film *The Miracle*. Faye Emerson and Skitch Henderson are having a rough patch in their marriage. Louella interviews John Wayne, who airs his anti-communist views; she presents him with a scroll from *The Motion Picture Herald.*

Photoplay Awards Dinner (ABC) (Special) February 13, 1951.

Winners of the Photoplay magazine readers' poll are awarded Gold Medals.

Lionel Barrymore, Bing Crosby, Cecil B. DeMille, Betty Hutton, John Wayne, Jane Wyman, Loretta Young.

City of Hope Hospital Dinner (ABC) (Special) February 17, 1951.

John Wayne appears in a cancer dramatization, *One in Five, One in Seven.*

Lee J. Cobb, Broderick Crawford, Douglas Fairbanks Jr., Cary Grant, Bert Parks, Rosalind Russell.

If Fight We Must (NBC) *The Ridgefield Affair* February 17, 1951.

When communist infiltration threatens a factory, a shop steward (John Wayne) attempts to mount a resistance. Written by Richard Allen Simmons. Directed by Warren Lewis.

Ben Wright, David Ellis, Tim Graham, Anne Diamond, Lou Krugman, Norman Field.

Lux Radio Theater (CBS) *She Wore a Yellow Ribbon* March 12, 1951.

Host: William Keighley. Announcer: John Milton Kennedy. The Rudy Schrager Orchestra.

Adaptation of John Wayne's 1949 film. Captain Nathan Brittles

(Wayne) is assigned one last patrol before his retirement from the US Cavalry. However, it turns out not to be a routine duty as the Arapaho Indians are planning an attack. Written for radio by S.H. Barnett, from the screenplay by Frank Nugent and Laurence Stallings, and *The Saturday Evening Post* magazine story by James Warner Bellah. Directed by Earl Ebi. The Intermission guest is RKO starlet Leslye Banning.

Lieutenant Cohill: Mel Ferrer. Olivia Dandridge: Mala Powers. Tyree: Barton Yarborough. The Major: Bill [William] Johnstone. Pennell: George Neise. Also: Wally Maher, Sandra Rogers, Norman Field, Dan Riss, Paul Dubov, Eddie Marr. Dorothy Lovett plays 'Libby Collins' in the Lux Soap commercials.

Hear It Now (CBS) March 30, 1951.

Host: Edward R. Murrow.

Senator Estes Kefauver holds hearings on organized crime in America. In the Korean Conflict, General Douglas MacArthur makes his own decisions. A look at the 1950 Academy Awards. John Wayne addresses the Motion Picture Alliance.

Judy Holliday, Jose Ferrer, Groucho Marx, Louella Parsons, Bob Hope, Mack Sennett, Sam Goldwyn.

Lux Radio Theater (CBS) *Movie Time, U.S.A.* September 24, 1951.

Host: William Keighley. Announcer: John Milton Kennedy. The Rudy Schrager Orchestra.

Seventeen stars re-enact scenes from eight movies (each representing one of the eight major studios) in a salute to the 50th anniversary of motion pictures. John Wayne plays Dan Kirby opposite Robert Ryan as Griff in a scene from *Flying Leathernecks* (RKO Radio). The other films and stars are *The Pride of St. Louis* (20th Century-Fox) with Dan Dailey and Joanne Dru; *Thunder on the Hill* (Universal-International) with Claudette Colbert and Ann Blyth; *An American in Paris* (Metro-Goldwyn-Mayer) with Gene Kelly and Leslie Caron; *Saturday's Hero* (Columbia) with John Derek and Donna Reed; *Wild Blue Yon-*

der (Republic) with Wendell Corey, Vera Ralston and Forrest Tucker; ***Distant Drums*** (Warner Brothers) with Gary Cooper and Mari Aldon; and ***Here Comes the Groom*** (Paramount) with Bing Crosby and Jane Wyman.

Also: Joseph Kearns, Eleanor Audley, Howard McNear, Bill [William] Johnstone, Gerald Mohr. Claudette Colbert, Ann Blyth, Joanne Dru and Donna Reed for Lux Soap.

Lieutenant General Albert Wedemeyer (NBC) (Special) November 2, 1952.

John Wayne introduces the Lieutenant General, author of a report on China and Korea, who speaks on behalf of General Dwight D. Eisenhower for President.

Salute to the Coast Guard Reserve (Syndicated) (Special) November 7, 1952.

A parade of entertainment notables take part in this tribute.

Bob Hope, John Wayne, Jane Russell, Marilyn Maxwell, Spike Jones & His City Slickers, Dorothy Shay, Jerry Colonna, Hy Averback, The Armed Forces Radio Service Orchestra.

House Party (CBS) August 11, 1953.

Host: Art Linkletter.

Daytime audience participation and variety. John Wayne guests.

House Party (CBS) September 1, 1953.

Host: Art Linkletter.

John Wayne pays Art and his studio audience another call.

Louella Parsons Program (CBS) April 27, 1954.

Host: Louella Parsons.

He-man Hollywood favorite, John Wayne, discusses his latest film, an aviation epic entitled ***The High and the Mighty***.

The Amos 'n' Andy Music Hall (CBS) July 25, 1955.

Stars: Freeman Gosden, Charles Correll.

The boys enter into an analysis of acting and singing styles with guests Jeanette MacDonald and John Wayne.

Monitor (NBC) October 2, 1955.

A program of news, sports special events and variety. Reporters visit a 'building bee' in Binghamton, New York. A ride on a Los Angeles streetcar in The Angel's Flight. An interview with a New York Madison Avenue bus driver. NBC microphones pick up an auction of old automobiles in Claremore, Oklahoma. The commissioning of the aircraft carrier Forrestal is reported from Portsmouth, Virginia. The construction of the Nyack-Tarrytown Bridge. Participants today include Maurice Chevalier, Jean Simmons, Milton Berle, John Wayne, Esther Williams, Myron Cohen, Betty von Furstenberg, Sonny Gale and The Burton Sisters.

Monitor (NBC) October 23, 1955.

Coverage of the North Carolina State Fair. A report on heart disease research. A talk on the new and revolutionary preventative for tooth decay. A horse race from Chicago. The bells of Rome. A talk with former US Senator William Benton about his recent trip to Russia. Today's guests include Tony Bennett, Jeanne Crain, Tyrone Power, Rosemary Clooney, John Wayne and The Ritz Brothers.

The Story of 'The Conqueror' (MBS) (Special) February 23, 1956.

Dick Powell, John Wayne and Susan Hayward tell how this motion picture was made.

Radio Journal (WBBM-Chicago, IL, dial 780 am) *'The Searchers' Premiere* May 17, 1956.

Howard Miller interviews the stars of the picture, John Wayne and Ward Bond. Miller also visits with Governor William Stratton of Illinois, singer Nat 'King' Cole and singer-actor Harry Belafonte.

Monitor (NBC) June 29, 1958.

Belgians discuss the coming visit of Herbert Hoover. Features with Janet Leigh and John Wayne.

Ingemar Johansson vs. Floyd Patterson (ABC) (Special) June 26, 1959.

A heavyweight championship prizefight from Yankee Stadium in New York City. Before the fight, Howard Cosell interviews John Wayne and William Holden, stars of the film ***The Horse Soldiers***. Sam Taub announces the fight and Les Kiter provides the blow-by-blow description.

Assignment (Canadian Broadcasting Corporation) June 29, 1961.

Host: Tony Thomas.

Tony interviews film star John Wayne.

John Wayne Interview (Voice of America) July 7, 1966.

Television Appearances

Cowboy Slim Theater (KTTV-Los Angeles, California, Channel 11) May 15, 1950.

John Wayne acts as emcee for an airing of his 1932 serial *The Shadow of the Eagle*. Also, *Funny Bunnies Meet the King*.

Camel Cigarette Commercials (All Networks) 1952.

John Wayne appears in a TV ad for R.J. Reynolds Tobacco Company.

The Red Skelton Show (NBC) October 26, 1952.

Star: Red Skelton. The David Rose Orchestra.

Guest: John Wayne. Red demonstrates how different people act when they walk against busy traffic at an intersection. British radio commentator Lord Beaverhead (Red) gives his version of the news. Clem Kadiddlehopper (Red) is mistaken by an ex-GI for the 'infamous' Lieutenant Muscles. Wayne appears as a vision and has no lines.

Jane Froman's USA Canteen (CBS) December 6, 1952.

Star: Jane Froman. The Peter Birch Dancers. Announcer: Allyn Edwards. The Alfredo Antonini Orchestra.

Musical half-hour set against the background of an armed services canteen. Tonight's guests include comedian Jackie Gleason, TV funnyman Jack Carter and actor John Wayne.

The Academy of Motion Picture Arts & Sciences 25th Annual Academy Awards (NBC) (Special) March 19, 1953.

Hosts: Bob Hope, Conrad Nagel. Announcer: Ronald Reagan. The Adolph Deutsch Orchestra.

Broadcast live from the RKO Pantages Theater in Hollywood and the International Theater in New York City. The first televised 'Oscar' awards. Hope is in Hollywood while Nagel presides from New York City, honoring outstanding achievement in 1952 motion pictures. Winners in major categories-**The Greatest Show on Earth** (Picture, Cecil B. De-Mille, presented by Mary Pickford); Gary Cooper (Actor, **High Noon**, presented by Janet Gaynor, John Wayne accepts the award for an absent Cooper); Shirley Booth (Actress, **Come Back Little Sheba**, presented by Ronald Colman); Anthony Quinn (Supporting Actor, **Viva Zapata!** Presented by Greer Garson, Katherine DeMille Quinn accepts for her absent husband); Gloria Grahame (Supporting Actress, **The Bad and the Beautiful**, presented by Edmund Gwenn); John Ford (Director, **The Quiet Man**, presented by Olivia de Havilland, John Wayne accepts the award for an absent Ford).

Irwin Allen (Documentary--Feature, **The Sea Around Us**, presented by Jean Hersholt); Edward C. Carfagno, Cedric Gibbons (Art Direction--Black and White, **The Bad and the Beautiful**, presented by Joan Fontaine and James Stewart); Frank Cavett, Frederick M. Frank, and Theodore St. John (Writing--Motion Picture Story, **The Greatest Show on Earth**, presented by Dore Schary); T. E. B. Clarke (Writing--Story and Screenplay, **The Lavender Hill Mob**, presented by Dore Schary); Merian C. Cooper, Bob Hope, Harold Lloyd, George Alfred Mitchell, Joseph M. Schenck (Honorary, presented by Charles Brackett); Cecil B. DeMille (Irving G. Thalberg Memorial Award, presented by Charles Brackett); Walt Disney (Short Subject--Two Reel, **Water Birds**, presented by Ray Milland and Jane Wyman); Harry Gerstad, Elmo Williams (Film Editing, **High Noon**, presented by Frank Capra); A. Arnold Gillespie (Special Effects, **Plymouth Adventure**, presented by Loretta Young); Keogh Gleason, Edwin B. Willis; (Set Decoration--Black and White, **The Bad and the Beautiful**, presented by Joan Fontaine and James Stewart); Winton C. Hoch, Archie Stout (Cinematography--Color; **The Quiet Man**, presented by Teresa Wright); The London Film Sound Department; (Sound Recording, **Breaking the Sound Barrier**, presented by Claire Trevor);

Norman McLaren (Documentary--Short Subject, *Neighbours*, presented by Ray Milland and Jane Wyman); Alfred Newman (Music--Scoring of a Musical Picture, ***With a Song in My Heart***, presented by Walt Disney); Fred Quimby (Short Subject--Cartoon, ***Johann Mouse***, presented by Ray Milland and Jane Wyman); Helen Rose (Costume Design--Black and White, ***The Bad and the Beautiful***, presented by Ginger Rogers); Charles Schnee; (Writing--Screenplay, ***The Bad and the Beautiful***, presented by Dore Schary); Paul Sheriff (Art Direction--Color, ***Moulin Rouge***, presented by Joan Fontaine and James Stewart); Robert Surtees (Cinematography--Black and White, ***The Bad and the Beautiful***, presented by Teresa Wright); Dimitri Tiomkin (Music--Song, *Do Not Forsake Me, Oh My Darlin'*, ***High Noon***, and also Music--Scoring of a Dramatic or Comedy Picture, ***High Noon***, presented by Walt Disney); Boris Vermont (Short Subject--One Reel, ***Light in the Window***, presented by Ray Milland and Jane Wyman); Marcel Vertes (Set Decoration--Color, ***Moulin Rouge***, presented by Joan Fontaine and James Stewart; and Costume Design--Color, ***Moulin Rouge***, presented by Ginger Rogers); Ned Washington (Music--Song Lyrics, *Do Not Forsake Me, Oh My Darlin'*, ***High Noon***, presented by Walt Disney). An Honorary Award was given to ***Forbidden Games*** (Best Foreign Film, presented by Luise Rainer). Produced by Johnny Green and Robert L. Welch. Directed by William A. [Bill] Bennington.

Nominated Songs: Celeste Holm performs: *Thumbelina* (composed by Frank Loesser), Bob Hope, Marilyn Maxwell: *Am I in Love* (Jack Brooks), Billy Daniels: *Because You're Mine* (Nicholas Brodszky; Sammy Cahn), Tex Ritter: *High Noon* (*Do Not Forsake Me, Oh My Darlin'*) (Dimitri Tiomkin; Ned Washington) (Academy Award Winner), Peggy Lee, Johnny Mercer: *Zing a Little Zong* (Harry Warren; Leo Robin).

Also: Edgar Bergen & 'Charlie McCarthy', Jacques Bergerac, Charles Coburn, Broderick Crawford, Joan Crawford, Donald Crisp, Jane Darwell, Bobby Driscoll, Jose Ferrer, Stewart Granger, Kim Hunter, Dean Jagger, Boris Karloff, Piper Laurie, Victor McLaglen, Terry Moore, Paul Muni, George Murphy, Gloria Swanson, Darryl F. Zanuck.

Seen in the audience: Rosemary Clooney, Tony Curtis, Eva Gabor, Zsa Zsa Gabor, Mitzi Gaynor, Edith Head, Janet Leigh, Mercedes McCambridge, Hugh O'Brian, Pat O'Brien, Merle Oberon, George Sanders, Elizabeth Taylor, Danny Thomas, Robert Wagner, Michael Wilding.

Art Linkletter's House Party (CBS) September 1, 1953.

Host: Art Linkletter.

Daytime talk, games and fun with guest John Wayne.

Three Lives (Syndicated) (Special) September 17, 1953 (when aired on WLW-A, Channel 7, Cincinnati, Ohio).

Narrator: John Wayne.

The United Jewish Appeal presents this drama of how the charity's work affected the lives of three individuals thanks to the support of the public. Written by Edna & Edward Anhalt. Directed by Edward Dmytryk. Music by Howard Jackson and William Lava.

Themselves: Arthur Franz, Charleton Heston, Randolph Scott, Jane Wyman. Dr. Stein: Leon Askin. Jim Adams: Phil Chambers. Zadok's Son: Joey [Joseph] Costarella. Rabbi: Eduard Franz. Reuben Zadok: Stacey [Stacy] Harris. Principal: Charles Meredith. Mrs. Adams: Elizabeth Patterson. Mrs. Vadney: Adeline de Walt Reynolds. Dr. Stein's Patient: Ruth Swanson. Mrs. Armstrong's Grandson: Stuart Torres. Mrs. Armstrong: Lurene Tuttle.

The Colgate Comedy Hour (NBC) October 11, 1953.

Host/Star: Jimmy Durante. Regulars: Eddie Jackson, Jules Buffano, Jack Roth, The Wanda Smith Cover Girls. The Roy Bargy Orchestra.

Guest: John Wayne. The Duke teaches Jimmy how to develop he-man qualities and become popular with the ladies. In a sketch, they send up Canadian Mountie movies. Directed by Fred Hamilton.

The Red Skelton Show (CBS) December 29, 1953.

Star: Red Skelton. Announcer: Bob Lemond. The David Rose Orchestra.

Guest: Jackie Gleason. Red spotlights Gertrude and Heathcliff in his monolog. He then brings John Wayne on stage to present him with *Modern Screen* magazine's award as Most Popular Actor of 1953. Sketches: The Saga of Cauliflower McPugg-A reporter tries to get the real story of the punch-drunk boxer from his manager (Jan Arvan); The Great White Hunter-Explorer McGumbo (Red) helps a woman search for her husband, who has gone missing in the jungle.

Jackie appears as his television character Reginald Van Gleason III. Directed by Seymour Berns. British Colonel: Hy Averback. Neil the Chimp: Himself (a chimpanzee).

The 26th Annual Academy Awards (NBC) (Special) March 25, 1954.

Hosts: Donald O'Connor (Hollywood), Fredric March (New York City). The Andre Previn Orchestra.

Broadcast live from the RKO Pantages Theater in Hollywood and the NBC Century Theater in New York City. Outstanding achievement in 1953 motion pictures is honored. Academy president Charles Brackett comments on technical and artistic innovations made during 1953 which reversed the thinking of many that "movies were on the way out". John Wayne is seen in the audience. Winners in major categories: Buddy Adler (Picture, **From Here to Eternity**, presented by Cecil B. DeMille); William Holden (Actor, **Stalag 17**, presented by Shirley Booth from Philadelphia, Pennsylvania); Audrey Hepburn (Actress, **Roman Holiday**, presented by Gary Cooper on film from Mexico); Frank Sinatra (Supporting Actor, **From Here to Eternity**, presented by Mercedes McCambridge); Donna Reed (Supporting Actress, **From Here to Eternity**, presented by Walter Brennan); Fred Zinnemann (Director, From Here to Eternity, presented by Irene Dunne).

Other winners include Charles Brackett, Richard Breen, and Walter Reisch (Writing--Story and Screenplay, **Titanic**, presented by Kirk Douglas); The Bell and Howell Company, Joseph I. Breen, Pete Smith, and 20th Century-Fox Corporation (Honorary, presented by Charles Brackett); Edward Carfagno and Cedric Gibbons (Art Direction--Black and White, **Julius Caesar**, presented by Marge and Gower Champion); George W. Davis and Lyle Wheeler (Art Direction--Color, **The Robe**, presented by Marge and Gower Champion); Walt Disney (Short Subjects--Cartoon, *Toot, Whistle, Plunk and Boom*, presented by Keefe Brasselle and Marilyn Erskine; Short Subjects--Two Reels, *Bear Country*, presented by Keefe Brasselle and Marilyn Erskine; Documentary--Short Subject, *The Alaskan Eskimo*, presented by Elizabeth Taylor and Michael Wilding, and Documentary--Feature, *The Living Desert*, presented by Elizabeth Taylor and Michael Wilding); Sammy Fain and Paul Francis Webster (Music--Song, "Secret Love" from *Calamity Jane*, presented by Arthur Freed); Paul S. Fox and Walter M. Scott (Set Decoration--Color, *The Robe*, presented by Marge and Gower Champion); Johnny Green (Short Subject--One Reel, *The Merry Wives of Windsor Overture*, presented by Keefe Brasselle and Marilyn Erskine); Loyal Griggs (Cinematography--Color, *Shane*, presented by Lex Barker and Lana Turner); Burnett Guffy (Cinematography--Black and White, *From Here to Eternity*, presented by Lex Barker and Lana Turner); Edith Head (Costume Design--Black and White, *Roman Holiday*, presented by Gene Tierney); Hugh Hunt and Edwin B. Willis (Set Decoration--Black and White, *Julius Caesar*, presented by Marge and Gower Champion); Bronislau Kaper (Music--Scoring of a Dramatic or Comedy Picture, *Lili*, presented by Arthur Freed); Charles LeMare and Emile Santiago (Costume Design--Color, *The Robe*, presented by Gene Tierney); John P. Livadary and the Columbia Sound Department (Sound Recording, *From Here to Eternity*, presented by Jack Webb); William Lyon (Film Editing, *From Here to Eternity*, presented by Esther Williams); Alfred Newman (Music--Scoring of a Musical Picture, *Call Me Madam*, presented by Arthur Freed); George Stevens (Irving G. Thalberg Memorial Award, presented by David O. Selznick); Daniel Taradash (Writing--Screenplay, *From Here to Eternity*, presented by Kirk Douglas); Dalton Trumbo (Writing--Motion Picture Story, *Roman Holiday*, presented by Kirk Douglas--the cited author, Ian McLellan Hunter, at the time was acting as a front for the blacklisted Trumbo); Chester Pate, Bob Springfield, Ken Strickfaden, A. Edward Sutherland and Barney Wolff (Special Effects, *The War of the Worlds*, presented by Merle Oberon).

Nominated Songs: Donald O'Connor and Mitzi Gaynor perform *The Moon Is Blue* (composed by Herschel Burke Gilbert and Sylvia Fine), Margaret Whiting: *My Flaming Heart* (Nicholas Brodszky and Leo Robin), Connie Russell: *Sadie Thompson's Song (Blue Pacific Blues)* (Lester Lee and Ned Washington), Ann Blyth: *Secret Love* (Sammy Fain and

Paul Francis Webster) (Academy Award Winner), Dean Martin: *That's Amore* (Harry Warren and Jack Brooks).

Also appearing: Phyllis Applegate, Marlon Brando, Raymond Burr, Linda Christian, Marla English, Grace Kelly, Deborah Kerr, Kim Novak, Geraldine Page, Thelma Ritter, Sol C. Siegel. Others seen in the audience: Julie Adams, Rory Calhoun, Jinx Falkenburg, Clark Gable, Lena Horne, Brenda Marshall, Virginia Mayo, Michael O'Shea, Ronald Reagan, Nancy Davis [Reagan]. Paul Douglas and Betty White for Oldsmobile Motors.

This Is Your Life (NBC) "William Wellman" December 8, 1954.

Host: Ralph Edwards. Announcer: Bob Warren.

John Wayne is among the guests who celebrate the life and career of William Wellman, noted motion picture director of such films as *Wings* (1927), *The Public Enemy* (1931), *A Star Is Born* (1937), *The Story of G.I. Joe* (1945), *Battleground* (1950) and *The High and the Mighty* (1954, which starred Wayne). Also on hand are film producers David O. Selznick and Robert Fellows; Hollywood columnist Hedda Hopper; actors James Cagney, Tab Hunter, Diana Lynn, Fred MacMurray, Jan Sterling and Teresa Wright; wife Dorothy Coonan Wellman and children William Jr., Kathleen, Maggie, Michael, Patricia, Tim, Celia and Cissy; Reginald 'Duke' Sinclair, member of the Lafayette Flying Corps during World War One; Arthur Wellman. Directed by Axel Gruenberg.

Sheilah Graham in Hollywood (NBC) January 31 thru February 4, 1955.

Host: Sheilah Graham.

Guest of the week is John Wayne, who is interviewed via film on location in San Francisco, California, while working on the film *Blood Alley*.

Gunsmoke (CBS) "Matt Gets It" September 10, 1955.

Stars: James Arness, Dennis Weaver, Milburn Stone, Amanda Blake.

John Wayne introduces the new series to viewers in a brief prologue. A gunman, hunted by a Texas sheriff, seeks refuge in Dodge City. US Marshal Matt Dillon (Arness) goes into action against this outlaw who shoots before he talks. Written for television by Charles Marquis Warren, from a story by John Meston. Directed by Charles Marquis Warren.

Dan Grat: Paul Richards. Sheriff Jim Hill: Robert Anderson. Bird: Malcolm Atterbury. Hotel Clerk: Howard Culver. Townsmen: Walter Bacon, Herman Hack, Chick Hannan, Bob Reeves.

Place the Face (NBC) September 13, 1955.

Host: Bill Cullen. Announcer: Jack Narz.

Celebrity contestants are asked to identify people from their past. Guests: John Wayne and singer Dorothy Shay. Final show of the series.

Warner Brothers Presents: Casablanca (ABC) *Who Holds Tomorrow?* September 27, 1955.

Host: Gig Young. Stars: Charles McGraw, Marcel Dalio, Dan Seymour, Michael Fox, Clarence Muse, Ludwig Stossel.

Trina (Anita Ekberg), a beautiful Swedish scientist, is carrying the secret of a powerful new weapon. Pursued by enemy agents, she goes to Rick's Café in Casablanca. John Wayne is seen with Gig in the "Behind the Scenes" segment spotlighting Wayne's Warner Brothers film **Blood Alley**.

The Milton Berle Show (NBC) September 27, 1955.

Star: Milton Berle. The Victor Young Orchestra.

First show of the season. Broadcast in color. Guests: Esther Williams and John Wayne. Esther joins Uncle Milty in a spoof of the movie **Summertime**. In a cameo, Dean Martin & Jerry Lewis appear in a sketch about a quiz show that bankrupts the network and Berle ends up as a prize; contestants Dean & Jerry win Uncle Milty. Written by Buddy Arnold, Bill Manhoff, Nate Monaster and Al Schwartz. Directed by Milton Berle.

The Mary Kaye Trio, Vaughn Monroe, Hal [Harold] Peary, The Herb Ross Dancers.

I Love Lucy (CBS) *Lucy Visits Grauman's* October 3, 1955.

Stars: Lucille Ball, Desi Arnaz, Vivian Vance, William Frawley, Joseph Michael Mayer. Announcer: Roy Rowan. Wilbur Hatch and the Desi Arnaz Orchestra.

First show of the season. Lucy is aghast when Ricky announces they are to return to New York upon completion of his film. In a last-minute tour of Hollywood, Lucy discovers that the cement slab of John Wayne's footprints at Grauman's Chinese Theater has come loose. Lucy steals it as a souvenir, but runs afoul of Ricky-who demands she return the slab. Unfortunately, the cement block drops and shatters into pieces. John Wayne appears as himself. Written by Jess Oppenheimer, Madelyn Pugh [Davis], Bob Carroll Jr., Bob Schiller and Bob Weiskopf. Directed by James V. Kern.

Tourist Couple: GeGe Pearson, Hal Gerard. Policemen: Clarence Straight, Ben Niems. Desi announces the show's sponsors: General Foods (Sanka Coffee) and Procter & Gamble (Lilt Home Permanents).

I Love Lucy (CBS) *Lucy and John Wayne* October 10, 1955.

Stars: Lucille Ball, Desi Arnaz, Vivian Vance, William Frawley, Joseph Michael Mayer. Announcer: Roy Rowan. Wilbur Hatch and the Desi Arnaz Orchestra.

Guest John Wayne appears on the scene to save Lucy from an embarrassing situation. He agreed to set his feet in new cement to replace the slab Lucy broke. However, Wayne must comply again when the new slab is ruined by guess who. Then, Little Ricky comes along and trudges across Wayne's latest effort. Can the wacky redhead cajole the Duke into planting his feet one more time? Highlight: Lucy posing as Wayne's masseur. Written by Jess Oppenheimer, Madelyn Pugh [Davis], Bob Carroll

Jr., Bob Schiller and Bob Weiskopf. Directed by James V. Kern.

George: Ralph Volkie. Man with Poster: Louis A. Nicoletti. Bellhop #1: Jack Chefe. Bellhop #2: Edwin Rochelle.

Producers' Showcase (NBC) *Dateline II* November 14, 1955.

Hosts: William Holden, Greer Garson. The George Bassman Orchestra.

John Wayne introduces the second annual variety show produced in cooperation with the Overseas Press Club and remarks on the theme, *Freedom of the Press.* Milton Berle provides comedy. Janet Blair sings *Funnies,* composed by Irving Berlin. To go with it, Tony Charmoli has fashioned a ballet on a *Li'l Abner* theme. Famed New England poet Robert Frost talks on *The Right to Know.* Irving Berlin has also contributed a new song titled *Free* performed by John Raitt. A playlet dramatizes an incident in the career of international correspondent Marguerite Higgins, starring Patricia Benoit as Higgins and Darren McGavin as Ed-the scene is a dugout near the front lines in the Korean War. A soldier brings in his seriously wounded buddy and tries desperately to keep him alive until the medics arrive. John Steinbeck contributes a eulogy of magazine photographer Robert Capa, who was killed in 1954 while in Indo-China. Peggy Lee sings *You're My Thrill* and *Swing Low, Sweet Chariot.* Written by Joseph Schrank (show script) and Donald Bevan (playlet). Directed by Alan Handley and Michael Case.

Additional Songs: Peggy, Janet, Greer: *How About You?*, Cast: *Free* (reprise).

The Colgate Variety Hour (NBC) November 27, 1955.

Host: Robert Paige. The Frank DeVol Orchestra.

Broadcast live from Hollywood. A telecast of Modern Screen magazine's annual awards taking place at the Cocoanut Grove at the Ambassador Hotel in Hollywood. Kirk Douglas and Louella Parsons present the awards. Providing entertainment are singer-actress Anna Maria Alberghetti, singer Eddie Fisher and singer-actor Gordon MacRae. Also participating are Claudette Colbert, Joan Collins, Bob Hope, Rock Hudson, Jimmy McHugh, Debbie Reynolds, Leigh Snowden, Russ Tamblyn, Lana Turner and John Wayne.

Screen Directors Playhouse (NBC) *Rookie of the Year* December 7, 1955.

Guest Director/Host: John Ford.

Small-town newspaper sports writer Mike Cronin (John Wayne) harbors an ambition to work for a big-city daily. He sees his chance to achieve his goal when attending the World Series. One of the rookies shows a style reminiscent of a former all-time great who was banned from baseball for accepting a bribe. Written for television by Frank [S.] Nugent, from a story by W.R. Burnett.

Ruth Dahlberg: Vera Miles. Larry 'Buck' Goodhue: Ward Bond. Lyn Goodhue: Pat [Patrick] Wayne. Ed Shafer: James Gleason. Mr. Cully: Willis Bouchey. Mr. White: Harry Tyler. Mr. Walker: William Forrest. Willie: Robert Leyden [Lyden]. Bobby: Tiger Fafara. Waiter: Chet Brandenburg. Phil: Charles Ferguson. Reporter: Rudy Germane.

Climax! (CBS) *The Louella Parsons Story* March 8, 1956.

Host: William Lundigan.

Broadcast live from Hollywood. Drama based on incidents in Louella Parsons' autobiography, *The Gay Illiterate*, tells of Parsons' career; Teresa Wright plays Louella Parsons. The time span is from the early 1920s to 1948. We see Parsons' early days as a newspaper reporter in Chicago. Here she loses her job and departs for New York. In the Big Apple she resumes her career, only to be stricken with tuberculosis. When she recovers from her illness, she meets the man who is to become her second husband, and her rise as a Hollywood columnist begins. Also, there is a tribute from stars of the movie industry, hosted by Jack Benny; Louella Parsons appears. Scheduled to visit are Eve Arden, Jean Pierre Aumont, Lex Barker, Joan Bennett, Charles Boyer, George Burns & Gracie Allen, Eddie Cantor, Dan Dailey, Howard Duff, Joan Fontaine, Zsa Zsa Gabor, Susan Hayward, Rock Hudson, Jack Lemmon, Ida Lupino, Jeanette MacDonald, Fred MacMurray, Robert Mitchum, Kim Novak, Merle Oberon,

Maureen O'Sullivan, Ginger Rogers, Gilbert Roland, Red Skelton, Robert Stack, Lana Turner, Robert Wagner, John Wayne. Written for television by Whitfield Cook. Directed by John Frankenheimer. Music by Leith Stevens. Whitfield Cook: Whit Bissell. Dr. Harry Martin: William Talman.

Also: Harriet Brest, Jeri Lou James, Sid Kane, Tyler McVey, Nestor Paiva, Marilee Phelps, Addison Richards, William Roerick, Helene Winston.

30th Annual Academy Awards (NBC) (Special) March 26, 1958.

Hosts: James Stewart, Bob Hope, Rosalind Russell, David Niven, Jack Lemmon.

Broadcast live from the RKO Pantages Theater in Hollywood. Honoring outstanding achievement in 1957 motion pictures. Academy president George Seaton opens the show with a few comments. Donald Duck (voice of Clarence Nash) narrates a cartoon history of movies. Married couples acting as 'custodians of Oscars' are Hope Lange and Don Murray; Janet Leigh and Tony Curtis; Natalie Wood and Robert Wagner. A medley of Oscar-winning songs from prior years features Mae West and Rock Hudson singing *Baby, It's Cold Outside*; Bob Hope and Jane Russell offering *Buttons and Bows*; Marge and Gower Champion rendering *The Continental*; Dean Martin and Kim Novak performing *The Way You Look*; Harry Belafonte singing *High Noon*; and Eddie Fisher vocalizing *Three Coins in the Fountain*. Burt Lancaster and Kirk Douglas team for a specialty number, *It's Great Not to Be Nominated* and winds up their bit with Douglas doing a handstand over Lancaster, who holds Douglas aloft while dancing offstage. After plugging his film, **The Barbarian and the Geisha** with help from Hope, John Wayne presents the Best Actress Award to Joanne Woodward for her performance in **The Three Faces of Eve**. Winners in major categories: Sam Spiegel (Picture, **The Bridge on the River Kwai**, presented by Gary Cooper); Alec Guinness (Actor, **The Bridge on the River Kwai**, presented by Cary Grant, Jean Simmons accepts the award for an absent Guinness); Red Buttons (Supporting Actor, **Sayonara**, presented by Lana Turner); Miyoshi Umeki (Supporting Actress, Sayonara, presented by Anthony Quinn); David Lean (Director, **The Bridge on the River Kwai**, presented by Sophia Loren). Malcolm Arnold (Music--Score, **The Bridge on the River Kwai**, presented by Anita Ekberg and Vincent Price); Pierre Boulle, Carl Forman, and Michael Wilson (Writing--Screenplay--Based on Material from Another Medium, *The Bridge on the River Kwai*, presented by Doris Day and Clark Gable); Ted Haworth (Art Direction, *Sayonara*, presented by Eva Marie Saint and Gregory Peck); Jack Hildyard (Cinematography, *The Bridge on the River Kwai*, presented by Joan Collins); Jerome Hill (Documentary--Feature, *Albert Schweitzer*, presented by Cyd Charisse and Ernest Borgnine); Larry Lansburgh (Short Subjects--Live Action, *The Wetback Hound*, presented by Jennifer Jones and Rock Hudson); Orry-Kelly (Costume Design, *Les Girls*, presented by Wendell Corey and Robert Ryan); Robert Priestley (Set Decoration, *Sayonara*, presented by Eva Marie Saint and Gregory Peck); Walter Rossi (Special Effects, *The Enemy Below*, presented by June Allyson); Edward Selzer (Short Subjects--Cartoon, *Birds Anonymous*, presented by Jennifer Jones and Rock Hudson); Peter Taylor (Film Editing, *The Bridge on the River Kwai*, presented by Joanne Woodward and Paul Newman); The Warner Bros. Studio Sound Department--George Groves, Sound Director (Sound Recording, *Sayonara*, presented by Dorothy Malone and Van Johnson); George Wells (Writing--Story and Screenplay--Written Directly for the Screen, *Designing Woman*, presented by Doris Day and Clark Gable); Charles Brackett, B.B. Kahane, Gilbert M. (Broncho Billy) Anderson, and the Society of Motion Picture and Television Engineers (Honorary, presented by Bette Davis); *The Nights of Cabiria* (Foreign Film (Italy), presented by Dana Wynter and Fred Astaire); Technical Awards presented by Hope Lange and Ronald Reagan.

Nominated Songs: Vic Damone (to Pier Angeli): *An Affair to Remember* (composed by Harry Warren, Harold Adamson and Leo McCarey), Dean Martin: *All the Way* (James Van Heusen and Sammy Cahn) (Academy Award Winner), Tommy Sands: *April Love* (Sammy Fain and Paul Francis Webster), Debbie Reynolds: *Tammy* (Ray Evans and Jay Livingston), Johnny Mathis: *Wild Is the Wind* (Dimitri Tiomkin and Ned Washington).

Also appearing: Zsa Zsa Gabor, Kim Novak, Giulietta Masina. Seen in the audience: Marlon Brando, Anthony Franciosa, Shelley Winters, Taina Elg, Betty Grable, Harry James, Ernie Kovacs, Sheree North, Maureen O'Hara, Robert Stack, Morris Stoloff, Diane Varsi.

Wide Wide World (NBC) *The Western* June 8, 1958.

Host: Dave Garroway. The David Broekman and James [Jimmie] Fagas Orchestras.

Today's live program traces the evolution of the western, which emerged from the pulp magazines to become a popular movie and television staple. Much of the program originates at Gene Autry's Melody Ranch, Newhall, California, where many western films and television series are shot. At the ranch, we meet John Wayne and Ricky Nelson, who are on location for the movie **Rio Bravo**. Gilbert 'Broncho Billy' Anderson, original cowboy star of the early silent screen, plays poker with Walter Brennan and George 'Gabby' Hayes. Character actor Chill Wills pays tribute to Will Rogers. Film director John Ford shows clips from his classic movie **Stagecoach**. Television producer Norman MacDonnell (**Gunsmoke**) talks about 'adult' westerns. Native American actor Rodd Redwing gives a shooting exhibition with a Colt .45 and a rifle-assisted by Gail Davis. Gary Cooper, Maria Schell and Karl Malden are seen at another location, Anchez, Washington, where they are making the film **The Hanging Tree**; the three actors and their director, Delmer Daves, comment on the current western trend. Filmed sequences show footage from TV westerns, also old and new Hollywood cowboy films with William S. Hart, Tom Mix, Hoot Gibson, Harry Carey [Sr.], Tim McCoy, Buck Jones, James Stewart, Gregory Peck and John Wayne in action. Also appearing are James Arness, star of TV's **Gunsmoke**; singing cowboy star and television producer Gene Autry; James Garner and Jack Kelly of TV's **Maverick**; writer Frank Gruber; stuntmen-actors Chuck Hayward and Chuck Roberson; Clayton Moore and Jay Silverheels of TV's **The Lone Ranger**; actors Ben Piazza and Big John Hamilton; and Warner Brothers Studio head Jack L. Warner. Written by Harold Azine. Directed by Van Fox. Music by David Broekman. Produced by Ted Rogers.

31st Annual Academy Awards (NBC) (Special) April 6, 1959.

Hosts: Bob Hope, Jerry Lewis, David Niven, Laurence Olivier, Tony Randall, Mort Sahl. The Lionel Newman Orchestra.

Broadcast live from the RKO Pantages Theater in Hollywood. Honoring outstanding achievement in 1958 motion pictures. William Holden and

John Wayne welcomes the television audience to the ceremonies. Kirk Douglas and Burt Lancaster perform *It's All Right with Us*, a reprise of last year's *It's Great Not to Be Nominated* including acrobatics: Kirk stands on Burt's shoulders and they both execute somersaults. Dana Wynter, Joan Collins and Angela Lansbury answer with *It's Bully Not to Be Nominated*. During the presentation of the Award for Best Costume, five actresses model gowns: Jayne Mansfield, Christine Carere, Joanna Moore, Victoria Shaw and Inger Stevens. Wayne joins Irene Dunne to present the Best Actor Award to David Niven for **Separate Tables**. Winners in major categories: Arthur Freed (Picture, **Gigi**, presented by Ingrid Bergman); Susan Hayward (Actress, **I Want to Live!** Presented by Kim Novak and James Cagney); Burl Ives (Supporting Actor, **The Big Country**, presented by Bette Davis and Anthony Quinn); Wendy Hiller (Supporting Actress, **Separate Tables**, presented by Shelley Winters and Red Buttons, accepted by Harold Hecht for an absent Hiller); Vincente Minnelli (Director, **Gigi**, presented by Millie Perkins and Gary Cooper).

Other winners: Preston Ames, William A. Horning (Art Direction--Black and White or Color--**Gigi**, presented by Vincent Price and Eddie Albert); Cecil Beaton (Costume Design--Black and White or Color, **Gigi**, presented by Wendell Corey and Ernie Kovacs); John W. Burton (Short Subject--Cartoon, **Knighty Knight Bugs**, presented by Janet Leigh and Tony Curtis); Maurice Chevalier (Honorary, presented by Rosalind Russell); Walt Disney (Short Subject--Live Action, **Grand Canyon**, presented by Janet Leigh and Tony Curtis); Adrienne Fazan (Film Editing, **Gigi**, presented by Jean Simmons and Louis Jourdan); Keogh Gleason, Henry Grace (Set Decoration--Black and White or Color, **Gigi**, presented by Vincent Price and Eddie Albert); Tom Howard (Special Effects, **Tom Thumb**, presented by Shirley MacLaine and Peter Ustinov); Sam Leavitt (Cinematography--Black and White, **The Defiant Ones**, presented by Doris Day and Rock Hudson); Alan Jay Lerner (Screenplay--Based on Material from Another Medium, **Gigi**, presented by Elizabeth Taylor, Dirk Bogarde, and Van Heflin); Alan Jay Lerner, Frederick Loewe (Music--Song, "Gigi", **Gigi**, presented by Sophia Loren and Dean Martin); Andre Previn (Music--Scoring of a Musical Picture, **Gigi**, presented by June Allyson and Dick Powell); Joseph Ruttenberg (Cinematography--Color, **Gigi**, presented by Doris Day and Rock Hudson); Ben Sharpsteen (Documentary--Short Subject, **AMA Girls**, and

Documentary--Feature, *White Wilderness*, presented by Natalie Wood and Robert Wagner); Nathan E. Douglas, Harold Jacob Smith, and Nedrick Young (Story and Screenplay--Written Directly for the Screen, *The Defiant Ones*, presented by Elizabeth Taylor, Dirk Bogarde, and Van Heflin); Jacques Tati (Foreign Film, *Mon Oncle*-- France, presented by Cyd Charisse and Robert Stack); Dimitri Tiomkin (Music--Scoring of a Dramatic or Comedy Picture, *The Old Man and the Sea*, presented by Eva Marie Saint and Anthony Franciosa); Todd-AO Sound Department, Fred Hynes--Sound Director (Sound, *South Pacific*, presented by Jane Wyman and Charlton Heston); Jack L. Warner (Irving G. Thalberg Memorial Award, presented by Buddy Adler). Technical Awards presented by Barbara Rush and Jacques Tati.

Nominated Songs: Anna Maria Alberghetti, Tuesday Weld, Connie Stevens, Nick Adams, Dean Jones, James Darren: *Almost in Your Arms* (*Love Song from Houseboat*) (composed by Jay Livingston and Ray Evans), John Raitt, danced by Marge and Gower Champion: *A Certain Smile* (Sammy Fain and Paul Francis Webster), Tony Martin, danced by Taina Elg: *Gigi* (Frederick Loewe and Alan Jay Lerner) (Academy Award Winner), Eddie Fisher: *To Love and Be Loved* (James Van Heusen and Sammy Cahn), Howard Keel and Rhonda Fleming: *A Very Precious Love* (Sammy Fain and Paul Francis Webster).

Also: James Algar, Dana Andrews, Frankie Avalon, Theodore Bikel, Honor Blackman, Lee J. Cobb, Fabian, Joan Fontaine, Steve Forrest, Martha Hyer, Dorothy Lamour, Joe Louis, Edmond O'Brien, Fess Parker, Louella Parsons, Laya Raki, Ron Randell, Ginger Rogers, Rosemarie Stack, Tom Tryon, Stuart Whitman, Cara Williams, Gig Young.

Hollywood-Ein Vovort in Vier Anekdoten (SDR) (Special) June 9, 1959.

Narrator: Michael Pfleghar.

Half-hour West German television feature spotlighting film personalities, including John Wayne. Written and directed by Michael Pfleghar.

Yul Brynner, Martine Carol, Mickey Hargitay, John Hart, Carol Hughes, Peggy Jacobson, Grace Kelly, Gina Lollobrigida, Jayne Mansfield, Jane Marie Mansfield, Milko Skofic, Lana Turner, Orson Welles.

The 32nd Annual Academy Awards (NBC) (Special) April 4, 1960.

Host: Bob Hope. The Andre Previn Orchestra.

Broadcast live from the RKO Pantages Theater in Hollywood. B.B Kahane, president of the Motion Picture Academy of Arts and Sciences, introduces Bob-who keep things moving as the ceremony honors outstanding achievement in 1959 motion pictures. John Wayne presents the Award for Best Director to William Wyler for **Ben-Hur**. Fred Astaire introduces the French star Yves Montand, who sings *Un Garcon Dansait* and dances to *The Continental.* Ella Fitzgerald sings a medley of George Gershwin tunes. During the presentation of the Costume Design Award-by Arlene Dahl and Fernando Lamas-gowns are modeled by Joan Blackman, Linda Hutchins, Barbara Lawson, Diane McBain, Yvette Mimieux, Jo Morrow, Maggie Pierce, Stella Stevens, Nancy Walters and Cindy Wood. Winners in major categories: Sam Zimbalist (Picture, **Ben-Hur**, presented by Gary Cooper, accepted by his widow, Mary Zimbalist); Charlton Heston (Actor, **Ben-Hur**, presented by Susan Hayward); Simone Signoret (Actress, **Room at the Top**, presented by Rock Hudson); Hugh Griffith (Supporting Actor, **Ben-Hur**, presented by Olivia de Havilland); Shelley Winters (Supporting Actress, **The Diary of Anne Frank**, presented by Edmond O'Brien). Other winners: Edward Carfagno, William A. Horning (Art Direction--Color, **Ben-Hur**, presented by Angie Dickinson and Richard Conte); Jacques-Yves Cousteau (Short Subject--Live Action, **The Golden Fish**, presented by Hope Lange and Carl Reiner); Ken Darby, Andre Previn (Music--Scoring of a Musical Picture, **Porgy and Bess**, presented by Gene Kelly); George W. Davis, Lyle R. Wheeler (Art Direction--Black and White, **The Diary of Anne Frank**, presented by Angie Dickinson and Richard Conte); John D. Dunning, Ralph E. Winters (Film Editing, **Ben-Hur**, presented by Barbara Rush); A. Arnold Gillespie, Milo Lory, Robert MacDonald (Special Effects, **Ben-Hur**, presented by Haya Harareet); Clarence Greene, Maurice Richlin, Russell Rouse, Stanley Shapiro (Writing--Story and Screenplay--Written Directly for the Screen, **Pillow**

Talk, presented by Janet Leigh and Tony Curtis); Bernhard Grzimek (Documentary--Feature, *Serengeti Shall Not Die*, presented by Mitzi Gaynor); Bert Haanstra (Documentary--Short Subject, *Glass*, presented by Mitzi Gaynor); Elizabeth Haffenden (Costume Design--Color, *Ben-Hur*, presented by Arlene Dahl and Fernando Lamas); Bob Hope (Jean Hersholt Humanitarian Award, presented by B.B. Kahane); John Hubley (Short Subjects--Cartoon, *Moonbird*, presented by Hope Lange and Carl Reiner); Hugh Hunt (Set Decoration--Color, *Ben-Hur*, presented by Angie Dickinson and Richard Conte); Lee DeForest, Buster Keaton (Honorary Awards); William C. Mellor (Cinematography--Black and White, *The Diary of Anne Frank*, presented by Edward Curtis); Metro-Goldwyn-Mayer Studio Sound Department, Franklin E. Milton, Director (Sound, *Ben-Hur*, presented by Natalie Wood and Robert Wagner); Orry-Kelly (Costume Design--Black and White, *Some Like It Hot*, presented by Arlene Dahl and Fernando Lamas); Neil Paterson (Writing--Screenplay Based on Material from Another Medium, *Room at the Top*, presented by Janet Leigh and Tony Curtis); Stuart A. Reiss, William M. Scott (Set Decoration--Black and White, *The Diary of Anne Frank*), presented by Angie Dickinson and Richard Conte); Miklos Rozsa (Music--Scoring of a Dramatic or Comedy Picture, *Ben-Hur*, presented by Gene Kelly); Robert L. Surtees (Cinematography--Color, *Ben-Hur*, presented by Edward Curtis).

Nominated Songs: Frankie Vaughan performs *The Best of Everything* (composed by Alfred Newman and Sammy Cahn), Joni James: *The Five Pennies* (Sylvia Fine), Frankie Laine: *The Hanging Tree* (Jerry Livingston and Mack David), Sammy Davis Jr.: *High Hopes* (James Van Heusen and Sammy Cahn) (Academy Award Winner), Gogi Grant: *Strange Are the Ways of Love* (Dimitri Tiomkin and Ned Washington).

Also: Ann Blyth, Jack Clayton, Wendell Corey, Joan Crawford, Felicia Farr, Eddie Fisher, George Hamilton, Dolores Hart, Susan Kohner, Machiko Kyo, Jack Lemmon, Nicole Maurey, Juanita Moore, Tony Randall, Aldo Ray, Russell Rouse, Robert Ryan, John Saxon, James Stewart, Elizabeth Taylor, Danny Thomas, Marlo Thomas, Robert Vaughn, Ed Wynn, Keenan Wynn.

The Jack Paar Show (NBC) September 26, 1960.

Host: Jack Paar. Announcer: Hugh Downs. The Jose Melis Orchestra.

Late-night talk and sketches with guests John Wayne and singer Jack Haskell.

The Ed Sullivan Show (CBS) November 13, 1960.

Host: Ed Sullivan. The June Taylor Dancers. The Ray Bloch Orchestra.

Walter Pidgeon and Beatrice Lillie do a comedy sketch. Dick Van Dyke and Chita Rivera perform scenes and sing selections from ***Bye, Bye, Birdie.*** British singer Shirley Bassey offers a tune. Comedy team Dan Rowan & Dick Martin do a bit. Ed introduces a German clown act, Le Bully Trio. A monologue from humorist Sam Levenson. Also, an appearance by John Wayne.

Songs: Beatrice: *Little White Bull*, Dick, teen trio: *We Love You, Conrad!*, Dick, Two Sad Girls: *Put On A Happy Face*, Chita: *Spanish Rose*.

Sad Girl: Sharon Lerit.

What's My Line? (CBS) November 13, 1960.

Host: John Daly. Panel: Arlene Francis, Joey Bishop (guest), Dorothy Kilgallen, Bennett Cerf. Announcer: Hal Simms.

Contestants are Elbert N. Carvel, governor-elect of Delaware (who also manufactures fertilizer); and Margaret Ballentyne, who is a bookie for horse races. The mystery guest is John Wayne, trying to throw the panel by disguising his voice in German.

Spirit of the Alamo (ABC) (Special) November 14, 1960.

John Wayne and a host of stars visit the site of the Battle of the Alamo. When Wayne finished work on his movie ***The Alamo***, he filmed the party that followed, on location in Texas, as the focal point of this show. Members of the film's cast, including Richard Widmark, Richard Boone and Linda Cristal, discuss their roles. Frankie Avalon, Ken Curtis and Joan

O'Brien sing from a local nightspot. Laurence Harvey reads Shakespeare Texas-style. Chill Wills attempts to sing. Carlos Aruza and Patrick Wayne stage a mock bullfight. Former US Vice-President John Nance Garner, in Uvalde, and authors J. Frank Dobie and Lon Tinkle, from Austin, talk about the Alamo. Wayne reads a letter written by Davy Crockett on the eve of the famous battle. Written by I. Salaman. Directed by Seymour Robbie. Music by Dimitri Tiomkin.

The Jack Benny Program (CBS) *John Wayne Show* November 20, 1960.

Stars: Jack Benny, Eddie 'Rochester' Anderson, Don Wilson, The Sportsman Quartet.

Videotaped in New York City. Guests: John Wayne, Frank Fontaine, and Jaye P. Morgan. Jack decides to emulate Ed Sullivan-he points out celebrities in the audience and comes up with Wayne and John L. C. Sivoney (Fontaine). Wayne is talked into subbing for Jack on a date with Jaye P., who sings *Won't You Come Home, Bill Bailey?* Wayne and Morgan go to a gypsy restaurant, where they are serenaded by a violin trio-including a disguised Jack, who is playing for tips. Written by George Balzer, Hal Goodman, Al Gordon, Sam Perrin, Howard Snyder and Hugh Wedlock Jr.

Howard K. Brawley: Milo Boulton. Betty Furness: Herself. Gypsy MC: Clarence Hoffman. Gypsy Fortune Teller: Zolya Talma.

Wagon Train (NBC) *The Colter Craven Story* November 23, 1960.

Stars: Ward Bond, Robert Horton, Frank McGrath, Terry Wilson.

Major Adams (Bond) and the train come across the disabled wagon of Dr. Colter Craven (Carleton [S.] Young) and his wife. Though Craven appears to be an alcoholic, Adams decides to give him a chance to become a useful member of the westbound party. Written by Tony Paulsen. Directed by John Ford.

Park Cleatus: John Carradine. General William T. Sherman: Michael Morris [John Wayne]. Allyris Craven: Anna Lee. General Ulysses S. Grant: Paul Birch. Kyle Cleatus: Ken Curtis. Creel Weatherby: Cliff Lyons. Quentin Cleatus: Chuck Hayward. Jamie: Dennis Rush. Mr. Grant:

Willis Bouchey. Jamie's Mother: Beula Blaze. Soldier: Danny Borzage. Colonel Lollier: Richard H. Cutting. Mrs. Grant: Annelle Hayes. Mrs. Jesse Grant: Mae Marsh. Tim Molloy: Jack Pennick. Junior: Chuck Roberson. Mort: Charles Seel. Townsman: Arthur Tovey. Hank: Hank Worden. Wagon Train Members: Tex Holden, Kermit Maynard, George Sowards.

Cinepanorama (Television Telerama) December 17, 1960.

Host: Francois Chalais.

Talk show with John Wayne, Sophia Loren, Raf Vallone, Marie Larforet.

Note: Loosely translated, the show's title means "A complete survey or presentation of the movie world".

Dateline (WBAP-Channel 5, Fort Worth-Dallas, Texas) February 1961.

Host: Bobby Wygant.

Talk show with guest John Wayne.

The 33rd Annual Academy Awards (ABC) (Special) April 17, 1961.

Host: Bob Hope. The Andre Previn Orchestra.

Broadcast from the Civic Auditorium in Santa Monica, California. Honoring outstanding achievement in 1960 motion pictures. Andre conducts the orchestra in a medley of Arthur Freed-Nacio Herb Brown tunes. Academy of Motion Picture Arts & Sciences president Valentine Davies introduces Bob. Vic Damone sings a medley of Oscar Hammerstein II songs. Juliet Prowse dances to *Fever*. Danny Kaye, Tony Curtis and Janet Leigh team for *Triplets*. William Wyler presents an Honorary Award to Gary Cooper, which is accepted by James Stewart on his behalf. Other Honorary Award winners are Stan Laurel (accepted on his behalf by Danny Kaye) and Hayley Mills. John Wayne is seen in the audience. Winners in major categories: Billy Wilder (Picture, **The Apartment**, presented by Audrey Hepburn; also Director, for the same film, presented by Gina Lollobrigida, and again for Writing-Story and Screenplay Written Directly for the Screen, presented by Kitty Carlisle and Moss Hart); Burt Lancaster (Actor, **Elmer Gantry**, presented by Greer Garson); Elizabeth Taylor (Actress, **Butterfield 8**, presented by Yul Brynner); Peter Ustinov (Supporting Actor, **Spartacus**, presented by Eva Marie Saint); Shirley Jones (Supporting Actress, **Elmer Gantry**, presented by Hugh Griffith). Tim Baar, Gene Warren (Special Effects, **The Time Machine**, presented by Polly Bergen and Richard Widmark); Ezra R. Baker (Short Subjects--Live Action, **Day of the Painter**, presented by Susan Strasberg and Wendell Corey); Ingmar Bergman (Foreign Film, **The Virgin Spring** [Sweden], presented by Eric Johnston); Edward G. Boyle (Set Decoration--Black and White, **The Apartment**, presented by Tina Louise and Tony Randall); Richard Brooks (Writing--Adapted Screenplay, **Elmer Gantry**, presented by Kitty Carlisle and Moss Hart); Freddie Francis (Cinematography--Black and White, **Sons and Lovers**, presented by Cyd Charisse and Tony Martin); Russell A. Gausman, Julia Herron (Set Decoration--Color, **Spartacus**, presented by Tina Louise and Tony Randall); Ernest Gold (Music--Scoring of a Dramatic or Comedy Picture, **Exodus**, presented by Sandra Dee and Bobby Darin); Alexander Golitzen, Eric Orbom (Art Direction--Color, **Spartacus**, presented by Tina Louise and Tony Randall); Edith Head, Edward Stevenson (Costume Design--Black and White, **The Facts of Life**, presented by Barbara Rush and Robert Stack); James Hill (Documentary--Short Subjects, **Giuseppina**, presented by Janet Leigh and Tony Curtis); Larry Lansburgh (Documentary--Feature, **The Horse with the Flying Tail**, presented by Janet Leigh and Tony Curtis); Stan Laurel (Honorary Award, presented by Danny Kaye and accepted on Laurel's behalf); Sol Lesser (Jean Hersholt Humanitarian Award, presented by Bob Hope); Daniel Mandell (Film Editing, **The Apartment**, presented by Betty Comden and Adolph Green); Russell Metty (Cinematography--Color, **Spartacus**, presented by Cyd Charisse and Tony Martin); Hayley Mills (Honorary Award, presented by Shirley Temple); Samuel Goldwyn Studio Sound Department, Gordon E. Sawyer, Director, and Todd-AO Sound Department, Fred Hynes, Director (Sound, **The Alamo**, presented by Paula Prentiss and Jim Hutton); William A. Snyder (Short Subjects--Cartoon, **Munro**, presented by Susan Strasberg and Wendell Corey); Morris Stoloff, Harry Sukman (Music--Scoring of a Musical Picture, **Song Without End**, presented by Sandra Dee and Bobby Darin); Bill Thomas, Valles (Costume Design--Color, **Spartacus**, presented by Barbara Rush and Robert Stack).

Directed by Richard Dunlap. Produced by Arthur Freed and Richard Dunlap.

Nominated Songs: The Hi-Los perform *The Facts of Life* (composed by Johnny Mercer), Sarah Vaughan: *Faraway Part of Town* (Andre Previn and Dory Langdon), The Brothers Four: *The Green Leaves of Summer* (Dimitri Tiomkin and Paul Francis Webster), Connie Francis: *Never on Sunday*" (Manos Hadjidakis) (Academy Award Winner), Jane Morgan: *The Second Time Around* (James Van Heusen and Sammy Cahn).

Also: Jack Bean, Jack Cassidy, Joan Crawford, I.A.L. Diamond, Peter Falk, Felicia Farr, Mel Ferrer, Eddie Fisher, Annette Funicello, Mitzi Gaynor, Johnny Grant, Laurence Harvey, Jean Hazelwood, Earl Holliman, Trevor Howard, Shirley Knight, Jack Kruschen, Hedy Lamarr, Peter Lawford, Jack Lemmon, Mara Massey, Gardner McKay, Sal Mineo, Ginger Rogers, Tommy Sands, Jean Simmons, Nancy Sinatra, Tuesday Weld, Chill Wills, Robert Young.

Here's Hollywood (NBC) July 24, 1962.

Hosts: Helen O'Connell, Jack Linkletter.

John Wayne, Elsa Martinelli, Red Buttons and Bruce Cabot relate anecdotes about their African location filming for the movie **Hatari!**

Alcoa Premiere (ABC) *Flashing Spikes* October 4, 1962.

Host: Fred Astaire.

Years ago, Slim Conway (James Stewart) was expelled from major-league baseball for accepting a bribe to throw a game. Now the past has come back to haunt him-he is accused of bribing his friend, young ballplayer Bill Riley (Patrick Wayne), whose error cost his team a World Series game. Written for television by Jameson Brewer, from a novel by

Frank O'Rourke. Directed by John Ford. Music by Johnny [John] Williams.

Commissioner: Jack Warden. Crab Holman: Edgar Buchanan. Gabby LaSalle: Tige Andrews. Mary Riley: Stephanie Hill. Rex Short: Carleton [S.] Young. Mayor: Willis Bouchey. Judge: Charles Seel. Hogan: Bing Russell. Man in the Dugout: Harry Carey Jr. Announcer: Vin Scully. First Reporter: Larry J. Blake. Second Reporter: Walter Reed. Nurse: Sally Hughes. Bush Umpire: Charles Morton. Bit Man: Cy Malis. Assistant Commissioner: William Henry. Marine Sergeant: Marion Morrison [John Wayne]. Series Umpire: Art Passarella. First Baseball Player: Vern Stephens. Second Baseball Player: Ralph Volkie. Third Baseball Player: Bud Harden. Fourth Baseball Player: Earl Gilpin. Fifth Baseball Player: Whitey Campbell. Comer: Don Drysdale.

The Dick Powell Theatre (NBC) *The Third Side of the Coin* March 26, 1963.

Guest Host: John Wayne.

Rosalind Cramer (June Allyson) has been dating her married boss, publisher William Kent (Hugh Marlowe), and now she demands $25,000 from him. Kent calls it blackmail, but Rosalind uses another word: compensation. Written by S. Lee Pogostin. Directed by Marc Daniels. Music by Joseph Mullendore.

Peter Kent: John Forsythe. Miriam Kent: Jeanne Bal. Joan Kent: Marta Kristen. John Kent: Donald Losby. Doorman: Larry J. Blake. Bellboy: Tommy Farrell. Also: Veronica Cartwright, Suzanne Cupito [Morgan Brittany].

Inside the Movie Kingdom (NBC) (Special) March 20, 1964.

Narrator: James Garner.

To take us 'inside' the international film world, producer Milton Fruchtman equips his crews with lightweight cameras making it possible for viewers to attend a Carroll Baker party, ride through Los Angeles with Sammy Davis Jr., stroll through Paris with Tony [Anthony] Perkins and enter closed movie sets across the globe. Written by Norman Corwin.

Also seen are Julie Andrews, Ingrid Bergman, Stephen Boyd, Claudia Cardinale, Melvyn Douglas, Henry Fonda, Gene Kelly, Jack Lemmon, Sophia Loren, Dean Martin, Steve McQueen, Melina Mercouri, Jeanne Moreau, Robert Morley, Paul Newman, Gregory Peck, Christopher Plummer, Anthony Quinn, Debbie Reynolds, Maximilian Schell, Romy Schneider, Omar Sharif, Peter Ustinov, Dick Van Dyke and John Wayne.

Cinepanorama (Television Telerama) September 26, 1964.

Host: Francois Chalais.

Guests: Barbara Bouchet, Kirk Douglas, Jill Haworth, Otto Preminger, John Wayne, Pierre Zimmer.

Cinepanorama (Television Telerama) December 26, 1964.

Host: Francois Chalais.

Guests: Kirk Douglas, Otto Preminger, John Wayne, Pierre Zimmer.

The Dean Martin Show (NBC) September 23, 1965.

Stars: Dean Martin, The Krofft Puppets. Pianist: Ken Lane. Les Brown and his Band.

Guests: John Wayne; singers Peggy Lee, Jack Jones; ventriloquist Shari Lewis; juggler Rudy Cardenas; and comic acrobat Walter Dare Wahl. Dean sings *Send Me the Pillow That You Dream On*. John joins Dean for *Don't Fence Me In* and *Everybody Loves Somebody*; the pair also talk about their movie ***The Sons of Katie Elder***.

Additional Songs: Peggy: *When a Woman Loves a Man, I'm Just Wild About Harry, Bill, Alright, Okay, You Win,* Jack: A medley of *Sound of Music, My Favorite Things, Climb Every Mountain.* Dean, Peggy, Jack: *I Can't Give You Anything But Love,* Shari: *The Name Game,* Dean, Puppets: *I've Got Your Number*, Puppets: *Tweedle Dee.*

Puppet voices: Joey Forman, Jane Kean. Also: Al Casey, Diane Davis, Margie Nelson, Larri Thomas.

23rd Annual Golden Globe Awards (NBC) (Special) February 28, 1966.

Host: Andy Williams. Miss Golden Globe: Cheryl Miller.

Broadcast from the Cocoanut Grove Nightclub, Ambassador Hotel, Los Angeles. Honoring outstanding 1965 film and television. John Wayne is winner of the Cecil B. DeMille Special Award. Additional winners: Julie Andrews (Actress-Comedy or Musical Film, **The Sound of Music**); Samantha Eggar (Actress-Drama Film, **The Collector**); Anne Francis (Female Television Star, **Honey West**); Elizabeth Hartman (Most Promising Newcomer, **Patch of Blue**); David Janssen (Male Television Star, **The Fugitive**); Maurice Jarre (Original Score, **Doctor Zhivago**); David Lean (Director, **Doctor Zhivago**); Lee Marvin (Actor-Comedy or Musical Film, **Cat Ballou**); Paul Newman (World Film Favorite-Male); Omar Sharif (Actor-Drama Film, **Doctor Zhivago**); Natalie Wood (World Film Favorite-Female). Also: Donna Butterworth, David McCallum, Robert Vaughn.

The Red Skelton Hour (CBS) March 1, 1966.

Star: Red Skelton. The Alan Copeland Singers. The Tom Hanson Dancers. Announcer: Art Gilmore. The David Rose Orchestra.

John Wayne hosts Red Skelton's Scrapbook, featuring Red in some of his favorite routines. In the Silent Spot Red plays a Gay Nineties bachelor. Dancer Melanie Alexander joins Red for a comic version of Michel Folkine's ballet, Spectre of the Rose. Wayne gives Red some tips on western-style courting. In The Upside-Down Room, drunken Willie Lump Lump (Red) awakens to find his bedroom rearranged. Red also does his famous doughnut-dunking routine. A series of blackouts sees Red as a man having Just One More Drink; a befuddled inventor; a kettledrum player; a math expert; a hunter; a man suffering a headache; and a guy taking medicine.

Written by Mort Green, Dave O'Brien, Robert Orben, Arthur Phillips, Martin Ragaway, Larry Rhine, Bob Schiller, Red Skelton and Bob Weiskopf. Directed by Bill Hobin. Bartender: Bob Duggan. Mrs. Lump Lump/ Gay '90s Lady Love: Chanin Hale. Carpenter Swanson/Policeman: Ray Kellogg. Ballerina: Roberta Lubell. Cranky Neighbor: Peggy Rea. Crabby Father: David Sharpe.

The Merv Griffin Show (Syndicated) March 2, 1966.

Host: Merv Griffin. Regular: Arthur Treacher. The Mort Lindsey Orchestra.

Today's show features the *Photoplay* magazine awards with guests: Joan Crawford and John Wayne. Rowlf the Muppet (voice of Jim Henson) sings *You and I and George*. Also: Marty Allen & Steve Rossi, Christopher Connelly, Patricia Morrow, Robert Vaughn, Peggy Wood.

The Dean Martin Show (NBC) October 27, 1966.

Star: Dean Martin. Pianist: Ken Lane. The Les Brown Orchestra.

Guests: John Wayne; Bill Cosby of TV's ***I Spy***; singer-dancer Joey Heatherton; and comedy team Dan Rowan & Dick Martin. Dean sings "The Shoe Goes on the Other Foot". Dean's daughter Gail makes her singing debut with "Rose of Washington Square". Wayne joins Dean for "I'm an Old Cowhand". Written by Harry Crane.

Additional Songs: Joey: *You Made Me Love You*; *Frankie and Johnnie*, Dean, Gail: *Bye, Bye, Blackbird*; *Mister Meadowlark*; *Back in Your Own Backyard*; Honey, Dean, Ken: *Red Sails in the Sunset*, All: *I've Got Tears in My Ears*; *Cry*. Al Casey.

The Lucy Show (CBS) *Lucy and John Wayne* November 21, 1966.

Stars: Lucille Ball, Gale Gordon, Roy Roberts, Mary Jane Croft. Announcer: Roy Rowan. The Wilbur Hatch Orchestra.

Mr. Mooney (Gordon) sends Lucy to deliver some financial papers to John Wayne's studio. Lucy's curiosity creates chaos on the star's western movie set when she becomes determined to meet Wayne in person.

Milton Berle makes a brief cameo appearance. Written by Bob [Robert] O'Brien. Directed by Maury Thompson.

Director: Joseph Ruskin. Pierce: Morgan Woodward. Assistant Director: Bryan O' Byrne. Waitress: Kay Stewart. Joyce: Joyce Perry. Accordionist: Danny Borzage. Barflies: Jerry Gatlin, Bill Hart, Boyd 'Red' Morgan, Chuck Roberson. Bartender: Victor Romito. Cameraman: Jerry Rush.

The Merv Griffin Show (Syndicated) November 30, 1966.

Host: Merv Griffin.

Guests: John Wayne, Kirk Douglas, Howard Keel, Hugh O'Brian. Merv visits with the four actors, who are making the picture *The War Wagon* on location in Mexico.

The Beverly Hillbillies (CBS) *The Indians Are Coming* February 1, 1967.

Stars: Buddy Ebsen, Irene Ryan, Donna Douglas, Max Baer Jr., Raymond Bailey, Nancy Kulp.

Granny (Ryan) prepares for an Indian attack while Jed and Mr. Drysdale (Ebsen, Bailey) plan a pow-wow with the tribe. It seems they have laid claim to the Clampetts' oil-rich land. John Wayne makes a cameo appearance. Written by Paul Henning and Buddy Atkinson. Directed by Joseph Depew.

Chief Running Wolf: Stanley Waxman. Little Fox: John Considine. Lawrence Chapman: Milton Frome. Indians: Vince [Vincent] St. Cyr, Morry Ogden.

The 24th Annual Golden Globes Awards" (NBC) (Special) February 15, 1967.

Host: Andy Williams. Miss Golden Globe: Corinna Tsopei.

Broadcast live from the Cocoanut Grove Nightclub, Ambassador Hotel, Los Angeles, California. Honoring outstanding achievement in 1966 film and television. Andy sings the Motion Picture Best Song Nominees: *A Man and a Woman*; *Alfie*; *Born Free*; *Georgy Girl* and *Strangers in the Night* (Golden Globe Award Winner). Television's Lassie delivers the envelope of winners' names to presenter John Wayne. Additional winners: Anouk Aimee (Actress-Film Drama, **A Man and a Woman**); Julie Andrews (World Film Favorite-Female); Alan Arkin (Actor-Comedy or Musical Film, **The Russians Are Coming**); Richard Attenborough (Supporting Actor-Film, **The Sand Pebbles**); Elmer Bernstein (Original Score--Film, **Hawaii**); Charlton Heston (Cecil B. DeMille Award); Jocelyn LaGarde (Supporting Actress-Film, Hawaii); Dean Martin (Male Television Star); Steve McQueen (World Film Favorite-Male); Marlo Thomas (Female Television Star); Fred Zinnemann (Director-Film, **A Man for All Seasons**). Additional presenters: Herb Alpert, Fred Astaire, Anne Baxter, Warren Beatty, James Coburn, Sandra Dee, Faye Dunaway, Samantha Eggar, Henry Fonda, James Garner, Richard Harris, Rex Harrison, Rita Hayworth, Rock Hudson, Sandy Koufax, David McCallum, Rachel Roberts, Jean Simmons, Elke Sommer, Catherine Spaak. Lesley Ann Warren. Also: Robert Culp, Ross Hunter, Geraldine Page, Vanessa Redgrave, Eva Marie Saint, Natalie Wood.

The Las Vegas Show (Syndicated) May 19, 1967.

Host: Bill Dana. Regular: Pete Barbutti. The Jack Sheldon Orchestra.

Variety with guests John Wayne, comedian Don Rickles, actress-singer-dancer Chita Rivera and actress-comedienne-singer Jo Anne Worley. Also: Tony Darryl, Ann Elder, Danny Meehan, Cully Richards, Jennie Smith.

Dateline: Hollywood (ABC) June 1, 1967.

Host: Joanna Barnes. Regular: Rona Barrett.

Daytime talk from the film capital. Joanna interviews John Wayne, Richard Egan and starlet Cami Sebring.

The Merv Griffin Show (Syndicated) February 21, 1968.

Host: Merv Griffin. Regular: Arthur Treacher. The Mort Lindsey Orchestra.

Merv interviews John Wayne and director John Huston. Other guests include comedian Morey Amsterdam, actor Maurice Evans, singer A.V. [Avelio] Falana, comic actress Barbara Nichols and Australian musician Robie Porter.

Rowan & Martin's Laugh-In (NBC) March 4, 1968.

Hosts: Dan Rowan & Dick Martin. Regulars: Judy Carne, Arte Johnson, Ruth Buzzi, Henry Gibson, Goldie Hawn, Larry Hovis, Roddy Maude-Roxby, Inga Neilsen, JoAnne Worley. Announcer: Gary Owens. The Ian Bernard Orchestra.

Guests: John Wayne; British comic Terry-Thomas; Sally Field of TV's *The Flying Nun*; Joby Baker of TV's *Good Morning, World*; comic and actor Godfrey Cambridge; and rock group The Bee Gees. Terry-Thomas plays Moses in a *News-of-the-Past* sketch. Sally appears as a futuristic phenomenon-a person made of spare parts. *Mod, Mod World* looks at England's past glory and present problems. Wayne sees a clip of Jerry Lewis stuttering and asks, *Was that Dean Martin?* The Bee Gees sing *Lemons Never Forget*. Wayne tells viewers, *"The program you have just seen is true. Only the writers will be changed to protect the innocent"*. Written by Paul Keyes, Hugh Wedlock [Jr.], Allan Manings, Chris Bearde, David Panich, Phil Hahn, Jack Hanrahan, Coslough Johnson, Marc London and Digby Wolfe. Directed by Gordon Wiles.

Rowan & Martin's Laugh-In (NBC) March 11, 1968.

Hosts: Dan Rowan & Dick Martin. Regulars: Eileen Brennan, Ruth Buzzi, Judy Carne, Henry Gibson, Goldie Hawn, Larry Hovis, Arte Johnson, Roddy Maude-Roxby, JoAnne Worley. Announcer: Gary Owens.

Guests: Barbara Feldon of TV's *Get Smart*; vocal duo Sonny [Bono] & Cher; ventriloquist Paul Winchell; comic Pat Morita; Anissa Jones of TV's *Family Affair*; John Wayne. Dan interviews a leprechaun (Barbara). Sonny presents a trained seal act. 'Mod, Mod World' peers into the supernatural. The cast does their 'salute' to former Alabama Governor George Wallace. Arte debuts his 'dirty old man' character, Tyrone. John Wayne tells viewers, *It's hard to believe this could happen in America*". Also, cameos by Jerry Lewis and Dinah Shore. Written by Paul Keyes, Hugh Wedlock [Jr.], Allan Manings, Chris Bearde, David Panich, Phil Hahn, Jack Hanrahan, Coslough Johnson, Marc London and Digby Wolfe. Directed by Gordon Wiles.

Rowan & Martin's Laugh-In (NBC) March 25, 1968.

Hosts: Dan Rowan & Dick Martin. Regulars: Pamela Austin, Ruth Buzzi, Judy Carne, Henry Gibson, Goldie Hawn, Larry Hovis, Arte Johnson, Roddy Maude-Roxby, JoAnne Worley. Announcer: Gary Owens. The Ian Bernhard Orchestra.

Guests: Sammy Davis Jr., Joey Bishop, John Wayne. Two Russian rockers (Sammy, Arte) sing *When the Saints Go Marching In*. The credibility gap gets a going-over as Sammy and Joey play Washington press officers. *Mod, Mod World* salutes the Olympic Games. Sammy debuts his *Here comes the judge* character. Dick uses *You bet your sweet bippy* phrase for the first time. John Wayne comments, *"I've shot men for less than that"* and *"That's as funny as an Indian attack"*. Also, appearances by Elgin Baylor, Harry Belafonte and Regis Philbin. Written by Paul Keyes, Hugh Wedlock [Jr.], Allan Manings, Chris Beard [Bearde], David Panich, Phil Hahn, Jack Hanrahan, Coslough Johnson, Marc London and Digby Wolfe. Directed by Gordon Wiles.

Rowan & Martin's Laugh-In (NBC) April 8, 1968.

Hosts: Dan Rowan & Dick Martin. Regulars: Pamela Austin, Eileen Brennan, Ruth Buzzi, Judy Carne, Henry Gibson, Goldie Hawn, Larry Hovis, Arte Johnson, David Lipp, Roddy Maude-Roxby, JoAnne Worley. Announcer: Gary Owens. The Ian Bernard Orchestra.

Guests: comedian Flip Wilson and comic-impressionist John Byner. Byner plays King George III discussing the American Revolution. Pamela interviews a religious leader (Flip). *Mod, Mod World* honors adventurers: the first American female in space (Judy) and first man to return from the moon (Larry). Other sketches include *Cocktail Party* and *USO dancers under attack.* Also, appearances by Paul Winchell, Hugh Downs, James Garner and John Wayne. Written by Paul Keyes, Hugh Wedlock [Jr.], Allan Manings, Chris Bearde, David Panich, Phil Hahn, Jack Hanrahan, Coslough Johnson, Marc London and Digby Wolfe. Directed by Gordon Wiles.

Rowan & Martin's Laugh-In (NBC) April 15, 1968.

Hosts: Dan Rowan & Dick Martin. Regulars: Eileen Brennan, Ruth Buzzi, Judy Carne, Henry Gibson, Goldie Hawn, Larry Hovis, Arte Johnson, Roddy Maude-Roxby, JoAnne Worley. Announcer: Gary Owens. The Ian Bernard Orchestra.

Guests: Kaye Ballard of TV's **The Mothers-In-Law**; comic-impressionist John Byner; vocal group The Curtain Calls. Byner interviews the richest woman in the world (Kaye). The *New Talent Showcase* features Judy on roller skates and Arte doing bird calls. *Mod, Mod World* looks at law and justice. The Curtain Calls sing *Sock It to Me, Sunshine.* Also, appearances by Harry Belafonte, Shelley Berman, James Garner, John Wayne and Flip Wilson. Written by Paul Keyes, Hugh Wedlock [Jr.], Allan Manings, Chris Bearde, David Panich, Phil Hahn, Jack Hanrahan, Coslough Johnson, Marc London and Digby Wolfe. Directed by Gordon Wiles.

Additional Songs: JoAnne: *My Mother's Eyes*; *They Call the Wind Maria*; *The Way You Look Tonight*, Arte: *By Myself*, Cast: *We Love the Law*; *The Law Was on Her Side*, Ruth: *When I Fall in Love*, Kaye: *I Just Kissed My Nose Goodnight.*

Rowan & Martin's Laugh-In (NBC) April 22, 1968.

Hosts: Dan Rowan & Dick Martin. Regulars: Eileen Brennan, Ruth Buzzi, Judy Carne, Henry Gibson, Goldie Hawn, Larry Hovis, Arte Johnson, Roddy Maude-Roxby, JoAnne Worley. Announcer: Gary Owens. The Ian Bernard Orchestra.

Guests: Barbara Feldon of TV's **Get Smart** and comic Tim Conway. Interviews take place with a space-age Noah (Tim) and a news-making taco maker (Barbara). Henry has a sermon on the state of television. A performance by vexed ventriloquist Lucky Pierre (Paul Winchell). A look at advertising in the *Mod, Mod World*. Tyrone and Gladys (Arte, Ruth) meet for the first time. Also, appearances by Shelley Berman, John Byner, Johnny Carson, Hugh Downs, John Wayne and Flip Wilson. Written by Paul Keyes, Hugh Wedlock [Jr.], Allan Manings, Chris Bearde, David Panich, Phil Hahn, Jack Hanrahan, Coslough Johnson, Marc London and Digby Wolfe. Directed by Gordon Wiles.

Songs: JoAnne: *Let's Call the Whole Thing Off*, Cast: *It Pays to Advertise.*

Rowan & Martin's Laugh-In (NBC) April 29, 1968.

Hosts: Dan Rowan & Dick Martin. Regulars: Eileen Brennan, Ruth Buzzi, Judy Carne, Henry Gibson, Goldie Hawn, Larry Hovis, Arte Johnson, Roddy Maude-Roxby, JoAnne Worley. Announcer: Gary Owens. The Ian Bernard Orchestra.

Guest: Tiny Tim. Tim submits to an interview by Dan and Dick; Tim sings *Tip Toe Through the Tulips. Mod, Mod World* salutes the American people and includes a singing tribute to the martini. Paul Winchell plays the upside-down man. Also, appearances by Sivi Aberg, Pamela Austin, Milton Berle, Shelley Berman, Joey Bishop, John Byner, Jill St. John, John Wayne and Flip Wilson. Written by Paul Keyes, Hugh Wedlock [Jr.], Allan Manings, Chris Bearde, David Panich, Phil Hahn, Jack Hanrahan, Coslough Johnson, Marc London and Digby Wolfe. Directed by Gordon Wiles.

Additional Songs: Cast: *God Bless You, Tiny Tim; It's a Sock It to Me, Very Interesting, Cuckoo, Laugh-In World; Here's to the Martini*, JoAnne: *Hava Nagila.*

The Joey Bishop Show (ABC) July 2, 1968.

Host: Joey Bishop. Announcer: Regis Philbin.

Late-night talk and variety with guests: John Wayne; vocal group The Mills Brothers; comic Pete Barbutti and singer Robin Wilson.

Your All-American College Show (Syndicated/KTVT-Channel 11, Dallas-Fort Worth, Texas) September 15, 1968.

Host: Dennis James.

Top college talent from around the country competes for recognition and prizes. Tonight's panel of celebrity judges is Peter Falk, Vera Miles and Ernest Borgnine. Guest presenter John Wayne awards the cash prize to the winner of the finals. Sponsored by Colgate-Palmolive Company.

Rowan & Martin's Laugh-In (NBC) September 16, 1968.

Hosts: Dan Rowan & Dick Martin. Regulars: Charlie Brill & Mitzi McCall, Chelsea Brown, Ruth Buzzi, Judy Carne, Henry Gibson, Goldie Hawn, Arte Johnson, Dave Madden, Pigmeat Markham, Alan Sues, Dick Whittington, JoAnne Worley. Announcer: Gary Owens. The Ian Bernard Orchestra.

First show of the season. Guests: Barbara Feldon of TV's **Get Smart**; John Wayne and *Playboy* mogul Hugh Hefner. Dan interviews Mrs. Sigmund Freud (Barbara), who analyzes her home life. Hugh appears in a party segment. President Johnson (Jack Riley) finds himself aboard a hijacked plane. *Mod, Mod World* surveys higher education. Rock group Mother Hubbard is the talent discovery. John Wayne visits the Joke Wall. Appearing in celebrity blackouts are Bob Hope, Jack Lemmon, Richard Nixon, Sonny Tufts and Zsa Zsa Gabor. Also: Billy Barnes, Byron Gilliam and Mayor John B. Whitney of Burbank, California. Written by Paul W. Keyes, Hugh Wedlock Jr., Allan Manings, Chris Bearde, David Panich, Coslough Johnson, Marc London, Dave Cox, Jim Carlson, Jack Mendelsohn, Jim Mulligan, Phil Hahn, Jack Hanrahan. Directed by Gordon Wiles.

Songs: JoAnne: *I Don't Want to Set the World on Fire*, Cast: *Up With Higher Education*, Arte: *No Matter Where You Go*.

Rowan & Martin's Laugh-In (NBC) September 23, 1968.

Hosts: Dan Rowan & Dick Martin. Regulars: Charlie Brill & Mitzi McCall, Chelsea Brown, Ruth Buzzi, Judy Carne, Henry Gibson, Goldie

Hawn, Arte Johnson, Dave Madden, Pigmeat Markham, Alan Sues, Jo-Anne Worley. Announcer: Gary Owens. The Ian Bernard Orchestra.

Guest: Eve Arden of TV's **The Mothers-In-Law**. A musical number features Eve as a Russian stripper. Dan and Dick present their *Discovery of the Week*-the director of the Burbank glee club. Arte plays Rabbi Shankar in a bit with Ruth. Henry reads a new poem. Charlie and Mitzi take a compatibility test. The cast offers a singing salute to the phone company. Also appearing are Herb Alpert, Arlene Dahl, Wild Man Fischer, Zsa Zsa Gabor, George Kirby, Jack Lemmon, Sonny Tufts, John Wayne and Patrick Wayne. Written by Paul W. Keyes, Hugh Wedlock Jr., Allan Manings, Chris Bearde, David Panich, Coslough Johnson, Marc London, Dave Cox, Jim Carlson, Jack Mendelsohn, Jim Mulligan, Phil Hahn, Jack Hanrahan.

Songs: Wild Man: *The Leaves Are Falling*; *Merry-Go-Round*, Cast: *Mother Bell*, Eve: *Bump and Grind*.

The Bob Hope Show (NBC) (Special) November 27, 1968.

Star: Bob Hope.

Bob presents a videotaped college concert in honor of the University of Southern California, broadcast from the Los Angeles Sports Arena. Guests: guitarist Glen Campbell, who begins a weekly television variety hour in January; Sergio Mendes and Brasil '66; singer Barbara McNair and singer-dancer Juliet Prowse. Also: sketches, comment on scenes on and off campus and words of encouragement for a superstar-USC's O.J. Simpson, a leading contender for the Heisman Trophy. Also: James Garner, John McKay, Fess Parker, Robert Stack, Marlo Thomas and John Wayne.

The Glen Campbell Goodtime Hour (CBS) February 5, 1969.

Star: Glen Campbell. Regulars: Pat Paulsen, Jack Burns, John Hartman. The Denny Vaughn Singers. The Ron Poindexter Dancers. Announcer: Roger Carroll. The Marty Paich Orchestra.

Guests: John Wayne, singer Jeannie C. Riley, rock group The Monkees.

Glen sings *Ann*; *Fate of Man*; *By the Time I Get to Phoenix*; *Sittin' on the Dock of the Bay*; and *Roll in My Sweet Baby's Arms*. In a spoof of Jeannie's hit song, *Harper Valley P.T.A.*, Pat plays a school principal with Glen, Jeannie and Jack as concerned parents. Pat performs comedy vignettes tied to the song *It Was a Very Good Year*. Wayne makes a cameo appearance talking about Glen's featured role in **True Grit**. The finale salutes telephones. Written by Jack Burns, Elias Davis, Gordon Farr, Jeff Harris, John Hartford, Bernie Kukoff, David Pollock, Rob Reiner, Cecil Tuck and George Yanok. Directed by Marty Pasetta.

Additional Songs: Jeannie: *The Girl Most Likely*, The Monkees: *Last Train to Clarksville*; *Tear Drop City*.

The Glen Campbell Goodtime Hour (CBS) February 19, 1969.

Star: Glen Campbell. Regulars: Pat Paulsen, Jack Burns, John Hartford. The Denny Vaughn Singers. The Ron Poindexter Dancers. Announcer: Roger Carroll. The Marty Paich Orchestra.

Guests: singer-comic Roger Miller; rocker Stevie Wonder. Glen sings *Mary in the Morning*; *Cold December in Your Heart*; *Words* and *Those Were the Days*. Pat struggles to break the language barrier that's blocking his efforts to date a gorgeous fraulein. The finale lampoons advertising. Also making appearances are John Wayne, Steve Allen, Jayne Meadows and Monty Hall. Written by Jack Burns, Elias Davis, Gordon Farr, Jeff Harris, John Hartford, Bernie Kukoff, Steve Martin, David Pollock, Rob Reiner, Cecil Tuck and George Yanok.

Additional Songs: Glen, Roger: *King of the Road*, Glen, Stevie: *Blowin' in the Wind*, Glen, Jim: *Memphis*, Roger: *Kansas City Star*, Stevie: *For Once in My Life*.

The Joey Bishop Show (ABC) August 6, 1969.

Host: Joey Bishop. Announcer: Regis Philbin.

Guests: John Wayne; country music group Buck Owens and the Buckaroos and comedian Guy Marks. Also: Gerri Granger.

The Red Skelton Hour (CBS) October 28, 1969.

Star: Red Skelton. Regulars: The Tom Hanson Dancers, The Jimmy Joyce Singers. Announcer: Art Gilmore. The David Rose Orchestra.

Guest: John Wayne. Red pays tribute (comic and serious) to the Duke, celebrating his fortieth year in films. Supplying musical pleasures are Julius Wechter and the Baja Marimba Band. Duke is the movie star as Red demonstrates various approaches of autograph hounds. Red plays Deadeye and Wayne is Rooster Cogburn in a sampling of what ***True Grit*** would have been like if Red had been cast in it. The Silent Spot-"*The Happy Irish Pub* with Red as a son of the 'auld sod' in his natural habitat-dancing a jig and smashing furniture. A little boy (Red) goes to a monster movie. Written by Fred S. Fox, Mort Greene, Seaman Jacobs, Dave O'Brien, Robert Orben, Arthur Phillips, Larry Rhine and Red Skelton. Directed by Bill Hobin.

Songs: Baja Marimba Band: *Brazilia*; *Coming Through the Back Door*; *Fresh Air*, Singers, Dancers: *Tonight*; *To the Movies We Go*.

Pub Patron: George Neise. Little Old Lady: David Sharpe. Also: Bob Duggan, Sam Edwards, Tommy Farrell, Chanin Hale, Brad Logan, Reta Shaw, Jan Arvan, Carol Worthington.

My Name Is George-Making of The Undefeated (ZDF) (Special) 1969.

Documentary made for West German television on the production of the film ***The Undefeated***, featuring appearances from its stars John Wayne and Rock Hudson; director Andrew V. McLaglen and stuntman Hal Needham.

Note: the network acronym ZDF stands for Zweites Deutsches Fernsehen ("Second German Television").

The Movie Game (Syndicated) March 16, 1970.

Host: Larry Blyden. Announcer: Johnny Gilbert.

Celebrities team with contestants in answering questions about films. Guests: Carl Reiner, Lizabeth Scott, Ann Sothern and John Wayne.

The 42nd Annual Academy Awards (ABC) (Special) April 7, 1970.
Broadcast live from the Dorothy Chandler Pavilion, Los Angeles, California. Academy president Gregory Peck introduces *Friends of Oscar* who present the Awards; they include Fred Astaire, Candice Bergen, Claudia Cardinale, Clint Eastwood, Elliott Gould, Bob Hope, James Earl Jones, Myrna Loy, Barbara McNair, Ali MacGraw, Cliff Robertson, Katharine Ross, Elizabeth Taylor, Jon Voight, John Wayne and Raquel Welch. Wayne presents the Award for Best Cinematography to Conrad Hall for ***Butch Cassidy and the Sundance Kid.*** Ingmar Bergman, Sergey Bondarchuk, Federico Fellini, Akira Kurosawa, David Lean, Mike Nichols, John Schlesinger and Franco Zeffirelli comment on new freedom and trends in film. Wayne receives the Award for Best Actor (***True Grit***) from Barbra Streisand. Burt Bacharach (Music--Original Score for a Motion Picture [Not a Musical], ***Butch Cassidy and the Sundance Kid***, presented by Barbara McNair and Cliff Robertson; and Music--Song, *Raindrops Keep Fallin' on My Head*, ***Butch Cassidy and the Sundance Kid***, presented by Candice Bergen); Herman Blumenthal, John De Cuir, Jack Martin Smith (Art Direction, ***Hello, Dolly!*** presented by Myrna Loy and Jon Voight); Francoise Bonnot (Film Editing, ***Z***, presented by Claudia Cardinale and James Earl Jones); Raphael Bretton, George Hopkins, Walter M. Scott (Set Decoration, ***Hello, Dolly!*** presented by Myrna Loy and Jon Voight); Bernard Chevry (Documentary--Feature, ***Arthur Rubinstein--The Love of Life***, presented by Fred Astaire and Bob Hope); Robert M. Fresco, Denis Sanders (Documentary--Short Subject, ***Czechoslovakia 1968***, presented by Fred Astaire and Bob Hope); Margaret Furse (Costume Design, ***Anne of the Thousand Days***, presented by Candice Bergen); William Goldman (Writing--Story and Screenplay--Based on Material Not Previously Published or Produced, ***Butch Cassidy and the Sundance Kid***, presented by Katharine Ross and Jon Voight); Cary Grant (Honorary Award, presented by Frank Sinatra); Lennie Hayton, Lionel Newman (Music--Score of a Musical Picture [Original or Adaptation], ***Hello, Dolly!*** presented by Elmer Bernstein and Shani Wallis); Ward Kimball (Short Subjects--Cartoon, ***It's Tough to Be a Bird***, presented by Myrna Loy and Cliff Robertson); George Jessel (Jean Hersholt Humanitarian Award, presented by Bob Hope); Robbie Robertson (Special Visual Effects, ***Marooned***, presented by Raquel Welch); Waldo Salt (Writing--Screenplay--Based on Material from Another Medium,

Midnight Cowboy, presented by Katharine Ross and Jon Voight); Jack Solomon, Murray Spivack (Sound, ***Hello, Dolly!*** presented by Candice Bergen and Elliott Gould); Joan Keller Stern (Short Subjects--Live Action, ***The Magic Machines***, presented by Myrna Loy and Cliff Robertson).

Also: Genevieve Bujold, Catherine Burns, Richard Burton, Dyan Cannon, Rupert Crosse, Hal David, Jane Fonda, Peter Fonda, Dennis Hopper, Sylvia Miles, Liza Minnelli, Vincente Minnelli, Jack Nicholson, Jacques Perrin, Michelle Phillips, Mickey Rooney, Jean Simmons, Larry Tucker, Roger Vadim, Billy Wilder, Susannah York. Written by Hal Kanter, Mary Loos and Frank Pierson. Directed by Jack Haley Jr. and Richard Dunlap. Produced by M.J. Frankovich and Richard Dunlap.

Nominated Songs: The Sandpipers perform *Come Saturday Morning* (composed by Fred Karlin and Dory Previn), Lou Rawls: *Jean* (Rod McKuen), B.J. Thomas: *Raindrops Keep Fallin' on My Head* (Burt Bacharach; Hal David) (Academy Award Winner), Glen Campbell: *True Grit* (Elmer Bernstein; Don Black), Michel LeGrand: *What Are You Doing the Rest of Your Life?*" (Michel LeGrand; Alan and Marilyn Bergman).

Raquel (CBS) (Special) April 26, 1970.

Star: Raquel Welch. The Don Randi Orchestra.

John Wayne, Bob Hope and Tom Jones are Raquel's leading men in this variety show. The hour was filmed around the world, with Raquel singing and dancing in colorful locales. The moods shift from dreamy to playful as Raquel takes a fantasy trip to Paris-where she sings *California Dreaming* aboard a barge on the Seine; London-at a discotheque, Raquel teams with Tom for a medley of Little Richard songs; Mexico-Raquel sings the Oscar-winning *Raindrops Keep Fallin' on My Head* beside a Mexico City fountain. On the Yucatan Peninsula, awesome Mayan ruins provide the setting for numbers from *Hair*. Academy Award Winner Wayne shows Raquel how to be a cowboy, and there's a brief clip from ***True Grit***; they also visit an orphanage in Mexico. Bob 'Sundance' Hope sings the John Lennon-Paul McCartney hit *Rocky Raccoon* with saloon hostess Raquel. Written by Douglas Tibbles, Larry Alexander and Jon [Jonathan] Axelrod. Directed by David Winters. Choreography by David Winters. Produced by David Winters, Patrick Curtis, Burt Rosen.

Additional Songs: Raquel: *Everybody's Talkin'*; *The Sound of Silence*; *Games People Play*; *Peaceful*; *Here Comes the Sun*; *Good Morning Starshine*, Tom: *I, Who Have Nothing*.

The Tonight Show Starring Johnny Carson (NBC) 1970.

Host: Johnny Carson. Announcer: Ed McMahon. The Doc Severinsen Orchestra.

Late-night talk and variety with guest John Wayne.

The Irv Kupcinet Show (NET) June 3, 1970.

Host: Irv Kupcinet.

Talk and interviews with guests John Wayne, Susannah York, Jon Voight. Also: Sammy Davis Jr., Lola Falana, Elke Sommer, William Wyler.

Note: the acronym NET stands for National Educational Television, the precursor to the Public Broadcasting Service (PBS).

Swing Out, Sweet Land (NBC) (Special) November 29, 1970.

Host: John Wayne. Announcer: Ed McMahon. The John Beal and Dominic Frontiere Orchestras.

Wayne's first television special is a journey through American history-with music, comedy and more than two dozen guest stars. Guests include Jack Benny as a citizen asking George Washington (Lorne Greene) about that dollar he supposedly hurled across the Potomac; Bob Hope and Ann-Margret entertaining the troops at Valley Forge; printer Red Skelton discussing dissent with apprentice Tom Smothers; Lucille Ball as the voice of Miss Liberty; Johnny Cash sings a salute to the men who built the railroads; and Bing Crosby as Mark Twain, philosophizing with freed slave Frederick Douglass (Roscoe Lee Browne). Also: Michael Landon as Peter Minuit, buying Manhattan Island from Indian Dan Blocker; Dean Martin as inventor Eli Whitney; Roy Clark playing banjo at Andrew Jackson's inaugural; Celeste Holm and Dennis Weaver as the parents of young Abe Lincoln; brothers David and Rick Nelson fighting on opposite sides in the Civil War; Phyllis Diller as 19th century Presidential candidate, Belva A. Lockwood; Dan Rowan & Dick Martin as the Wright Brothers; and George Burns as himself. Written by Paul Keyes and John Aylesworth. Directed by Stan Harris. Choreography by Jaime Rogers. Produced by William O. Harbach, Nick Vanoff and Paul W. Keyes.

Songs: Johnny Cash performs *Ribbon of Steel*, Ann-Margret: *It Was Good Enough for Grandma*, Glen Campbell: *This Is a Great Country*, Roy Clark: *Oh, Susannah*, Leslie Uggams: *Clementine*, Doodletown Pipers: *The Declaration*, All: *God Bless America*.

Alexander Hamilton: Ross Martin. Crispus Attucks: Greg Morris. Thomas Jefferson: Hugh O'Brian. John Adams: William Shatner. Saloon Singer: Leslie Uggams. Confederate Soldier's Wife: Cathy Baker. Bud: Lisa Todd. Father: Arthur Tovey. Bartender: Ed McMahon. Colorado: Jesse Vint. Missouri Representative: Owen Bush. Illinois Representative: Harry Hickox. Mississippi Representative: Kay E. Kuter. Maine Representative: Forrest Lewis. Alabama Representative: Orville Sherman. James Caldwell: Patrick Wayne. Florida Representative: Dan White. Iowa Representative: Hal Williams.

Plimpton! Shoot-Out at Rio Lobo (ABC) (Special) December 9, 1970.

Writer George Plimpton-America's professional amateur-offers a behind-the-scenes look at his movie debut. Plimpton is playing one of the bad guys in **Rio Lobo**, a John Wayne western being filmed in Arizona. Director Howard Hawks has given him just one line of dialogue, *"This here's your warrant, Mister"*-and he wants it without any trace of Plimpton's Harvard accent. Cameras follow George's progress from wardrobe and makeup to encounters with Wayne, veteran heavy Jack Elam and the special-effects men. Plimpton's big scene: he walks into the Rio Lobo saloon and gets the drop on Wayne and the sheriff...but not for long. Plimpton visits with fellow movie newcomer Joe Namath (who was filming **C.C. and Company** nearby) and film clips trace the careers of Wayne and director Hawks. The Jack K. Tiller Orchestra. Written by William Kronick and George Plimpton. Directed by William Kronick. Music by

Walter Scharf. Produced by William Kronick and Conrad Holzgang for David L. Wolper Productions.

Also: A.D. Flowers, Victor French, David Huddleston.

The Super Comedy Bowl (CBS) (Special) January 10, 1971.

Entertainment, with comedy and music, featuring top stars of pro football and show business in a tongue-in-cheek salute to the gridiron world. The players who appear include Kermit Alexander (Los Angeles Rams), Emerson Boozer (New York Jets), Dick Butkus (Chicago Bears), Ben Davidson (Oakland Raiders), Roman Gabriel (Rams), Mike Garrett (San Diego Chargers), Roosevelt Grier (Rams), Deacon Jones (Rams), Alex Karras (Detroit Lions), John Mackey (Baltimore Colts), Joe Namath (Jets), Dave Robinson (Green Bay Packers), Gale Sayers (Bears) and O.J. Simpson (Buffalo Bills). Performing with the players are Lucille Ball, Carol Burnett, Judy Carne, Tina Cole, Norm Crosby, Teresa Graves, Charlton Heston, David Huddleston, Marty Ingels, Arte Johnson, Jack Lemmon, Art Metrano, Pat O'Brien, Charles Nelson Reilly, Jill St. John, Alan Sues, Leslie Uggams and John Wayne. Directed by Marty Pasetta.

The Merv Griffin Show (Syndicated) January 27, 1971.

Host: Merv Griffin. Regular: Arthur Treacher.

Merv conducts an interview with John Wayne from the actor's ranch in Stanfield, Arizona.

The Tonight Show Starring Johnny Carson (NBC) February 8, 1971.

Star: Johnny Carson. Announcer: Ed McMahon. The Doc Severinsen Orchestra.

Late-night talk and variety with guests: singer-actress Ann-Margret; comedians Jack Benny and Red Skelton; actors John Cassavetes, Peter Falk, Ben Gazzara and John Wayne. Written by Hank Bradford, Michael Barrie, Joe Bigelow, Stan Daniels, Stan Dreben, Jim Mulholland and Ed Weinberger.

Everything You Always Wanted to Know About Jack Benny-But Were Afraid to Ask (NBC) (Special) March 10, 1971.

Star: Jack Benny. Announcer: Bill Baldwin.

A funny look at Jack Benny's past. Joining Jack are Lucille Ball, George Burns, Phil Harris, John Wayne, Bob Hope and Dionne Warwick. Briefly kibitzing is Dr. David Reuben, author of Everything You Always Wanted to Know About Sex. The show presents Benny's own view of his Hollywood career…it's the forties and Benny is filmdom's biggest star, giving advice to a chorus boy (Wayne) and trying to seduce a star-struck Goldwyn Girl (Ball). George Burns gives a more objective view of Jack's career. Phil tries to sing That's What I Like About the South with little or no help from Jack. Jack sings About a Quarter to Nine and picks up his violin for Mendelssohn's Concerto in E Minor. Dionne offers I Got Love and Who Gets the Guy? Written by Hal Goodman, Hilliard Marks, Bucky Searles and Hugh Wedlock Jr. Directed by Norman Abbott. Music arranged and conducted by Jack Elliott and Allyn Ferguson. Produced by Irving Fein and Norman Abbott.

Film Director: Tommy Farrell. Vaudeville Agent: Remo Pisani. Also: David Westberg.

V.I.P.-Schaukel (ZDF/Folge 37) September 12, 1971.

Host: Margaret Dunser.

Combination documentary-news-talk-family show from West Germany, with guests Myriam Bru, Beatrice Buchholz, Christopher Buchholz, Horst Buchholz, David Cameron, Arlene Dahl, Rhonda Fleming, Glenn Ford, Louis Feraud, Jean Gabin, Zsa Zsa Gabor, Mary Hopkin, Hildegard Knef, Elsa Martinelli, David Niven, Prince Bernhard of the Netherlands, Prince Philip of Great Britain, Queen Elizabeth II of Great Britain, Eva Renzi, Carroll Richter, Gunter Sachs, Christian Gunnar Sachs, Mirja Sachs, Gertrude Schilling, Simone Signoret, John Wayne and Ilse Werner. Written by Margaret Dunser. Directed by Edgar Von Heeringen.

Songs: Mary: *Let My Name Be Sorrow*, Elsa: *Solarium Transatlantique*.

Note: This show's title translates to English as "V.I.P.-Swing".

The Glen Campbell Goodtime Hour (CBS) September 14, 1971.

Star: Glen Campbell. Regulars: Dom DeLuise, Eddie Mayehoff, R.G. Brown, Larry McNeeley, Jerry Reed. The Mike Curb Congregation. Announcer: Roger Carroll. The Marty Paich Orchestra.

Guests: John Wayne, comic-actor Tim Conway, rockers Three Dog Night. Glen sings *Close to You*; *Sooner or Later*; *Tenderly*; *Take Me Home, Country Roads* and *He Ain't Heavy, He's My Brother*. Glen and the Duke parody their **True Grit** roles. Tim makes a comic visit to Tap Dancers Anonymous. Wayne displays memorabilia of his long career. A sketch, *Sergeant Swell*, is a stop-motion spoof of old-time westerns. Carol Burnett makes a cameo appearance. Written by Bob Arnott, John Bradford, Rich Eustis, John Hartford, Ray Jessel, Coslough Johnson, Sandy Krinski, Marty Leshner, Steve Martin, Al Rogers, Frank Shaw and Cecil Tuck. Directed by Jack Shea.

Additional Songs: Three Dog Night: *Joy to the World*; *Just an Old-Fashioned Love Song*, Children's Chorus: *Sing*.

The Glen Campbell Goodtime Hour (CBS) October 5, 1971.

Star: Glen Campbell. Regulars: Dom DeLuise, Eddie Mayehoff, R.G. Brown, Jerry Reed, Larry McNeeley, John Hartford. The Mike Curb Congregation. Announcer: Roger Carroll. The Marty Paich Orchestra.

A salute to fifty years of movie-making includes the 50th Annual *Photoplay* Magazine Awards. Glen and Shirley Jones do a medley of Oscar-winning songs. Dom spoofs famous screen lovers. Award winners scheduled to appear include **Love Story** author Erich Segal; Jack Benny and Debbie Reynolds, winners for their charitable endeavors; and David Cassidy and Susan Dey (most popular new stars) of TV's **The Partridge Family**. Also seen are Bing Crosby, Phyllis Diller, Bob Hope, John Marley, Maureen O'Hara, Danny Thomas, John Wayne, Flip Wilson, Jane Wyman and Robert Young. Written by Rich Eustis, John Hartford, Steve Martin and Cecil Tuck.

Rowan & Martin's Laugh-In (NBC) November 1, 1971.

Hosts: Dan Rowan & Dick Martin. Regulars: Ruth Buzzi, Larry Hovis, Alan Sues, Ann Elder, Lisa Farringer, Lily Tomlin, Johnny Brown, Dennis Allen, Barbara Sharma, Richard Dawson, Moosie Drier. Announcer: Gary Owens. The Ian Bernard Orchestra.

A reunion of ex-regulars celebrates the series' 100th show. Guest John Wayne recites poetry ala visiting ex-regular Henry Gibson. Arte Johnson does his Dirty Old Man and the German Soldier. Teresa Graves joins Tiny Tim's harem. Also on hand are *sock-it-to-me* girl Judy Carne and Jo-Anne Worley as a virus. Written by Paul W. Keyes, Marc London, David Panich, Jim Mulligan, Gene Farmer, John Rappaport, Stephen Spears, Don Reo, Allan Katz, Rowby Greeber [Goren], Gene Perret, Bill Richmond and Jack Wohl. Directed by Mark Warren.

The Bob Hope Show (NBC) (Special) November 7, 1971.

Star: Bob Hope. Les Brown and his Band of Renown.

Guests: Jack Benny, Debbie Reynolds, John Wayne, The Osmond Brothers. In a western spoof of TV's **All in the Family**, Wayne is a bigoted sheriff whose meathead son (Bob) falls for an Indian princess. *Carnal College* is a movie take-off about an irresistible college senior (Jack), an innocent freshman (Bob) and a girl who can't say no (Debbie). Directed by Dick McDonough.

Songs: Bob, Osmonds: *I Want a Girl*, Debbie: *I Want to Be Happy*; *Forget Your Troubles*, Osmonds: *Down by the Lazy River*, Donny Osmond: *Hey, Girl*. Also: JoAnna Cameron, Allison McKay.

The American West of John Ford (CBS) (Special) December 5, 1971.

Clips from John Ford's westerns are the gems in this tribute to the veteran director. Ford has won six Oscars; ironically, none of them for westerns. However, his mastery of the genre and affection for legends of the west shine through his scenes ranging from the chase in **Stagecoach** (1939) to the showdown in **The Man Who Shot Liberty Valance** (1962). One of the most famous legends is the gunfight at the O.K. Corral. A clip from *My Darling Clementine* (1946) shows Ford's reenactment of the shoot-out based on an account given to him by Wyatt Earp. Henry Fonda, James Stewart and John Wayne swap anecdotes with Ford and narrate the films (many of which they appeared in). Ford also shoots a scene with them in Monument Valley. Other clips are from ***Three Bad Men*** (1926), ***Fort Apache*** (1948), ***She Wore a Yellow Ribbon*** (1949), ***Rio Grande*** (1950), ***The Searchers*** (1956) and ***Cheyenne Autumn*** (1964). Ford also sings *The Whiffenpoof Song*. Written for television by Dennis H. Vowell, from a format by Daniel Sargent Ford. Directed by Dennis Sanders. Music by Jack Marshall. Produced by Bob Banner, Daniel Sargent Ford, Tom Egan and Britt Lomond. Also appearing are Andy Devine, Olive Carey, Jeffrey Hunter, John Qualen, Mickey Simpson and Chuck Hayward.

The Tonight Show Starring Johnny Carson (NBC) January 14, 1972.

Star: Johnny Carson. Announcer: Ed McMahon. The Doc Severinsen Orchestra.

Guests: comedienne Totie Fields; singer Johnnie Ray; actor-director Mark Rydell; movie cowboy John Wayne.

Rowan & Martin's Laugh-In (NBC) January 31, 1972.

Hosts: Dan Rowan & Dick Martin. Regulars: Ruth Buzzi, Alan Sues, Lily Tomlin, Dennis Allen, Johnny Brown, Barbara Sharma, Larry Hovis, Moosie Drier, Richard Dawson, Ann Elder, Lisa Farringer. Announcer: Gary Owens. The Ian Bernard Orchestra.

Guests: Jack Carter, Chad Everett, Paul Lynde, Mona Tera, John Wayne. Wayne recites more poems and goes through the wall. In a sketch, Chad plays a doctor who is fooling around with his nurse (Barbara). Jack is in a solid, high-powered spot as a used-car salesman. The *Mod World* takes a look at the world of economics. Written by Paul W. Keyes, Marc London, David Panich, Jim Mulligan, Gene Farmer, John Rappaport, Stephen Spears, Don Reo, Allan Katz, Rowby Greeber [Goren], Gene Perret, Bill Richmond and Jack Wohl. Directed by Mark Warren.

The Lee Philip Show (WBBM-Chicago, Illinois, Channel 2) February 12, 1972.

Host: Lee Philip.

Lee interviews actor John Wayne.

Rowan & Martin's Laugh-In (NBC) March 13, 1972.

Hosts: Dan Rowan & Dick Martin. Regulars: Ruth Buzzi, Alan Sues, Lily Tomlin, Dennis Allen, Johnny Brown, Barbara Sharma, Richard Dawson, Ann Elder, Lisa Farringer, Larry Hovis. Announcer: Gary Owens.

Guests: JoAnn Pflug, Steve Allen, Carol Channing, Gene Hackman, Charles Nelson Reilly, Terry-Thomas, John Wayne. Pflug is seen in a running bit where she takes a bath and is seemingly interrupted by the whole world. As for Wayne's appearance, the Big Duke recites pretty poetry. Written by Paul W. Keyes, Marc London, David Panich, Jim Mulligan, Gene Farmer, John Rappaport, Stephen Spears, Don Reo, Allan Katz, Rowby Greeber [Goren], Gene Perret, Bill Richmond and Jack Wohl.

Harry Jackson: A Man and His Art (Syndicated) (Special) April 30, 1972.

Narrated by John Wayne.

Documentary about American artist Harry Andrew Jackson, who worked in the abstract, expressionist, realist and American Western styles. Jackson's friend, Wayne, was the subject of Jackson's 1969 sculpture *The Marshal*.

The David Frost Show (Syndicated) June 5, 1972.

Host: David Frost.

David interviews John Wayne.

The Tonight Show Starring Johnny Carson (NBC) June 7, 1972.

Star: Johnny Carson. Announcer: Ed McMahon. The Doc Severinsen Orchestra.

Johnny presents the *Photoplay* magazine Gold Medal Awards. Guest John Wayne is one of the winners. Other guests include singer-actress Ann-Margret; actress-singer-dancer Sandy Duncan; actors Gary Grimes and Christopher Mitchum; Harvey Korman of TV's ***The Carol Burnett Show***; and Al Traina. Written by Nick Arnold, Hank Bradford, Michael Barrie, Bob Howard, Ted Lang, Jim Mulholland and Mickey Rose.

Zenith Presents: A Salute to Television's 25th Anniversary (ABC) (Special) September 10, 1972.

Announcer: Dick Tufeld. The Zenith Singers and Dancers.

Film clips from more than 400 shows (from the conquests of **Boston Blackie** to the antics of Sonny & Cher) are culled for this tribute, which also features elaborate production numbers and a host of celebrities scheduled to accept awards for their roles in television's success story: Judith Anderson, James Arness, Lucille Ball, Milton Berle, Sid Caesar, Perry Como, Dave Garroway, Lorne Greene, Bob Hope, George C. Scott, Rod Serling, Dinah Shore, The Smothers Brothers, Ed Sullivan, John Wayne, Robert Young and Efrem Zimbalist Jr. The cast of TV's ***Your Hit Parade*** (Gisele MacKenzie, Snooky Lanson, Russell Arms, Eileen Wilson) sings a '50s medley of *Shrimp Boats*; *Shanghai*; *Love Is Sweeping the Country*; *Doggie in the Window* and *This Old House*. Written by John Bradford, Lennie Weinrib and Bob Wells. Directed by Marty Pasetta. Produced by Bob Finkel, Duane Bogie and Marty Pasetta.

Additional Songs: Jimmy Durante: *September Song*, Florence Henderson: *How Sweet It Is*, George Chakiris: *They Went Thataway*.

Also: Maria Cole, Dewey Murrow, Harry Reasoner, Edward M. Davis.

Rowan & Martin's Laugh-In (NBC) September 11, 1972.

Hosts: Dan Rowan & Dick Martin. Regulars: Ruth Buzzi, Lily Tomlin, Dennis Allen, Richard Dawson, Brian Bressler, Patti Deutsch, Sarah

Kennedy, Jud Strunk, Willie Tyler, Donna Jean Young, Lisa Farringer, Moosie Drier, Tod Bass. Announcer: Gary Owens. The Ian Bernard Orchestra.

First show of the season. Guest John Wayne camps it up as a flop-eared bunny and parodies his movie roles. A salute to the summer of '72. Edith Ann (Lily) has stories of going to school. Ruth as Shakuntala the Klutz taking a dancing lesson. Lily with a new character, the Ghetto Mother. Cameos by Isaac Hayes, Jill St. John, Martin Milner, Kent McCord. Written by Paul W. Keyes, Marc London, David Panich, Jim Mulligan, Gene Farmer, John Rappaport, Stephen Spears, Don Reo, Allan Katz, Rowby Greeber [Goren], Bill Richmond, Bob DeVinney, Bob Howard and Jack Douglas. Directed by Bill Foster. Also: Army Archerd, Meredith Bernhart, Mike Caldwell, Kyra Carlton, Rosie Cox Gitlin, Joy Ribeiro, Frank Welker, Janice Whitby, Adele Yoshioka.

The Wayne Train (All Networks) (Commercial) 1973.

A TV trailer promoting John Wayne's film **The Train Robbers**.

The Merv Griffin Show (Syndicated) (WNEW-TV, channel 5, New York City) February, 1973.

Host: Merv Griffin.

John Wayne is interviewed. He reveals his favorite starring role and sings *The Shadow of Your Smile"* with Merv. Other topics include Wayne's *Singing Sandy* role in B westerns, his admiration of Marlon Brando, his love for Harry Carey Sr., his close relationship with his own father, the popularity of the western and his own philosophy of life on and off the screen.

Rowan & Martin's Laugh-In (NBC) February 12, 1973.

Hosts: Dan Rowan & Dick Martin. Regulars: Ruth Buzzi, Lily Tomlin, Dennis Allen, Richard Dawson, Patti Deutsch, Jud Strunk, Donna Jean Young, Lisa Farringer, Tod Bass, Brian Bressler, Moosie Drier, Sarah

Kennedy, Willie Tyler. Announcer: Gary Owens. The Ian Bernard Orchestra.

A Sherlock Holmes spoof with cameo guest Ernest Borgnine as Watson opposite Dennis' Holmes. Other cameos are made by John Wayne, Don Rickles, Arthur Godfrey and Slappy White. The *Cocktail Party* takes off in a simulated 747. Dick sells maps to movie stars' homes in a satirical salute to California. *Robot Theater* features Ruth and Dennis. Written by Paul W. Keyes, David Panich, Marc London, Jim Mulligan, Gene Farmer, John Rappaport, Stephen Spears, Don Reo, Allan Katz, Rowby Goren, Bill Richmond, Bob Howard, Bob DeVinney and Jack Douglas. Directed by Bill Foster.

Merv Griffin's St. Patrick's Day Special (Syndicated) March, 1973.

Talk show host Griffin spotlights the Irish holiday with guests including John Wayne.

The Tonight Show Starring Johnny Carson (NBC) March 22, 1973.

Star: Johnny Carson. Announcer: Ed McMahon. The Doc Severinsen Orchestra.

Guests: John Wayne; James Franciscus of TV's **Waterworld**; actors Charles Grodin and Danny Thomas; pop singer-actress Jaye P. Morgan; vocalist-actor John O'Banion; and magician the Amazing [James] Randi. Written by Hank Bradford, Bob Howard, Ted Lang, Tom Moore, Jim Mulholland and Mickey Rose.

Cavalcade of Champions (NBC) (Special) March 27, 1973.

Host: Bob Hope.

A sports award show honoring outstanding professional and amateur athletes. Presenters Sammy Davis Jr., Barbara Eden, Mitzi Gaynor, Darren McGavin, Dinah Shore, Fred MacMurray, Danny Thomas and John Wayne introduce the winners, selected by sports fans from across the country. Also: film clips of the nominees in action. Included: Dick Allen, Johnny Bench and Steve Carlton (baseball); Kareem Abdul-Jabbar, Wilt Chamberlain and Jerry West (basketball); Larry Brown, Franco Harris and Earl Morrall (football); Jack Nicklaus, Gary Player and Lee Trevino (golf); and in other categories, Muhammad Ali, Bobby Orr, Mark Spitz, Chris Evert and Billie Jean King.

The American Film Institute Salute to John Ford (CBS) (Special) April 2, 1973.

Host: Danny Kaye. The Nelson Riddle Orchestra.

A tribute to director John Ford, veteran of a fifty-six-year movie career. Highlights include clips from Ford's famous films and words of tribute from Charlton Heston, Jack Lemmon, Maureen O'Hara, Gregory Peck, Frank Sinatra, James Stewart, John Wayne, Charles Bronson, Yul Brynner, Clint Eastwood, Henry Fonda, Cary Grant, Bob Hope, Grace Kelly, Lee Marvin, Roddy McDowall, President Richard M. Nixon, Rosalind Russell, Steven Spielberg, George Stevens Jr., Leslie Uggams, Robert Wagner and Richard Widmark. In the audience: Peter Bogdanovich, Frederick Brisson, Gary Collins, Dani Crayne, Richard Crenna, Robert Evans, Chad Everett, Felicia Farr, Sylvia Fine, Linda Harrison, Rock Hudson, Burl Ives, Maggie Johnson, Jennifer Jones, Mary Jones, Henry Kissinger, Jeanne Martin, Frank McCarthy, Mary Ann Mobley, Ryan O'Neal, Tatum O'Neal, Veronique Peck, Donna Reed, Nelson Rockefeller, Eileen Schauler, Norton Simon, Jules C. Stein, Rod Taylor, Forrest Tucker, Liv Ullmann, Jack L. Warner, Stuart Whitman, Billy Dee Williams, Jonathan Winters, Natalie Wood, William Wyler, Richard D. Zanuck, Fred Astaire, Jack Benny, Walter Cronkite, Kirk Douglas, Irene Dune, Zsa Zsa Gabor, Jill Ireland, Kate Jackson, David Janssen, Fred MacMurray, Robert Mitchum, Patricia Neal, Pat Nixon, Nancy Reagan, Ronald Reagan, Cybill Shepherd.

RCA's Opening Night (NBC) (Special) September 13, 1973.

Hosts: Dan Rowan & Dick Martin. Announcer: Vin Scully. The Ian Bernard Orchestra.

A vaudeville-style hour down memory lane…Ruby Keeler tap dances in sync with a clip from *42nd Street*; Bob Newhart does his sixties' monologue about a friend's obnoxious dog; and Harry Belafonte sings "Jamaica Farewell". The big comic moment is the "Hollywood Boys Glee Club" singing "Row, Row, Row Your Boat"-Edward Asner, Ernest Borgnine, Jack Carter, Howard Cosell, Glenn Ford, Redd Foxx, Kent McCord, Martin Milner, Charles Nelson Reilly and John Wayne. Comedian Jimmie Walker joins Olympian Cathy Rigby on the balance beam and uneven parallel bars. Written by Allan Katz, Paul Keyes, Marc London, David Panich and Don Reo. Directed by Bill Foster.

Additional Songs: Tony Orlando & Dawn: *Sweet Gypsy Rose*, Porter Wagoner and Dolly Parton: *If Tear Drops Were Pennies*.

Parkinson (BBC) February 1, 1974.

Host: Michael Parkinson. The Harry Stoneham Five.

British talk show with guest John Wayne.

Note: The acronym BBC stands for British Broadcasting Corporation.

John Wayne and Glen Campbell and the Musical West (NBC) (Special) March 8, 1974.

With Wayne as his special guide, Glen and his guests-Burl Ives and Michele Lee-explore the history and folklore of the American West in song and story. Glen sings such tunes as *This Land Is Your Land* and joins Burl and Michele for ***Wagon Wheels***". Wayne talks about legendary figures. A folklore medley on Billy the Kid and Jesse James is sung by Glen and Burl. Written by Marty Farrell. Directed by Dwight Hemion. Music by Dennis McCarthy and conducted by the Jack Parnell Orchestra. Produced by Nick Sevano, Dwight Hemion and Gary Smith.

The American Film Institute Salute to James Cagney (CBS) (Special) March 18, 1974.

Host: Frank Sinatra.

A testimonial dinner in honor of James Cagney, recipient of the AFI Life Achievement Award. Tributes come from Doris Day, Jack Lemmon, Bob Hope and Ronald Reagan. Clips from Cagney's movies are shown as some of his co-stars take bows from the audience: Joan Blondell, Mae Clarke, Allen Jenkins and Frank McHugh. Charlton Heston, Cicely Tyson and George Stevens Jr. speak on behalf of the American Film Institute. Reagan announces that the AFI archive has preserved copies of every Cagney film. Frank Gorshin, Kirk Douglas and George Segal sing *Give My Regards to Broadway* and Sinatra offers *My Way*. Directed by Bill Foster. Produced by George Stevens Jr., Rita Burton and Paul Keyes.

Also: Shirley MacLaine, George C. Scott, John Wayne, Ralph Bellamy, Tom Bradley, Frances Cagney, Clint Eastwood, Mick Jagger, Danny Kaye, Gene Kelly, John Lennon, A.C. Lyles, Ali MacGraw, Steve McQueen, Paul Newman, Carroll O'Connor, George Raft, Nancy Reagan, Joanne Woodward.

Maude (CBS) *Maude Meets the Duke* September 9, 1974.

Stars: Beatrice Arthur, Bill Macy, Adrienne Barbeau, Conrad Bain, Rue McClanahan.

John Wayne visits his loyal fan Arthur (Bain) while he is in town filming a movie, unaware that the indomitably liberal Maude waits in ambush for the conservative Duke. Written by Robert Hilliard, Bob Schiller and Bob Weiskopf. Directed by Hal Cooper. Philip Traynor: Brian Morrison. Liz: Elisabeth Fraser. Child Fan: Robert Cokjlat.

The Dean Martin Celebrity Roast: Bob Hope (NBC) (Special) October 31, 1974.

Dean turns Bob over the comedy flames. Guests include Flip Wilson, James Stewart, Howard Cosell, Jack Benny, General Omar Bradley, Phyllis Diller, Milton Berle, Neil Armstrong, Rich Little, Ginger Rogers,

Reverend Billy Graham, Johnny Bench, Foster Brooks, Ronald Reagan, Nipsey Russell, Don Rickles, Sugar Ray Robinson, Mark Spitz, Zsa Zsa Gabor, Henry Kissinger, Dolores Hope, John Wayne (whose jokes come in a pre-recorded message). Written by George [Arthur] Bloom, Stan Burns, Harry Crane, Peter Gallay, Don Hinkley, Mike Marmer, Milt Rosen and Tom Tenowich. Produced and directed by Greg Garrison.

The Don Rickles Show-Mr. Warmth (CBS) (Special) January 19, 1975.

Comedy special with the insult master hosting guests Jack Klugman, Dean Martin, Jaye P. Morgan, Bob Newhart, Helen Reddy, Frank Sinatra, Loretta Swit, John Wayne, and appearances by Charlie Callas, Rip Taylor and Steve Landesburg. Written by Paul W. Keyes, Marc London, Bob Howard, Bob O'Brien and Terry Hart. Directed by Bill Foster. Music by Nelson Riddle. Produced by Joseph Scandore and Herbert F. Solow.

The 17th Annual TV Week Logie Awards (Nine Network) (Special) March 7, 1975.

Host: Bert Newton.

Australian television awards show broadcast from Melbourne. American actors William Conrad, Farrah Fawcett, Lee Majors and John Wayne are guest presenters. Wayne presents Gold Logie Awards to Ernie Sigley (Most Popular Male Personality on Australian Television, ***The Ernie Sigley Show***) and to Denise Drysdale (Most Popular Female Personality on Australian Television, ***The Ernie Sigley Show***).

Bunny Brooke, Debra Byrne, Richard Carleton, Diane Cilento, Cul Cullen, Michele Dotrice, Ted Dunn, Pat Evison, Margaret Anne Ford, Bob Francis, Paul Hogan, George Mallaby, Rosemary Margan, John Meillon, Keith Michell, Jeff Newman, Sandy Palmer, Tom Payne, Bill Peach, Barbara [Barbie] Rogers, Paul Sharrat, Rhonda Sharrat, Mike Walsh, John Waters, Anne Wills, Edward Woodward.

The 47th Annual Academy Awards (NBC) (Special) April 8, 1975.

Hosts: Sammy Davis Jr., Bob Hope, Shirley MacLaine, Frank Sinatra. Announcer: Hank Sims.

Broadcast live from the Dorothy Chandler Pavilion in Los Angeles, California. Highlights include special tributes and awards to director Jean Renoir, director Howard Hawks (presented by John Wayne) and the Jean Hersholt Humanitarian Award to Arthur B. Krim. Sammy gives a musical salute to Fred Astaire. Winners in major categories: Francis Ford Coppola (Picture, Director and Writing-Screenplay Adapted from Another Medium, *The Godfather Part II*, Picture Award presented by Warren Beatty, Director Award presented by Goldie Hawn and Robert Wise, Writing Award presented by James Michener); Art Carney (Actor, *Harry and Tonto*, presented by Glenda Jackson); Ellen Burstyn (Actress, *Alice Doesn't Live Here Anymore*, presented by Jack Lemmon, accepted by Martin Scorsese for an absent Burstyn); Robert De Niro (Supporting Actor, *The Godfather Part II*, presented by Ryan and Tatum O'Neal, accepted by Francis Ford Coppola for an absent De Niro); Ingrid Bergman (Supporting Actress, *Murder on the Orient Express*, presented by Peter Falk and Katharine Ross). Other winners: Robert Towne (Writing-Original Screenplay, *Chinatown*, presented by James Michener); Mario Puzo (Writing-Screenplay Adapted from Another Medium, *The Godfather Part II*, presented by James Michener); Fred Koenekamp and Joseph Biroc (Cinematography, *The Towering Inferno*, presented by Jon Voight and Raquel Welch); Dean Tavoularis and Angelo Graham (Art Direction, *The Godfather Part II*, presented by Susan Blakely); George R. Nelson (Set Decoration, *The Godfather Part II*, presented by Susan Blakely); Theoni V. Aldredge (Costume Design, *The Great Gatsby*, presented by Lauren Bacall); Ronald Piece and Melvin Metcalfe Sr. (Sound, *Earthquake*, presented by Joseph Bottoms and Deborah Raffin); Harold F. Kress and Carl Kress (Film Editing, *The Towering Inferno*, presented by Macdonald Carey and Jennifer O'Neill); Nino Rota and Carmine Coppola (Music-Original Dramatic Score, *The Godfather Part II*, presented by Diahann Carroll and John Green); Nelson Riddle (Music-Scoring: Original Song Score and/or Adaptation, *The Great Gatsby*, presented by Gene Kelly); Will Vinton and Bob Gardiner (Short Film-Animated, *Closed Mondays*, presented by Roddy McDowall and Brenda Vaccaro);

Paul Claudon and Edmond Sechan (Short Film-Live Action, *One-Eyed Men Are Kings*, presented by Roddy McDowall and Brenda Vaccaro); Robin Lehman (Documentary-Short Subject, *Don't*, presented by Lauren Hutton and Danny Thomas); Peter Davis and Bert Schneider (Documentary-Feature, *Hearts and Minds*, presented by Lauren Hutton and Danny Thomas); Frank Brendel, Glen Robinson and Albert Whitlock (Special Achievement Award-Visual Effects, *Earthquake*, presented by Bob Hope). Directed by Marty Pasetta. Produced by Howard W. Koch.

Nominated Songs: Aretha Franklin, Jack Jones and Frankie Laine perform *Benji's Theme* (*I Feel Love*), Aretha, Jack, Frankie: *We May Never Love Like This Again* (composed by Al Kasha and Joel Hirschhorn) (Award Winner from *The Towering Inferno*, presented by Gene Kelly), Frankie: *Blazing Saddles*, Jack: *Little Prince*, Aretha: *Wherever Love Takes Me*.

Also: Irwin Allen, Fred Astaire, Jeff Bridges, Lloyd Bridges, John Cassavetes, Joan Collins, Valentina Cortese, Laura Dern, Michael Douglas, Faye Dunaway, Robert Evans, Felicia Farr, Michael V. Gazzo, Ronald S.Kass, Diane Ladd, Walter Mirisch, Ricardo Montalban, Jack Nicholson, Valerie Perrine, Helen Reddy, Gena Rowlands, Talia Shire, Lee Strasberg, Jeff Wald, Paul Williams, Anjelica Huston. Peter Ustinov for Gallo Wines.

Bob Hope on Campus (NBC) (Special) April 17, 1975.

Star: Bob Hope. Les Brown and His Band of Renown.

John Wayne, Flip Wilson, Aretha Franklin and rock group America guest star with Bob, who visits UCLA, Columbia University, Vassar, Florida Southern College and Howard Payne University. Bob interviews students and presents comedy sketches: Wayne portrays basketball coach John Wooden, with Bob as his successor; Hope plays a prissy zoology major with a swinging roommate (Flip), whose lifestyle prompts Bob to appeal to the dean (Wayne) for a change. Flip also does a routine as the Reverend Leroy of the Church of What's Happening Now. Produced by Elliott Kozak. Sponsored by Sears, Roebuck and Company.

Backstage in Hollywood (CBS) July 24, 1975.

Host: David Sheeman.

Talk show with guests John Wayne, Kirk Douglas, Clint Eastwood, Charles Bronson.

Saturday Night Live with Howard Cosell (ABC) September 27, 1975.

Host: Howard Cosell. The Elliott Lawrence Orchestra.

Howard takes viewers around the world for the latest and best in entertainment, sports and news. America's number one rock group, The Eagles, and singer Linda Ronstadt appear in a special remote from San Diego, California. Muhammad Ali and Joe Frazier are seen via satellite from Manila, the Philippines, on the eve of their forthcoming World Heavyweight Championship fight; Howard talks with Ali and Frazier about their strategies, conditioning and fight predictions. Redd Foxx of TV's Sanford and Son performs one of his stand-up routines. Barbara Walters offers her candid impressions of the many celebrities she has interviewed. Wayne talks with Howard about his life, career, his present health and his plans-both cinematic and otherwise-for the future. Harry Blackstone Jr. demonstrates his outstanding magic skills. John Byner is also on hand with some of his celebrity impressions.

Songs: Linda: *Heat Wave*, Eagles: *Best of My Love*; *Already Gone*.

The Tonight Show Starring Johnny Carson (NBC) October 15, 1975.

Host: Don Rickles (subbing for an absent Johnny Carson). Announcer: Ed McMahon. The Doc Severinsen Orchestra.

Guests: comedian Bob Hope; singer-actor Bing Crosby; actor John Wayne; Adrienne Barbeau of TV's Maude; and singer Pat Boone.

Texaco Presents: A Quarter Century of Bob Hope on Television (NBC) (Special) October 24, 1975.

On Easter Sunday, 1950, a famous star of motion pictures and radio made his television debut. Tonight, that same star shares his treasury of television memories with the nation's viewers. Highlights of Bob's twenty-five years on the small screen are featured on the show. On hand to talk with Bob about their own segments from shows of the past are guests Frank Sinatra, Bing Crosby and John Wayne. In all, eighty-eight celebrities are seen in kinescopes and clips from the comedian's past programs. Bob gets things rolling with a new monologue, and he shows excerpts from monologues about Presidents of the US, from Harry S Truman (who was in office when Hope's first show aired on April 9, 1950) to Gerald Ford. Clips include a 1956 sketch with Lucille Ball, Desi Arnaz, William Frawley and Vivian Vance from TV's *I Love Lucy* in which Hope imagines he is married to Lucy. In a scene from Bob's first show, he and Dinah Shore sing *Baby, It's Cold Outside*. Other musical performers include John Denver, Olivia Newton-John, The Carpenters, Maurice Chevalier, Diana Ross, Ray Charles, Aretha Franklin and Barbra Streisand. Other seen are Jack Benny, Ingrid Bergman, Carol Burnett, James Cagney, Glen Campbell, Eddie Cantor, Johnny Carson, Perry Como, Sammy Davis Jr., Angie Dickinson, Jimmy Durante, Redd Foxx, Jackie Gleason, Shirley MacLaine, Ann-Margret, Steve McQueen, Dean Martin, David Niven, Burt Reynolds, Ed Sullivan, Danny Thomas, Raquel Welch, Flip Wilson and Ed Wynn. Written by Gig Henry, Paul W. Keyes and Charles Lee. Produced by Bob Hope and Paul W. Keyes.

The Tonight Show Starring Johnny Carson (NBC) January 8, 1976.

Host: Johnny Carson. Announcer/Regular: Ed McMahon. The Doc Severinsen Orchestra.

Guests: John Wayne; actor James Hampton; actor-writer-comedian Buck Henry; and actress-singer Phyllis Newman.

The People's Choice Awards (CBS) (Special) February 19, 1976.

Hosts: Jack Albertson, Army Archerd.

The most popular entertainers in America receive awards as determined by the results of a scientific survey of the public. Guest presenters include Robert Blake, Carol Burnett, Kirk Douglas, Henry Fonda, Bob Hope, Mary Tyler Moore, Valerie Perrine, Telly Savalas, Roy Scheider and John Wayne.

The Dean Martin Celebrity Roast: Dean Martin (NBC) (Special) February 27, 1976.

Host: Don Rickles.

Singer-actor Dean is the recipient of zingers from dais guests Orson Welles, Bob Hope, John Wayne, Muhammad Ali, Rich Little and Angie Dickinson.

Dick Cavett's Backlot U.S.A. (CBS) (Special) April 5, 1976.

A sentimental journey down Hollywood's memory lane. Touring Paramount Studios, Dick Cavett is the guide, as musical numbers and conversations with stars recall the old days of movie-making. After a brief *interview* segment with dog star Won Ton Ton, Dick meets Mickey Rooney on a city street lot, where Mickey and a children's chorus sing and dance to *We Got Us*. Dick visits with some movie extras. On a buckboard traveling through an old west set, John Wayne recalls his career. Dick has a walking interview with Gene Kelly, who gets rained on while *Singin' in the Rain* softly plays in the background. The highlight of the show is a closing segment with Mae West. Costumed as Diamond Lil, one of her '30s roles, the 82-year-old Miss West regales Dick with some double-entendres and sings sultry versions of *Frankie and Johnny* and *After You've Gone*. She also talks about discovering Cary Grant and working with W.C. Fields.

Kup's Show (PBS) 1976.

Host: Irv Kupcinet.

Irv promotes the *lively art of conversation* with guest John Wayne.

The Great American Picture Star: John Wayne (BBC) (Special) July 8, 1976.

This British television special shows how Americans feel about John Wayne and how he feels about them. Wayne takes a ride on his converted minesweeper *The Wild Goose*. Produced by Janet Hoenig and Jain Johnstone.

Donahue (Syndicated) 1976.

Host: Phil Donahue.

Talk and interview session with guest John Wayne.

The Mike Douglas Show (Syndicated) August 13, 1976.

Host: Mike Douglas. Guest Co-Host: Danny Thomas.

Mike has a cowboy theme with rodeo champ Larry Mahan, stunt rider J.W. Stoker and film actor John Wayne. Other guests are actress Marge Redmond, vocalist Diana Trask and actor Jack Weston.

The Mike Douglas Show (Syndicated) September 20, 1976.

Host: Mike Douglas. Guest Co-Host: Wayne Rogers.

Guests: John Wayne, Adrienne Barbeau of TV's Maude; musical group LaBelle and vocalist Peter Lemongello.

The Mike Douglas Show (Syndicated) September 21, 1976.

Host: Mike Douglas. Guest Co-Host: Wayne Rogers.

Guests: John Wayne; comedienne Julie McWhirter; missionary nun Mother Teresa and vocalist Maxine Nightingale.

The Mike Douglas Show (Syndicated) September 22, 1976.

Host: Mike Douglas. Guest Co-Host: Wayne Rogers.

Mike receives another visit from John Wayne. Other guests: restauranter Rocky Aoki; golfer Lonnie Koch; musicians the Preservation Hall Jazz Band; ballet dancer Dennis Wayne and actress Joanne Woodward.

The Merv Griffin Show (Syndicated) 1976.

Host: Merv Griffin.

Talk program with guest John Wayne.

Bob Hope's World of Comedy (NBC) (Special) October 29, 1976.

Star: Bob Hope.

A fascinating and funny look back at Bob's career through segments covering slapstick, vaudeville, foreign stars, animal skits and so on. Guest appearances are made by Lucille Ball, Big Bird of TV's Sesame Street, Norman Lear, Don Rickles, Neil Simon and John Wayne.

An All-Star Tribute to John Wayne" (ABC) (Special) November 26, 1976.

Host: Frank Sinatra.

A roster of celebrity guests celebrates John Wayne's career in film. Testimonials come from Bob Hope, Charles Bronson, Angie Dickinson, Claire Trevor, James Stewart, Lee Marvin, Ron Howard, Henry Winkler, John Byner, Sammy Davis Jr., Monty Hall, Dan Rowan & Dick Martin. Highlights include a western spoof of Wayne's movies and film clips from **True Grit** and **The Quiet Man**. Songs are offered by Glen Campbell and Maureen O'Hara. Written by Paul W. Keyes and Marc London. Directed by Dick McDonough. Music by Nelson Riddle. Produced by Paul W. Keyes. Presented by Sears, Roebuck and Company.

CBS Salutes Lucy: The First 25 Years (CBS) (Special) November 28, 1976.

A two-hour retrospective of the first lady of American television comedy. Clips are shown of her three TV series (***I Love Lucy***, ***The Lucy Show***, and ***Here's Lucy***) and specials. Guests include Desi Arnaz Sr., Milton Berle, Carol Burnett, Richard Burton, Johnny Carson, Sammy Davis Jr., Gale Gordon, Bob Hope, Danny Kaye, Dean Martin, James Stewart and John Wayne.

Bob Hope's Comedy Christmas Special (NBC) (Special) December 13, 1976.

Star: Bob Hope.

John Wayne, Neil Sedaka, Dyan Cannon, Lola Falana and Kate Jackson celebrate Christmas with Bob; he also presents Miss America 1977 (Dorothy Benham), Miss Teenage America 1977 (Becky Reid) and Diane Ramaker-1977 Tournament of Roses Queen-and her court. Bob takes a meeting with the 1976 Associated Press All-America Football Team: Ricky Bell, Tony Dorsett, Tommy Kramer and Dennis Thurman. Neil sings some rock songs. Lola has some beat numbers. Bob chats with Wayne. Directed by Dick McDonough. Old Lady: Ted Zeigler.

Super Night at the Super Bowl (CBS) (Special) January 8, 1977.

Hosts: Andy Williams, Sammy Davis Jr., Elliott Gould.

Broadcast live from the Rose Bowl in Pasadena, California, where Super Bowl XI (Oakland Raiders versus Minnesota Vikings) will be played. Appearances by Jack Albertson, Johnny Bench, Natalie Cole, Angie Dickinson, Joe Frazier, Werner Herzel, Abbe Lane, Ken Norton, Charley Pride, Don Rickles, Chita Rivera, Sha-Na-Na, O.J. Simpson, The Sylvers, The Borden Twins, the USC Trojan Marching Band and John Wayne. Written by Gordon Doyle and Buz Kohan. Produced and directed by Marty Pasetta.

Jimmy Carter's Inaugural Gala (CBS) (Special) January 19, 1977.

Honoring President-elect Jimmy Carter and Vice President-elect Walter Mondale, from the John F. Kennedy Center for the Performing Arts in Washington DC. Chevy Chase presents a satire for the occasion. A Broadway cast renders songs from **Porgy and Bess**. Also, appearances by Hank Aaron, Donnie Ray Albert, Muhammad Ali, Lauren Bacall, Warren Beatty, Leonard Bernstein, Billy Carter, Jimmy Carter, Lillian Carter, Clamma Dale, Bette Davis, James Dickey, Redd Foxx, Aretha Franklin, John Lennon, Shirley MacLaine, Elaine May, Paul Newman, Mike Nichols, Jack Nicholson, Linda Ronstadt, Beverly Sills, Shirley Temple and John Wayne. Directed by Marty Pasetta. Produced by James Lipton.

Sinatra and Friends (ABC) (Special) April 21, 1977.

Star: Frank Sinatra.

Sinatra presents a mostly musical program with some *acquaintances*: John Denver, Loretta Lynn, Robert Merrill, Leslie Uggams, Tony Bennett, Natalie Cole, Dean Martin and John Wayne.

Johnny, Weil Du Geburtstag Hast (ZDF) (Special) June 7, 1977.

West German television presentation honoring John Wayne's 70th birthday (which was May 26, 1977).

Note: The English translation of this special's title is "Johnny, Because It's Your Birthday".

Oscar Presents the War Movies and John Wayne (ABC) (Special) November 27, 1977.

John Wayne is host and narrator of this portrait of wartime America as reflected in the movies made before, during and after World War II.

An All-Star Tribute to Elizabeth Taylor (CBS) (Special) December 1, 1977.

In a career that has included over fifty films, Taylor is recognized as one of the all-time leading ladies. Friends and fellow actors pay tribute to the two-time Academy Award winner in a cast party atmosphere. Guests include Robert Blake, Debbie Boone, Michael Caine, Henry Fonda, Frank Gorshin, Monty Hall, Bob Hope, Rock Hudson, Paul Newman, Peter Lawford, James Lydon, Roddy McDowall, Carroll O'Connor and John Wayne.

ABC's Silver Anniversary Celebration (ABC) (Special) February 5, 1978.

Host: Dick Clark.

Twenty-five years of the programs shown on the American Broadcasting Company are reviewed through live entertainment and clips from past shows. Barry Manilow sings *It's a Miracle*. John Wayne presents the category of westerns and shows how the genre has changed over the years. Hal Linden covers police series. Julie Andrews handles variety shows. Alan King brings up the subject of some of ABC's failures in TV programming. Robert Young and Vince Edwards do a reprise of various medical series. Marlo Thomas and Henry Winkler oversee the segment devoted to comedy series. Kate Jackson, Jaclyn Smith and Cheryl Ladd introduce a retrospective on adventure series. Howard Cosell remembers outstanding ABC sports events. Jim McKay touches on highlights of Olympics coverage. Keith Jackson has NCAA and NFL football as his territory. News coverage is reported on by Harry Reasoner and Barbara Walters. Hal Holbrook and Brenda Vaccaro look at historical dramas. Monty Hall hosts the contest programs segment. John Travolta and Billy Dee Williams unspool *Movies of the Week*. Edward Asner and Nick Nolte spotlight mini-series. Eight attractive ladies sing the theme to **Rocky**.

Also appearing: Edie Adams; Michael Ansara; John Astin; Pearl Bailey; Robert Blake; Ray Bolger; Ernest Borgnine; Tom Bosley; James Brown; Paul Burke; The Captain & Tennille; The Carpenters; David Carradine; Charo; Michael Cole; Tina Cole; Chuck Connors; Robert Conrad; Richard Crenna; Dennis Cross; Billy Crystal; John Denver; Howard Duff;

Patty Duke; Barbara Eden; Lola Falana; Norman Fell; Steve Forrest; John Forsythe; Jodie Foster; Redd Foxx; Annette Funicello; Frank Gifford; Lee Grant; David Hartman; David Hedison; Katherine Helmond; Ron Howard; David Janssen; Gabe Kaplan; Kaptain Kool and the Kongs; Jack Kelly; The King Cousins; Cissy King; Eartha Kitt; Bernie Kopell; The Lennon Sisters; Peggy Lipton; Paul Lynde; Dotty Mack; Gavin MacLeod; Fred MacMurray; Penny Marshall; Pamela Sue Martin; Ed McMahon; Kristy McNichol; Clayton Moore; Vic Morrow; Rick, David & Harriet Nelson; Hugh O'Brien; Donny & Marie Osmond; Patti Page; Vincent Price; Donna Reed; John Ritter; Cliff Robertson; Cesar Romero; David Soul; Robert Stack; Connie Stevens; Peter Strauss; Danny Thomas; Leslie Uggams; Karen Valentine; Rudy Vallee; Ben Vereen; Abe Vigoda; Clint Walker; Burt Ward; Lawrence Welk; Adam West; Anson Williams; Cindy Williams; Clarence Williams III; Efrem Zimbalist Jr.

Written by Robert Arthur, Stuart Bloomberg, Phil Hahn and Bill Lee. Directed by Perry Rosemond. Music by Lenny Stack. Produced by Dick Clark and Bill Lee.

John Wayne for Great Western Savings (ABC) 1978.

Wayne participates in this commercial for the Great Western Savings Company of California. Directed by Haskell Wexler.

The American Film Institute Salute to Henry Fonda (CBS) (Special) March 15, 1978.

Announcer: Hank Simms.

A black-tie testimonial dinner for the noted actor. Also seen is footage of Fonda's memorable films spanning a period of almost fifty years. Paying tribute are Jane Alexander, Lucille Ball, Richard Burton, Bette Davis, Kirk Douglas, Jane Fonda, Peter Fonda, James Garner, Lillian Gish, Charlton Heston, Ron Howard, Jack Lemmon, Fred MacMurray, Marsha Mason, Dorothy McGuire, Lloyd Nolan, Gregory Peck, Barbara Stanwyck, James Stewart, John Wayne, Richard Widmark and Billy Dee Williams. Written by Hal Kanter. Directed by Marty Pasetta. Produced by George Stevens Jr. and Eric Lieber.

Seen in the audience: Eddie Albert, Dana Andrews, Lucie Arnaz, Richard Benjamin, Marisa Berenson, Jacqueline Bisset, Robert F. Blumofe, Tom Bradley, Charles Bronson, Michael Caine, John Carradine, Stockard Channing, Richard Crenna, Angie Dickinson, Louise Fletcher, Bridget Fonda, Shirlee Fonda, Troy Garity, Lee Grant, Joel Grey, Mark Hamill, Henry Hathaway, Tom Hayden, Jill Ireland, Jack Klugman, Norman Lear, Mervyn LeRoy, Fiona Lewis, Jack Lord, Shirley MacLaine, Karl Malden, Walter Matthau, Guy McElwaine, Burgess Meredith, Gary Morton, Jack Nicholson, Nick Nolte, Merle Oberon, George Peppard, Paula Prentiss, Charles 'Buddy' Rogers, Kim Schmidt, Neil Simon, George Stevens Jr., Leigh Taylor-Young, John Travolta, Brenda Vaccaro, Vanessa Vadim, Raquel Welch, Billy Wilder, Henry Winkler, Robert Wise, Natalie Wood, Joanne Woodward, William Wyler, Jane Wyman and Gig Young.

Oscar's Best Actors (ABC) (Special) May 23, 1978.

Hosts: William Holden, Gene Kelly, Marsha Mason, John Wayne.

A salute to the fifty men who have won the Academy Award for Best Actor. Highlights include film clips of actors in their Oscar-winning roles; Oscar night acceptance speeches by winners, including those made by Wayne, Holden and recent winner Richard Dreyfuss. Also shown is a rarely-seen clip of James Stewart's touching tribute to the gravely ill Gary Cooper on the Academy Award show in 1961.

Happy Birthday, Bob (NBC) (Special) May 29, 1978.

Star: Bob Hope. Les Brown and His Band of Renown.

Hope is honored on his 75th birthday. Included are clips from his films, newsreel footage from his Christmas shows overseas and a tribute to Bob's friendship with Bing Crosby. Musical numbers feature Pearl Bailey, Lynn Anderson, Lucille Ball, Charo, Mac Davis, Sammy Davis Jr., K.C. and the Sunshine Band, Carol Lawrence, Tony Orlando, Donny & Marie Osmond and David Soul. Comedy is provided by the Muppets, Redd Foxx, Alan King, Charles Nelson Reilly, Don Rickles, Robert Shields &

Lorene Yarnell, Danny Thomas and Fred Travalena. Also making appearances are Christie Brinkley, George Burns, Johnny Carson, Jimmy Carter, Lynda Carter, Bert Convy, Howard Cosell, Kathryn Crosby, Michael S. Davison, Phyllis Diller, Elliott Gould, Dolores Hope, Julio Iglesias, Peter Isacksen, The Carl Jablonski Dancers, Peter Jay, Ann Jillian, Dorothy Lamour Loretta Lynn, Fred MacMurray, Barbara Mandrell, Dudley Moore, George C. Scott, Tom Selleck, Red Skelton, Elizabeth Taylor, Cheryl Tiegs, Tommy Tune, Twiggy, John Wayne and Flip Wilson. Written by Bob Arnott and James Lipton. Directed by Bob Wynn. Produced by James Lipton, Gerald Rafshoon and Bob Wynn.

The Road to Eltham (Thames Television) (Special) May 29, 1978.

British television movie featuring appearances by George Burns, Michael Caine, Joan Collins, Perry Como, Rhonda Fleming, Bob Hope, Dorothy Lamour, Fred MacMurray, Bob Monkhouse, Jane Russell, John Wayne, Raquel Welch and archive footage of Bing Crosby. Directed by Terence Dixon. Produced by Terence Dixon and Charles Thompson.

Donny and Marie (ABC) September 22, 1978.

Stars: Donny & Marie Osmond. Regulars: The Osmond Brothers, Johnny Dark, The Disco Dozen, Jim Connell, Larry Larsen.

First show of the season. Musical variety with guests Bob Hope, singer-actress Olivia Newton-John and K.C. & The Sunshine Band. Donny, Marie and the Band perform *Groove Line*, *Boogie Shoes* and *You're the One That I Want*. The comedy highlight is a sketch about King Tut. Cameo appearances are made by John Wayne, Robert Conrad, Betty White, Dick Van Patten and Lassie.

Additional Songs: Olivia: *Hopelessly Devoted to You*, K.C & The Band: *Do You Feel Alright?*

General Electric All-Star Anniversary (ABC) (Special) September 29, 1978.

John Wayne is host for this variety salute to America's past 100 years. Period stills and film clips lend a documentary flavor to the show, which skims history's highpoints-beginning with Thomas Alva Edison's development of the first commercially successful incandescent lamp in 1879. Suzanne Somers kicks up her heels to *Yankee Doodle Dandy*. Cheryl Ladd performs *Baby Face* in a Ziegfeld-style sequence. Lucille Ball appears as a flapper in a Roaring Twenties spot. Monologues are offered by Bob Hope and Jimmie Walker. James Whitmore gives an impersonation of Will Rogers. Albert Brooks holds open auditions to find a new national anthem. Dramatic vignettes include James Stewart as Mark Twain and Pat Hingle as Thomas Edison. Sha Na Na performs a 1950s song medley. Leslie Uggams offers a tribute to US cities. Henry Winkler does a recitation of John F. Kennedy's inaugural address. Alex Haley covers Martin Luther King's *I Have a Dream* speech. Red Skelton performs a mime sketch of an old man watching a parade. There are also appearances by Elizabeth Taylor, Henry Fonda, Michael Landon, Cindy Williams, Penny Marshall, John Ritter, Denise McKenna and Nelson Riddle. Written by Paul Keyes, Bob Howard, Monty Aidem and Jeffrey Barron. Directed by Dick McDonough. Produced by Paul W. Keyes.

Additional Songs: Charley Pride: *When I Stop Leaving*, Donny & Marie Osmond: *Certified Honey*.

All-Star Party for James Stewart (CBS) (Special) December 7, 1978.

Host: Monty Hall.

Taped at the Burbank Studios in California, Variety Clubs International offers this tribute to veteran actor Stewart by numerous friends and associates: General Omar Bradley, Carol Burnett, Johnny Carson, Angie Dickinson, Farrah Fawcett, Henry Fonda, Glenn Ford, Shirley Jones, Rich Little, Fred MacMurray, Ricardo Montalban, Elizabeth Taylor, John Wayne and Robin Williams. Seen in the audience: June Allyson, Frank Capra, John Carradine, Ellen Corby, William Demarest, Joanne Dru, Kathryn Grant, June Haver, Brian Keith, Strother Martin, Andrew V. McLaglen, Una Merkel and Robert Stack.

This Is Your Life (Thames Television) December 13, 1978.

Host: Eamonn Andrews.

In this British version of the American human-interest series, highlights of guest Patricia Neal's life are augmented with visits by family and friends: husband Roald Dahl; daughters Lucy, Ophelia and Tessa Dahl; son Theo Dahl; granddaughter Sophie Dahl (on film); mother Eula Neal; lifelong friend and fellow actress Helen Horton-she and Neal shared an apartment in New York City while looking for acting jobs in 1945. Builder Wally Saunders, who helped remodel Neal and husband Dahl's house in Great Missenden, Buckingham County, England; Joseph Cotten and his wife Patricia Medina; Elaine Stritch-who appeared several times in Roald Dahl's television series *Tales of the Unexpected*; actors Kenneth Haigh, Marius Goring, Richard Greene and Wendy Hiller. Kirk Douglas and John Wayne send their regards on film-both actors co-starred with Neal in the movie *In Harm's Way*.

Perry Como's Early American Christmas (ABC) (Special) December 13, 1978.

Star: Perry Como. The Ray Charles Singers.

Guests: John Wayne; violinist Eugene Fodor; Diana Canova of TV's *Soap*; Miss America Kylene Barker; The William and Mary Choir. Perry hosts a Christmas show filmed at Colonial Williamsport, Virginia. A look at 18th Century American and English Yuletide traditions. Perry sings *Ave Maria*; *The Little Drummer Boy* and *Home for the Holidays*; he also performs a medley of colonial songs with Wayne, backed by the William and Mary Choir. Eugene is accompanied by a harpsichordist. Perry and the townspeople of Williamsburg offer *The Twelve Days of Christmas*. Produced by Bob Banner, Stephen Polliot and Ron Miziker.

The Barbara Walters Special (ABC) March 13, 1979.

Host: Barbara Walters.

Barbara interviews John Wayne at his home in Laguna Beach, California, and on his boat. She asks him about his life, career and political views. Other segments feature Jane Fonda and Carroll O'Connor with his wife, Nancy.

The 51st Annual Academy Awards (ABC) (Special) April 9, 1979.

Host: Johnny Carson. The Jack Elliott and Allyn Ferguson Orchestra.

Broadcast live from the Dorothy Chandler Pavilion, Los Angeles, California. Honoring outstanding achievement in 1978 motion pictures. John Wayne presents the Oscar for Best Picture, ***The Deer Hunter***, to producer Michael Cimino. Robin Williams and Woody Woodpecker (voice of Grace Stafford) present an Honorary Award to animator Walter Lantz. Cary Grant presents another Honorary Award to Laurence Olivier. Audrey Hepburn presents a third Honorary Award to director King Vidor. The fourth and final Honorary Award of the evening is presented to the Museum of Modern Art by Gregory Peck. Sammy Davis Jr. and Steve Lawrence perform *Oscar's Only Human* and *Not Even Nominated*. Winners in major categories: Jon Voight (Actor, ***Coming Home***, presented by Ginger Rogers and Diana Ross); Jane Fonda (Actress, ***Coming Home***, presented by Richard Dreyfuss and Shirley MacLaine); Christopher Walken (Supporting Actor, ***The Deer Hunter***, presented by Dyan Cannon and Telly Savalas); Maggie Smith (Supporting Actress, ***California Suite***, presented by George Burns and Brooke Shields); Michael Cimino (Director, ***The Deer Hunter***, presented by Francis Ford Coppola and Ali MacGraw). Other winners: Nancy Dowd, Waldo Salt and Robert C. Jones (Writing-Screenplay Written Directly for the Screen, ***Coming Home***, presented by Lauren Bacall and Jon Voight); Oliver Stone (Writing-Screenplay Based on Material From Another Medium, ***Midnight Express***, presented by Lauren Bacall and Jon Voight); Nestor Almendros (Cinematography, ***Days of Heaven***, presented by James Coburn and Kim Novak); Paul Sylbert and Edwin O' Donovan (Art Direction, ***Heaven Can Wait***, presented by Shirley Jones and Ricky Schroder); George Gaines (Set Decoration, ***Heaven Can Wait***, presented by Shirley Jones and Ricky Schroder); Anthony Powell (Costume Design, ***Death on the Nile***, presented by Ray Bolger and Jack Haley); Richard Portman, William McCaughey, Aaron Rochin and Darin Knight (Sound, ***The Deer Hunter***, presented by Margot Kidder and Christopher Reeve); Peter Zinner (Film Editing, *The Deer Hunter*, presented by Dom De Luise and Valerie Perrine); Giorgio Moroder (Music-Original Score, *Midnight Express*, presented by Dean Martin and Raquel Welch); Joe Renzetti (Music-Original Song Score and Its Adaptation or Best Adaptation Score, *The Buddy Holly Story*, presented by Dean Martin and Raquel Welch); Eunice Macaulay and John Weldon (Short Films-Animated, *Special Delivery*, presented by Robby Benson and Carol Lynley); Taylor Hackford (Short Films-Live Action, *Teenage Father*, presented by Robby Benson and Carol Lynley); Jacqueline Phillips Shedd and Ben Shedd (Documentary-Short Subject, *The Flight of the Gossamer Condor*, presented by Mia Farrow and David L. Wolper); Arnold Shapiro (Documentary-Feature, *Scared Straight!* Presented by Mia Farrow and David L. Wolper); Les Bowie, Colin Chilvers, Denys Coop, Roy Field, Derek Meddings and Zoran Perisic (Visual Effects, *Superman*, presented by Steve Martin); Leo Jaffe (Jean Hersholt Humanitarian Award, presented by Jack Valenti). Written by Michael Barrie, Johnny Carson, Hal Goodman, Larry Klein, Buz Kohan, Jim Mulholland, Tony Thomas and Rod Warren. Directed by Marty Pasetta. Produced by Jack Haley Jr., Stu Bernstein, Eytan Keller and Michael B. Seligman.

Nominated Songs: Olivia Newton-John sings *Hopelessly Devoted to You* (composed by John Farrar), Donna Summer: *Last Dance* (Paul Jabara) (Academy Award Winner), Johnny Mathis, Jane Oliver: The Last Time I Felt Like This (Marvin Hamlisch and Alan & Marilyn Bergman), Barry Manilow: *Ready to Take a Chance Again* (Charles Fox and Norman Gimbel), Debby Boone: *When You're Loved* (Richard M. Sherman and Robert B. Sherman).

Also: Warren Beatty, Ellen Burstyn, Gary Busey, Jill Clayburgh, Bruce Dern, Richard Farnsworth, Jerome Hellman, John Hurt, Diane Keaton, Paul Mazursky, Penelope Milford, Geraldine Page, Alan Parker, Anthony Ray, Meryl Streep, Armand Assante, Troy Garity, Tom Hayden, Robert Stack, Robert Wagner.

Hollywood (Thames Television/HBO) *Out West* March 4, 1980.

Narrator: James Mason.

The development of the film western in the silent era is reviewed and tonight's installment takes a look at the work of William S. Hart, Tom Mix, Harry Carey Sr. and others, along with interviews. Written and directed by Kevin Brownlow and David Gill. Music by Carl Davis. Executive Producer: Mike Wooller. Producers: Kevin Brownlow and David Gill. Associate Producers: Susan McConachy and Raye Farr. Karl Brown, Yakima Canutt, Olive Carey, Iron Eyes Cody, Lefty [R.L.] Hough, Al Hoxie, Henry King, Jesse L. Lasky Jr., Colonel Tim McCoy, Colleen Moore, Harvey Parry, Blanche Sweet, John Wayne.

Note: McCoy's and Wayne's interviews appeared posthumously.

Sources

The Columbia Story by Clive Hirschhorn, Crown Publishers, Inc., 1989.

The Complete Directory of Prime Time Network and Cable TV Shows, 1946-Present, 9th Edition, By Tim Brooks and Earle Marsh, Ballantine, 2007.

Encyclopedia of American Short Films, 1926-1959 by Graham Webb, McFarland & Company, Inc., 2020.

Films of the Seventies, A Filmography of American, British and Canadian Films, 1970-1979 by Marc Sigoloff, McFarland Classics, 1984.

The Films of 20th Century-Fox, A Pictorial History by Tony Thomas and Aubrey Solomon, The Citadel Press, 1979.

Hollywood Song, The Complete Film & Musical Companion, 3 Volumes, by Ken Bloom, Facts on File, 1995.

Inside Oscar, The Unofficial History of the Academy Awards by Mason Wiley & Damien Bona, Ballantine Books, 1987.

Internet Movie Database, website at www.imdb.com.

John Wayne: American by Randy Roberts and James S. Olson, The Free Press, 1995.

The MGM Story, The Complete History of Fifty-Seven Roaring Years by John Douglas Eames, Crown Publishers Inc., 1982.

The Monogram Checklist, The Films of Monogram Pictures Corporation, 1931-1952 by Ted Okuda, McFarland & Company, Inc., 1987.

Movie Time, A Chronology of Hollywood and the Movie Industry from Its Beginnings to the Present by Gene Brown, Macmillan, 1995.

Navarro's Silent Film Guide, A Comprehensive Look at Silent Cinema by Dan Navarro, El Dorado Books, 2005.

Newspaper Archive, Internet website at www.NewspaperArchive.com.

The Paramount Story by John Douglas Eames, Crown Publishers, Inc., 1985.

Performers' Television Credits, 3 volumes, By David M. Inman, McFarland & Company, Inc., 2001.

The Republic Pictures Checklist, Features, Serials, Cartoons, Short Subjects and Training Films of Republic Pictures Corporation, 1935-1959 by Len D. Martin, McFarland & Company, Inc., 1998.

The RKO Story by Richard B. Jewell with Vernon Harbin, Arlington House, 1982.

70 Years of Oscar, The Official History of the Academy Awards by Robert Osborne, Abbeville Press, 1999.

Sound Films, 1927-1939, A United States Filmography by Alan G. Fetrow, McFarland & Company, Inc., 1992.

Television Variety Shows, Histories and Episode Guides to 57 Programs by David Inman, McFarland & Company, Inc., 2006.

Turner Classic Movies Presents Leonard Maltin's Classic Movie Guide, 3rd Edition, edited by Leonard Maltin, Plume/Penguin Random House LLC, 2015.

TV Guide magazine, various issues, 1953-1980, Triangle Publications.

The United Artists Story by Ronald Bergan, Crown Publishers, Inc., 1986.

The Universal Story by Clive Hirschhorn, Crown Publishers, Inc., 1983.

The Warner Bros. Story by Clive Hirschhorn, Crown Publishers, Inc., 1979.

Wikipedia, the Free Encyclopedia, Internet website at http://en.wikipedia.org.

Also from BearManor Media

The Complete Filmography
of Audrey Totter

The Complete Filmography
of Richard Carlson

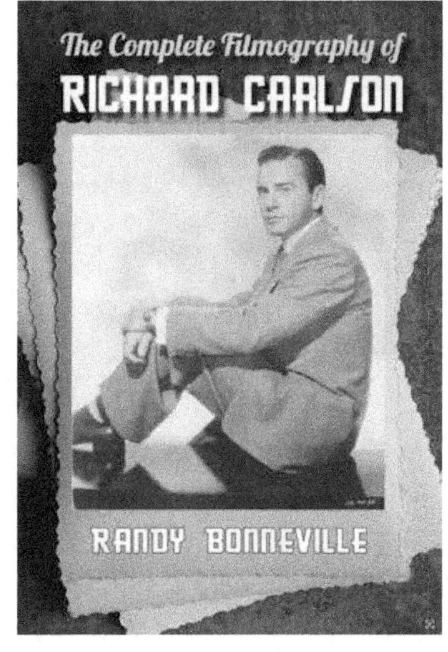

The Buckskin Western TV Log